BUSINESS ECONOMICS

BUSINESS ECONOMICS

by

JAMES BATES
Lecturer in Economics, University of Bristol

and

J. R. PARKINSON
Professor of Economics, The Queen's University, Belfast

BASIL BLACKWELL
OXFORD
1963

PRINTED IN GREAT BRITAIN IN THE CITY OF OXFORD
AT THE ALDEN PRESS
AND BOUND BY THE KEMP HALL BINDERY

CONTENTS

TABLES AND DIAGRAMS

Page

TABLES

DIAGRAMS

PREFACE

The idea of writing this book occurred to us independently. If it had been an individual project it would, of course, have been different: that it has been possible to align our thoughts is mainly due to the fact that the need for the book was felt in attempting to teach economics to students in industrial administration at Glasgow University. The final decision to write it was taken at the bar of the Gleneagles Hotel during a conference organized by the British Institute of Management, so that the book owes its origins to attempts to educate managers in more ways than one.

Those who have attempted to teach short courses in economics to students in industrial administration will appreciate how necessary it is to be selective in choosing material. Economics as it is taught is concerned largely with the economy as a whole and its organization and management; the theory of the firm is scarcely more than a step in this process; and much of what is taught in economics seems to have small relevance to the problems of those in business—particularly those in small business. A knowledge of the factors making for a high level of demand, an efficient exchange of commodities in international trade and the organization of world finance are sometimes relevant to the success of large businesses and can be considered by expert economic sections in relation to the general policy of the firm; but the small firm can seldom rise to these refinements and to a young general manager economics often seems to be either obvious in elementary exposition, inapplicable to real-life situations in its more sophisticated forms, or just plainly irrelevant. It is not easy to defend economics against these criticisms by arguing that the best form of education for management is general education, and that relevance is a secondary matter. Education for management covers a wide field and some, at least, of the matter imparted must be of use in a narrow technical sense in addition to contributing to general education.

In this book we have attempted to extract from the general body of economic thought some parts that seem to us to be particularly relevant to taking decisions in business. We do not, of course, think that we have covered every aspect of economics with relevance to business decisions; and we have deliberately abstained from treating some subjects of importance, for example, wages and industrial relations. We did not think that a short treatment of these subjects would be very helpful; much of the subject lies outside the usual boundaries of economics, and could not easily have been integrated with the main tenor of development of the book. For other reasons we have omitted other things: for example we have not included a discussion of the theoretical and quantitative aspects of production functions, largely because a reasonable discussion of these would involve technical economic and statistical considerations beyond the scope of this book. Similarly we have omitted decision theory, game theory, activity analysis and other recent developments in mathematical economics which are relevant to business economics but which could not be usefully discussed in a book of this nature.

The theme of the book is that while the economic situation is always changing, and the businessman is therefore operating in an uncertain world, it is nevertheless possible to take business decisions in a systematic fashion, and by using appropriate techniques and ways of thought to reduce the uncertainties involved. We anticipate that in future numerical analysis is likely to play an increasingly important part in the taking of business decisions; this is why we have devoted a section of the book to elementary quantitative analysis. This section is intended only to introduce readers to the possibilities of numerical analysis mainly by illustration, and does not, of course, take the matter very far, though we are conscious that, nevertheless, it does not make easy reading.

In the process we have attempted to achieve a certain mixing of the ways of thought and techniques used by economists, econometricians and accountants. Probably the resulting blend will suit no one; but there does appear to be a border area in the three subjects of study where those engaged should be discussing common problems from a common point of view.

In these and other ways the book is something in the nature of an experiment. We should like to acknowledge assistance from a number of people, and to start with Professor A. K.

Cairncross (as he then was) who encouraged us in the project and gave us the benefit of his advice on an early draft of the table of contents. We should also like to thank Mr Jim Houston and Mr Jim McGregor of Honeywell Controls Ltd who supplied us with some valuable information and extremely useful comments on early drafts of some of the chapters. Mr J. B. Stevenson, lecturer in Accountancy at Glasgow University made useful comments on some of the accounting aspects raised in the book. He is not, of course, responsible for the no doubt unorthodox remarks which still appear. Mr Gordon Fisher offered valuable comments on the chapter on forecasting, and other chapters on quantitative analysis; here again the faults that remain are our own. We should also like to thank Mr Peter Hart for comments on these and other chapters and Mr N. Robertson for helpful criticism of the chapter on demand. Again the remaining faults are our own.

We are grateful to our wives for their forbearance and help during the writing of this book; we also gratefully acknowledge the typing assistance of Miss A. Allen, Miss K. MacDonald and Mrs D. Ryder.

RECOMMENDED READING

In general we have followed the practice of recommending further reading at appropriate places in the text, and the reader who wishes to follow up particular topics will find that these references provide a useful starting point.

In addition there are a number of books which, between them cover in greater detail approximately similar ground to that covered in this book: a brief selection of these is included for guidance.

W. J. Baumol *Economic Theory and Operations Analysis.* (Prentice Hall, 1961)

Joel Dean *Managerial Economics* (Prentice Hall, 1951)

R. S. Edwards and H. Townsend *Business Enterprise* (Macmillan 1958)

P. Sargant Florence *The Logic of British and American Industry* (Routledge and Kegan Paul, 1953)

A. Merrett and G. Bannock *Business Economics and Statistics* (Hutchinson 1962)

M. H. Spencer and L. Seigelman *Managerial Economics* (Richard Irwin, 1959)

Introduction

THE NATURE OF INDUSTRIAL CHANGE

Change is the essence of industrial development. The Industrial Revolution in Great Britain and later in other countries of the Western World was both a cause and consequence of change; it brought about changes in living standards, tastes and habits, trading patterns, political strength, moral standards and indeed most aspects of life; and it was in itself a consequence of the technological and scientific changes of the eighteenth and nineteenth centuries.

Change is particularly relevant to business economics: business reacts to changes in population, tastes and techniques, and an analysis of these and other changes contains a large part of the explanation of business behaviour; but it is also in part the function of business to bring about or stimulate changes in order better to achieve its objectives. Business behaviour can in fact be seen as a process of initiating change and responding to it.

THE IMPACT OF INDUSTRY

The Industrial Revolution in Britain started in the second half of the eighteenth century; the process probably started as one of technological change, which came first in agriculture, spread to the all-important textile industry and, by the end of the eighteenth century, had so transformed the pattern of industry and life in Britain that it was completely unrecognizable. The population of England and Wales increased from 5½ million in 1700 to 9 million in 1800. Britain was still predominantly agricultural, but her industry had undergone radical changes in its organization, techniques and methods of production. In transport most of our canals had been constructed and a network of usable roads had been laid. In manufacturing industry the steam engine had arrived as a practical proposition; the iron industry, now able to use coal instead of charcoal, was growing rapidly and had already established itself in Staffordshire, South Wales, Clydeside and South Yorkshire; the textile industry had developed from a cottage-based industry to a mechanized factory industry.

It was really in the years following the Napoleonic Wars that Britain became the first industrialized nation in the world. During the nineteenth century industrial output increased fourteen times, whilst the proportion of the population engaged in agriculture and fishing fell from over one-third to less than a tenth. At the same time there was a corresponding activity in commerce and distribution linked with growing foreign and domestic trade; railways and steamships were added to the canals and roads of the previous century and provided a comprehensive and effective system of communications; and industrial and commercial finance developed from rudimentary beginnings to a complex and highly organized market; these developments stemmed from and made possible the Industrial Revolution. It was during this period that the economy was founded on its three great basic industries: coal, iron and steel (including shipbuilding) and textiles.

Beside this great technological and commercial change other far-reaching changes were taking place, not the least of which was the emergence and growth, late in the nineteenth century, of two major competitors, the United States and Germany. From then on Britain's massive lead in industrialization and technical superiority was to be progressively cut, and she was eventually to drop behind in the industrial and commercial race. Newer technologies were also developing—notably in chemicals, engineering, fuel and power and, as the First World War approached, motor vehicles—and British industry was slow to adapt to these (partly, it must be supposed, because Britain seemed to be doing fairly well on the old basis).

Although in 1913 British industry appeared to be riding the crest of the wave, there was in fact room for a great deal of misgiving, and the industrial structure of Britain was already seriously maladjusted to world trends. The basic industries which had been responsible for the prosperity of Britain were, from 1919 onwards, to be a major cause of embarrassment; and up to the outbreak of the Second World War the newer industries proved inadequate to make good the deficiencies of the old.

The 1920s and 1930s were a period of stagnation and decline for a large part of British industry. The Great Depression hit the world in the 1930s, and Britain suffered along with everyone else, but the troubles of the British economy were more deep-rooted; they were due to the fundamental changes in world markets and competitors, and not entirely to the fluctuations of the Trade Cycle. Consumers abroad were no longer demanding the goods on which Britain had grown great, and this loss of overseas markets goes a long way towards explaining the chronic problem of some sections of British industry. Output from British shipyards fell by about 40 per cent between 1929 and 1937, whilst at the same time foreign output was doubling; exports of woollen goods fell by 20 per cent, cotton piece goods by 50 per cent, largely because of Japanese competition; coal exports fell by 40 per cent, steel exports by a like amount (though in the case of the latter industry the growth of the motor vehicle industry and rearmament more than compensated for the fall in exports, and total production in fact increased). The contrast between Britain and other industrial nations is highlighted by the fact that, although the United States suffered even more severely from the depression than Britain, she has continued to draw away rapidly from Britain during the present century; other nations have drawn level.

Not all of the changes were unfavourable, however. There were many technological advances, some new industries were growing up and there was some adaptation to changes; and the attitude of the State was changing from one of complete non-interference (or *laissez-faire*) to one of responsibility and a realization that the problems of industry were not solely the problems of the sectors immediately concerned.

Since the Second World War industrial change and technological progress have continued rapidly in Britain. New raw materials, the growing use of synthetics, and the growth of new power supplies (in the form of oil and nuclear power), large expenditures by the Government on research and development, innovations in the motor industry, the aircraft industry, chemicals and electronics have all had a considerable impact on Britain's industrial structure. Again Britain has probably been slower to adapt to technological change, and her industrial growth has been slower than that of many of her competitors but, by comparison with the 1930s, many of the changes have been in the right direction if not of the right magnitudes.

The basic industries, with the exception of textiles and (more recently) shipbuilding, have prospered. This has been due largely to the new and better conditions of the post-war period, with higher and more evenly distributed incomes, the avoidance of major depressions, and the increasing demand for capital goods which started with the reconstruction boom and continued for most of the period. Government policy, too, has helped these industries: some, notably the fuel and power industries and railways, have been nationalized; others have received protection from the imports of foreign competitors and substitute products.

Technological change has favoured the basic industries too, not merely in their own productive processes but also because so many of the new industries have created demands for the products of the constructional and associated industries. The growth of oil refining in Britain, for example, has meant a demand for the products of the construction trades in the building of large-scale refineries.

The technological changes have been brought about partly by the War and the large defence programmes which have followed it and have become a familiar part of the industrial scene. The changes have also been a response to new demands brought about by material shortages, labour shortages, currency shortages and rising labour costs, which have caused new industries to develop to supply labour-saving machinery and alternative materials. The growing affluence of British society has brought with it an increasing demand for the more expensive consumer durable goods, and for the technological development which is a feature of the market for such goods.

ASPECTS OF CHANGE

Business economics is a study of the behaviour of firms in theory and practice, and in both cases the interesting and significant aspects of behaviour are the dynamic ones. The main difference between the firm which merely potters along and the dynamic growing firm lies not only in their reaction to changes in the demand and supply conditions which face them, but in the ways in which they themselves contribute to the change by research and new developments and by the satisfaction and even creation of new demands. This reaction to change is implicit in the analysis and description which make up the remainder of this book, but it is as well to spell out and examine the more important aspects of change in their own right. These represent the climate in which firms have to operate.

One of the main changes in the nineteenth and twentieth centuries has been the shift of centres of economic development and consequent changes in the location of industry. Location of industry tends to be affected mainly by supplies of materials, labour components and ancillary trades, power or markets (and in some cases, such as the shipbuilding and coal industries, by sheer physical limitations). Before the development of efficient and cheap transport the tendency was for industry to establish itself near to one of its raw materials. The steel industry grew up on the coalfields because of the cost advantages of doing so, but has tended during this century to move towards the iron ore deposits, largely because low-grade iron ore is relatively more expensive to transport than coal. Nowadays the locational pull of most of these factors has declined in importance. One of the consequences of the regional specialization of industry, which was determined by locational factors, has been the growth of depressed areas and regional economic problems resulting from the decline of the industries on which the regions rely. Scotland, Wales, Tyneside, Merseyside and Northern Ireland are all suffering now from these difficulties, and Government policy[1] has been increasingly concerned with solving the problems caused by over-specialization.

London and the Midlands have experienced a different kind of locational pull. This has been partly due to the existence of mass markets in these areas and partly to the existence of manpower resources (this has in recent years developed into a problem of labour shortage). The growth of ancillary trades, such as component manufactures for the motor industry, has helped to keep industry in this area; such movements develop a momentum of their own which tends to perpetuate locational patterns. Today's depressed areas were the prosperous ones of the last century.

These changes are still in progress and Government action in

[1] See Appendix to Chapter VII.

this field has been mainly concentrated on attempts either to minimize the effects of the changes or, in specific cases, to reverse them. The attempt to get industry to go to the depressed areas is one example of such Government policy, which has had limited success. The declining industries are another facet of the problem. One of the consequences of change, whether it be dynamic and resulting from expansion, or whether it results from depression and decline, is the shift of resources from one employment to another. Some industries adapt fairly readily to change—light engineering and the small metal trades are good examples, largely because neither the machinery nor the skills of these trades are specific or tied too closely to a particular product or market—but others do not.

Unfortunately for Britain, most of her basic industries were of a type which could not adapt readily to industrial change—there are few alternative uses for cotton mills, coal mines or shipyards, and they usually represent such high capital expenditure that, whatever the evidence, owners are reluctant to abandon them. Labour becomes highly specialized and specific to certain tasks, so does equipment; and, as depression continued in these industries in the 1930s there were severe problems of unemployment and surplus capacity, which led in turn to a falling off in capital expenditure, the gradual departure and run-down of able and efficient management, and a corresponding decline in industrial efficiency. This dismal pattern was all too familiar in the staple British trades in the 1930s.

The reaction of industry to these changes was naturally defensive, and in the attempt to preserve the declining industries and to minimize the effects of the depression, several schemes were tried, many of them ill-conceived. In the coal-mining industry, for example, wages were reduced and the industry also tried to restore its fortunes (with the aid of legislation such as the 1930 Coal Mines Act) by regulating output and sales: the real need was to re-organize the industry into larger, more efficient units and to get rid of the less efficient units, but little progress was made along these lines. The steel industry received import duty protection which, although it was granted on condition that the industry put its house in order, in fact provided a disincentive to reorganization. One of the major economic consequences of the depression of the 1930s was a tendency towards monopoly and cartelization of the declining industries. It is true that at the same time there was a healthier reaction in some quarters, towards 'rationalization'[2] (the grouping of productive units into larger organizations in order to achieve economies of scale and remove surplus capacity), but this movement had limited success. By the outbreak of the Second World War surplus capacity still existed in the staple trades in Britain, and their failure to adapt to change was painfully obvious. The changes had been so drastic that adaptation of thinking and methods of production was too big a job.

Since the Second World War, however, the basic trades have fared rather better. The cotton industry and the shipbuilding industry are still faced with a long-term decline in the demand for their products, and their problems are still far from being solved; but the steel industry has been able to share in the prosperity of the economy as a whole. The coal industry, with surplus capacity in the inter-war years, has faced the opposite problem for most of the post-war period and has had to strive hard to meet a high level of demand for coal whilst at the same time undertaking vast capital expenditure and reorganization; and, although it is clear that the long-term trend of decline in the demand for coal has not been halted, the industry is now in a better position to face this problem.

The problem of change is less severe for the expanding industries, presenting, as it does, a challenge in the form of possibilities of increased activity and profits rather than the reverse. The existence of the European Economic Community presents one such challenge. Many firms, and even whole industries, fail to react to this sort of challenge, but to those who do the rewards are great. The chemical industry, the aircraft industry, motor vehicles, electronics, light engineering, have all reacted to the challenge of change and have grown in so doing. The challenge of increasing international competition for the products of British industry in all fields will bring about further changes.

The result of all this change has been a change in the composition of the output of the British economy illustrated in Table 1. Forty-three per cent of the employed population is now engaged in the vehicles, engineering, shipbuilding, electrical,

[2] See Chapter III.

chemical and metal industries, compared with 12 per cent half a century ago; by comparison only just over twenty-seven per cent work in the mining, textile and clothing trades compared with fifty-four per cent in 1907.

TABLE I

CHANGE IN THE COMPOSITION OF BRITISH INDUSTRY

Trade	*Change in size (Nos. employed) 1907 = 100*	*Change in relative share Percentage of employed population 1907*	*1957*
Rapid growth		*Increasing share*	
Vehicles	1,090	1.5	10.2
Engineering, Shipbuilding, Electrical goods	707	5.2	22.9
Chemicals	326	2.3	4.7
Metal goods	284	3.0	5.3
Other manufactures	517	0.9	2.7
Medium growth			
Precision instruments	194	1.3	1.5
Paper and printing	164	6.0	6.0
		Declining share	
Metal manufacture	139	7.4	6.4
Treatment of mining products	136	4.1	3.5
Food, drink and tobacco	127	8.5	6.7
Wood and cork manufactures	112	4.4	3.0
Leather	110	1.0	0.7
Decline			
Mining	87	17.6	9.6
Textiles	74	22.9	10.5
Clothing	72	13.8	6.1
ALL TRADES	161	100.0	100.0
TOTAL EMPLOYMENT		5,470	8,834

Source: *Census of Production,* and Dunning and Thomas, *British Industry, Change and Development in the Twentieth Century* (Hutchinson, 1961).

The changes in industrial structure lightly sketched in these paragraphs were themselves the results of changes in the economic forces affecting industry. The growth of foreign competition for the basic trades of the British economy, helped in many cases by restrictions imposed on trade by competitors, was bound to affect these industries, even at times when total world demand was increasing. One of the penalties of being first in the field in industrial development is that competitors when they eventually come along (as they inevitably do if the opportunities for profit are sufficiently attractive) can take advantage of developments. They can spot and avoid the mistakes of the pioneer, and usually have the additional advantage of newer and up-to-date equipment.

The growth of competition brought about changes in the pattern of world trade: no longer, for example, is Britain the world's major supplier of cheap textiles, machine tools, heavy iron or steel goods or ships, Japan and Germany in particular have been ousting Britain from that position; and Britain's share of world trade in manufactures has declined progressively since the end of the Second World War (see Table 2). The volume of world trade continues to increase as more nations develop and add both to the demand for and supply of traded products. The former primary producing countries, who specialized in the production of foodstuffs and raw materials for the industrial nations, are themselves industrializing; and not only are they providing competition in international markets, they are also protecting their own growing industries and keeping out the goods of former suppliers. For a nation such as Britain, which is highly dependent on international trade for the maintenance and improvement of its standard of living, such changes have far-reaching effects. Imports of raw materials account for almost two-thirds of Britain's import bill, and it has been estimated[3] that almost a quarter of the selling value of manufactured goods in Britain is accounted for by the cost of imported raw materials. Well over 80 per cent of Britain's exports are manufactured goods, and these represent 37 per cent of the net product of manufacturing industry.

Tariff barriers and other restrictions on trade have kept British goods out of traditional markets. This may well change as the principles of the General Agreement on Tariffs and Trade are applied and as larger Free Trade blocks, such as the European Economic Community and the European Free Trade Association grow up. But as tariffs are removed on British goods sold abroad, so they are removed on foreign goods coming into Britain. Some industries gain from this, others lose: the results of a study by the Economist Intelligence Unit[4] suggest that the

[3] See J. H. Dunning and C. J. Thomas, *British Industry, Change and Development in the Twentieth Century* (Hutchinson, 1961), Chapter VII.

[4] Economist Intelligence Unit, *Britain and Europe* (1957).

liberalization of European trade would bring gains for the motor industry, wool, engineering, rubber, iron and steel, hosiery and clothing (59 per cent of total net output), probable gains for metal manufactures, aircraft, ore refining, building materials and glass (22 per cent of total net output), losses for cotton, man-made fibres, paper, leather, watches and clocks (10 per cent of net output), probable losses for china, footwear and toys (3 per cent of net output), whilst railway vehicles, furniture and jute would be little affected.

TABLE 2

SHARES OF WORLD TRADE IN MANUFACTURED GOODS

	Percentage of total value	
	1950	*1959*
United Kingdom	25·5	17·3
Western Germany	7·3	19.1
Japan	3·4	6.7
U.S.A.	27·3	21.3
France	9·9	9·2
Others	26.6	26.4
World manufacturing production (1953 = 100)	83	127
World trade in manufactures	86	158

Source: Adapted from Dunning and Thomas, *British Industry, Change and Development in the Twentieth Century* (Hutchinson, 1961), Table 20, p. 209; and from data in *Board of Trade Journal* (July 28th, 1956), and *National Institute Economic Review* (May 1960).

There are many other aspects of change. The growth of population increases demand, not merely in the obvious way of increasing the total demand for goods already produced, but also, to an extent depending on the location, types and habits of the new population, it also affects the structure of demand. The large population growth of India and China does not mean that there will be a proportionately increasing demand for motor cars and consumer durable goods, but for foodstuffs and the raw materials of the industrial progress which these nations are intent on achieving. World trade changes, not merely in total, but in direction and structure.

Changes in income, both in total and in its distribution among various groups and classes, create new demand patterns which force further changes in industry. As incomes per head increase, consumers develop new demands, for more expensive clothes and foods, for higher standards of accommodation, for more expensive consumer durable goods such as furniture, household equipment, motor cars, etc. And as more and more people receive higher incomes, and inequalities are reduced, so does the production of these goods on a larger and more economical scale become feasible, and the pattern of industry changes. In the early days of the motor industry, not only were cars themselves expensive to make, but the number of people with the standard of living which was associated with the ownership of private personal transport was also small. Henry Ford broke through this circle and mass produced cars at relatively low prices; the industry still had to wait for growing incomes before it became the giant it is today, but the growth had started. We are in the midst of such a revolutionary income change in the United Kingdom at the moment; incomes are growing, and whether or not they are more equally distributed, the lower income groups are getting higher real incomes (partly as a result of increasing productivity) and the pattern of British industry is changing in consequence. The Western world continues to develop along these lines and industry both adapts to meet the changes and helps to bring them about. The underdeveloped nations have not yet experienced this, but one of the aims of international economic policy is to bring these changes about.

Probably the biggest change of all (though not necessarily individually the most important) has been technological. In the period since the outbreak of the Second World War there has been a second Industrial Revolution, and we witnessed more technological change in two decades than in the preceding two centuries. This period has seen the development of nuclear power, a new field of human endeavour in space research, the growth of the electronics industry and automation, startling developments in chemicals and plastics, motor vehicles, and aircraft. This is an era of inventions and scientific progress and the emphasis on research and development continues to increase.[5] The Second World War and the large

[5] Britain still only spends about one-fifth as much as the United States on research and development, however. See G. Freeman, *Research and Development: A Comparison between British and American Industry*, National Institute Economic Review, No. 20 (May 1962).

defence programmes which are now a major part of our lives have provided the main impetus, and Government-sponsored research in these fields accounts for a major part of the expenditure, but there are other reasons. Full employment and rising labour costs have encouraged the search for labour-saving methods of production in industrialized nations; political requirements and balance of payments problems have led in Britain to the search for alternative sources of energy and raw materials to replace imports of these products; British industry has also been affected by the new technologies and consumption patterns of other nations (notably the United States).

As a result of this technological change the emphasis of growth in the British economy has been on the science-based industries. Not only has this meant a change in structure and employment of resources; it has also meant that there is a greater interdependence between industries. Most of these new industries rely on several, formerly independent industries: automation relies on the electronics industry, the machine tool industry and the instrument industry; the textile industry is no longer based exclusively on natural materials but is coming increasingly to rely on the chemical industry. The old dividing lines between industries, never very clear, are becoming impossible to discern.

CHANGE AND THE INDIVIDUAL FIRM

The history of business and industry is the history of adaptation to changing circumstances; and business economics is to some extent a study of the way in which firms behave in response to changes in techniques, markets, economic structures, organization, habits and tastes; and how they themselves bring about change. A static description of business behaviour does not make sense in real life, however useful it may be as a theoretical abstraction or as a starting point for more realistic analysis. A firm thrives and continues to do so, not because it was originally set up and developed in some 'correct' way, but because it constantly adapts itself and adjusts its scope, its products, its methods of manufacture, its organization and its management. Firms either grow or decline, they rarely stand still.

This book is an analysis of the way in which firms behave; seen, not particularly from the point of view of the professional economist, but from the point of view of the person engaged in the business.

NOTE

The foregoing pages are merely an illustrative sketch of the outlines of industrial change intended as a perspective against which the problems of business policy must be viewed. More detail of the structure and development of British industry will be found in the following books:

1. G. C. Allen, *The Structure of Industry in Britain* (Longmans, 1961).
2. J. H. Dunning and C. J. Thomas, *British Industry: Change and Development in the Twentieth Century* (*Hutchinson*, 1961).

Chapter I

POLICY AND THE SUCCESSFUL FIRM

OBJECTIVES

Nearly all businessmen assert, when questioned, that the object of their firm is to make a profit. This is a natural reply from those in private industry even if their actions frequently belie the full implications of their assertions. But the aims of businessmen are complex; the money to be got out of business is only one reason for being in it; and non-financial considerations are more important than is often imagined.

An important reason for setting up a business has always been the desire for personal independence; and the service gratuities paid at the end of the war were often used to found small businesses for precisely this reason. But many ex-service men found that the way of the small business is hard; it is not easy to get established and it is difficult to expand. Larger firms benefit from economies of scale and because of this they can often buy at lower prices or produce more cheaply. Personal supervision often does not suffice to offset these advantages and many small proprietors get less from their businesses than they would be able to earn in alternative paid occupations. It might be right to describe them as trying to maximize the net advantages that can be obtained from business, but the net advantages are compounded of the value of independence coupled with a reasonable income. It would be wrong to regard them as struggling to maximize monetary earnings alone.

Much the same kind of consideration applies in the case of a proprietor whose business is successful and has scope for expansion, but who prefers to keep it at its present size. Expansion requires effort; it involves worry and risk; the rewards are cut by taxation; and if present profitability is sufficient to provide for an acceptable and customary standard of living in line with the family position and the aspirations of neighbours, there may be no desire to expand further. This attitude of mind, while understandable, and perhaps even commendable as denoting a refusal to be preoccupied with material considerations, is at odds with the evolution of society. It is often said that a business must either expand or die and there is a strong element of truth in the assertion. In an expanding economy, the economic scene changes rapidly. Output may increase by 3 per cent or more per annum and double in the space of 25 years. In this sense, the economy is made-over every generation and a business that cannot think in these terms will ultimately lose its place if the forces of competition are effective. It will be better for the community if this happens sooner rather than later; for the continued presence of inefficient firms struggling for existence in an industry keeps profit margins low and discourages more efficient firms from expanding their output or entering the market for the first time because they are afraid of pouring good money after bad. Those doubting the deadening effects of gradual erosion as opposed to speedy elimination of firms on the edge of bankruptcy, have only to look at the demise of the cotton industry and contrast it with the growing efficiency of the jute industry protected from the full impact of foreign competition. Slow erosion of the stagnant firm is all the more to be feared because, through interrelations between firms, it exerts a cumulative effect on the community. Once the number of stagnant or declining firms increases beyond a certain point, it becomes difficult to establish offsetting points of growth. Many observers of the Scottish scene think that this has been an important cause of the slow growth of Scottish industry in recent years.

When businesses expand, the reasons are not always economic. The tycoon bent on expansion may be at least as concerned with the prestige, political influence and power conferred by control of a large business. At this stage in the development of an enterprise, seeking to maximize profits by expansion may give way to achieving expansion even at the expense of profit. But the reason for expansion may also be predominantly altruistic. Mr Thomas Coughtrie, Chairman of Belmos, started to expand his business with the intention of creating employment in Lanarkshire during the depression; he was so successful that expansion became essential in order to retain young managers of promise and promote them to positions of responsibility. The profit motive may be secondary in such cases.

Profit is often regarded as the test of business efficiency. But is only one of a number of possible tests. It is true that no enterprise can expect to flourish if it cannot pay its way, and profits, but not necessarily maximum profits, are a condition of survival. But the level of profits may be quite an inappropriate test of the management of certain enterprises. It would be wrong to test the performance of a nationalized industry by the level of profits that was being made and certainly inappropriate to suggest that its objective should be to maximize profits irrespective of other consideration. Nationalized industries are expected to provide a service to the community, and to have some regard to the public good when conducting their operations; they are not expected to exploit their monopolies in order to maximize profits; indeed, when industries were nationalized at the end of the war they were generally directed to break even financially taking the good years with the bad. More recently there has been a change of view about the appropriate financial objectives of nationalized industries in the direction of their attempting to secure an adequate return on the capital invested in them, as would be expected of private industry. It has also been suggested that they should seek to make provision at least for the full depreciation of their assets measured at replacement cost and, perhaps, for the additional capital needed to expand their activities and adopt new productive techniques.

If nationalized industries are expected to conduct their operations in the interests of the public good, efficiency must be judged by other tests than making profits. These include comparisons with similar industries elsewhere, evidence of a progressive outlook and the maintenance of an adequate quality of service. Similar tests may also be applied to private industry. Amongst businessmen themselves profitability is only one test of success and there is high regard for the firm that is known to be progressive, technically advanced, and receptive to ideas. Indeed, a firm that makes substantial profits and even succeeds in expanding its activities may still be judged to be lacking if it fails by the above criteria.

All this is apparent to most businessmen and is reflected in the conduct of business and in the direction of firms. The largest firms must certainly have regard to the public interest as well as to the interest of their shareholders. This is bound to give rise to some conflict of interest between making maximum profits and serving the ends of the community. Many business decisions do involve moral judgments and such decisions are often difficult to make because a balance has to be struck between different interests. What is true of large business is equally true of small: maximization of profit is not likely to override all other considerations. Private industry is likely to exploit monopoly situations to some degree but, irrespective of fears of retaliatory action from potential competitors or of regulation by the government, a company may deliberately attempt to refrain from exploiting its monopoly position to the full, preferring to follow some concept of a fair or reasonable price. Charging what the market will bear is regarded as profiteering and a lower price based on cost may therefore be charged on ethical grounds.[1] For similar reasons a firm's policy in relation to, say, redundancy may be more generous than would be dictated solely by considerations of self-interest.

Much economic analysis, and particularly the theory of the firm, has been founded on the assumption that firms strive to maximize their profits. This is a very useful starting-point for analysis and we do not propose any radical departure from it in this book. But it is an assumption that must be made with caution. If firms always strive to maximize their profits they can be assumed to take profitable opportunities when they see them, or even when these exist; but in fact they do not. The firm that is earning a high return on the capital employed in it will have every incentive to expand and increase profit still further, but, if the owner of the firm is satisfied with what he has got, expansion is unlikely. Maximization of profits as an operating criterion in a competitive environment might also be expected to give rise to a process of natural selection that would ensure the most efficient firms gradually superseding the less efficient, but as we have seen the process is uncertain, protracted and indecisive in the case of a declining industry. When demand for an industry's products is increasing, however, the competitive process may be effective in allowing the more efficient and progressive firms to increase their share of the market.

To concentrate economic analysis on the working of the profit motive may also be to ignore many of the factors that do affect

[1] See P. J. D. Wiles, *Price, Cost and Output* (Blackwell, 1962).

the growth and decline of firms. Some interesting work by Dr Barna[2] suggests that economic factors may have been overstressed in explaining the performance of firms and, therefore, the evolution of economies. It is not easy to explain the growth and decline of individual firms exclusively in terms of economic factors; it is often much easier to understand the dynamics of industry by studying businessmen themselves. Good management can ensure that firms prosper and develop in apparently unfavourable conditions; and the expansion of firms may depend far more on the satisfaction to be obtained from doing a good job than on consideration of pecuniary reward. Business is also creative; it is not only nursing and teaching in which a sense of vocation may appear to be more important than pecuniary considerations alone. There are many dedicated businessmen serving the community who rank the satisfaction to be obtained in business with that obtained from practising in the professions. Indeed, there is an increasing tendency to regard management as a profession, partly because so many professions are represented in business operations. But it is also due to the divorce of ownership and control of business that Burnham pointed to in his book *The Managerial Revolution*.[3]

COMPANY CONTROL

In the small business the question of the divorce of ownership and control seldom arises, but in the large company it may be complete. Legally, ownership of a company is vested in the ordinary shareholder. Nominally slightly more than half the votes conferred by the ownership of shares is necessary to ensure control; but in practice control may be secured with a much smaller proportion of votes. A substantial block of votes may be all that is needed unless opposition to policies is organized effectively in order to mobilize all opposition votes. Control can be extended to subsidiary companies without the need for personal ownership of more than half their shares: control of the parent company may be ensured by holding 51 per cent of the shares; this company in turn may control a subsidiary company by holding 51 per cent of its shares; and so on. At the

[2] *Investment and Growth Policies in British Firms* (Cambridge University Press), 1962.
[3] James Burnham, *The Managerial Revolution* (Penguin, 1962).

end of such a chain a shareholder controlling a subsidiary company may have subscribed indirectly through the parent company's holdings for only a very small percentage of the subsidiary company's shares, but may, nevertheless, have as complete a control as if he owned all the issued shares.

Legal control is only one aspect of control, because most decisions in business are not made by the legal owners of the firms. Professor Sargant Florence[4] has shown that it is usual for Boards of Directors to hold only a small proportion of ordinary shares in the companies they direct. In very large companies the shares held by the Board of Directors exceeded 1 per cent of total shares in only 43 per cent of the companies examined, and exceeded 20 per cent of total shares in only 13 per cent of companies, while there was only an average of one and a half directors amongst the largest twenty shareholders of large companies. From the analysis made by Professor Sargant Florence it appears that at least two-thirds of large British companies are not owner-controlled as judged by the absence of a predominant voteholder or of a concentration of ordinary shares in the hands of directors.

The existence of interlocking directorates and this form of control over subsidiary companies further complicates the question. The Directors of I.C.I. take major policy decisions but many important decisions are made by companies that I.C.I. controls or in which it has invested capital; the powers of local managers of I.C.I. companies may also be sufficient to enable them to exercise a considerable measure of autonomy. It may be that subsidiary companies will find themselves subject to close control on some matters and completely free on others. If the character of a firm is decided by the right to make decisions rather than by ownership it becomes very difficult to be precise about what is meant by the firm. In fact, for different matters the firm may alter its composition. In law it may have one constitution; in trade union bargaining another; and for the purpose of investment decisions still another identity may be involved.

As we have seen, the majority of directors are not among the largest shareholders and 'most of these relatively shareless directors are probably full-time "inside" executive officers of

[4] In *Ownership, Control and Success of Large Companies* (Sweet & Maxwell, 1961).

the company and the holding of office is certainly a more frequent ground for appointment to directorships than shareholding, particularly where boards are small'.[5] Succession to the board thus tends to be arranged within the firm by existing directors, and while formal approval must be obtained this is often no more than a formality when shareholdings are widely diffused and the votes of shareholders are assigned to existing directors as proxies. It is not unusual for institutions to work in this way; many of them are self-perpetuating and indeed must often be so if continuity in operations and management is to be assured.

The composition of a company board is highly variable; it may include direct representatives of the owners of the companies and directors appointed for their professional skills. The attitudes and aptitudes of those appointed should be such that the board constitutes a well-balanced team of specialists with sufficiently wide experience to be able to see the company as a whole. But even if no director has a substantial stake in the enterprise, at least one must have the outlook and personality of an entrepreneur: of a pioneer in the business, of one who is not content to let matters rest but who is constantly looking for something new to try. An eminent authority in the field of administration, Professor T. T. Paterson, sees industrial development very much as a process of change, reorganization and consolidation: if these three steps are essential to development it seems desirable that the board of directors should include individuals who are particularly adept at guiding the enterprise through the various stages.[5a] The qualities of directors capable of initiating change may well be different from those who are most capable of putting the changes into effect, and the responsibility of supervising the period of consolidation might well fall on a third type of director, possibly an older man with the patience and experience needed for putting the finishing touches to some innovation.

CHANGE

If businesses are to succeed they must be capable of initiating and absorbing change. Sometimes the changes involved will be radical, such as the introduction of a new product or process or

[5] Sargant Florence, op. cit., p. 105.

[5a] See 'Administration of Research', *Nature*, vol. 198, May 11th, 1963, p.521.

a major extension of plant. Sometimes new departures will be involved, but often change and reorganization will be no more than an attempt to catch up with what competitors have already done. A readiness to accept what is new to the firm is often as important as the ability to trace a new path.

We saw earlier how much the industrial world has changed since the Industrial Revolution could have been said to have begun. The advanced countries of the world have moved from being predominantly agricultural to being predominantly industrial in not much more than a century. Change in even the last 50 years has been prodigious: we have reached a stage of industrial development where many things are out of date almost as soon as they have been produced, and often before quantity production has been started. One of the problems of preparing production programmes during the war was that after production had started successive modifications were needed, particularly to fighter aircraft, and that any programme was always an uneasy compromise between producing small quantities of the latest models and larger quantities of older models already out of date. In aircraft production this kind of dilemma still persists. But in the older branches of production change is more gradual—at least in this country—and does not prevent articles being produced in large numbers.

Change does not concern only minor modifications to current models or the decision to introduce a new model in the same progression. It can be much more radical and much more disruptive. One has only to look at the history of the Glasgow area to see how change can alter the outstanding characteristics of a trading and industrial environment. In Glasgow, first tobacco, then textiles and later heavy industry offered opportunities of enrichment to merchants and manufacturers. But in each instance something occurred to increase the comparative advantages of other areas in these spheres and activity moved elsewhere. The tobacco trade collapsed with the revolt of the American colonies, and many of the merchants failed in consequence, but the experience that had been acquired in trading and the capital that had been amassed enabled other industries, particularly textiles, to grow. Textiles remained of predominant importance until the outbreak of the American Civil War disrupted cotton supplies. The Scottish industry never recovered from this setback, partly because the English mills had been less affected and were better equipped and more efficient. A century later the shipbuilding industry, which had been a pillar of Glasgow's subsequent prosperity, also found itself struggling against competition from shipyards abroad and in other parts of the United Kingdom,[6] and new opportunities were being sought in light industry and vehicle production.

There were, of course, successful transitions from one source of economic activity to others by firms and individuals in the Glasgow area. But if an entrepreneur failed in one activity his business activities were often over. The same would probably be true today for the smaller firm but it would not necessarily be so for the mammoth company, even if its endeavours were centred largely in one industry. Management skills are not peculiar to any one industry: much the same skills are needed to conduct a business in tobacco as are needed for the textile industries or for heavy industry. The technical requirements are of course different, but the managerial skills are not.

PRODUCTION OPPORTUNITIES

One of the key management skills is that of sensing an opportunity. To some extent this does call for practical insight and even intuition, but as with many other management skills an analytical approach can contribute a great deal to finding the answer that is sought, and in discerning unsuspected opportunities. The function of economic intelligence divisions in larger firms is not just to deal with day-to-day events; they are more often asked for long-term studies in the hope that these will suggest where profitable opportunities may be found in the future.

Nothing is more difficult than attempting to anticipate some new need perhaps as yet unfelt by those for whom a product is intended; new departures are fraught with difficulty and no one can be sure that they will be successful; but if the initial difficulties can be overcome a period of expansion to meet developing markets may open up increasingly profitable opportunities; and the scope of these is illustrated in the following chapter.

[6] For an account of industrial and commercial developments in the Glasgow area reference may be made to the essay of this title by John B. S. Gilfillan and H. A. Moisley, included in *The Glasgow Region*, prepared for the meeting of the British Association in Glasgow, 1958.

However, all innovators have their imitators and emulators; and once the flush of newness is over the advantages of other centres of development may become more apparent and competitors gain an increasing share of the market, or profitable opportunities may disappear for other reasons. The loss of advantage may be fast or slow. The prosperity of the cotton textile industry in the United Kingdom lasted for more than a century; even as late as 1912–14 the industry was enjoying a phenomenal peak of prosperity, and spindle capacity was being increased immediately after the First World War—mistakenly as it proved. But newer industries such as electronics have reached a point where the initial impetus given by being early in the field has been lost much sooner; while in the production of refrigerators, production capacity has been developed in recent years more rapidly than any likely immediate increase in demand. It is not just newness that matters but the ability to keep one step ahead of competitors. When competition is effective profitable opportunities, once observed, are likely to disappear as new producers start production. Often they may be more strongly placed than those first in the field because they have not been put to the cost of developing new processes or can take a fresh look at what is needed and develop better production facilities.

There are no golden rules for identifying favourable market opportunities. But economic reasoning can be helpful in eliminating unlikely possibilities; it is clear, for example, that the textile industries in this country are under pressure from underdeveloped countries. It would seem to be unnecessarily hazardous to establish a new company in textiles when so many existing companies are doing so badly; but there may be special circumstances, for example, entrepreneurs with outstanding talent for textile production, or a partially protected market in some speciality, or some new process that would minimize the importance of cheap labour. For those already in the textile industry withdrawal may be neither desirable nor easy. It is a question of making the best of existing circumstances even if this may mean that new money has to be invested to salvage something out of a going concern. It is always difficult to know what to do in such circumstances, whether to improve existing production processes while continuing to manufacture the same products, whether to adopt some radically new method of production or attempt to produce some new product. Many firms in declining industries recognize that they are operating in unfavourable circumstances, and attempt to diversify their activities. Thus a firm producing domestic boilers may branch out into the provision of canteen equipment, perhaps by the acquisition of a subsidiary, and another engaged in textiles may decide to supplement its activities by producing plastic materials. Likewise, shipbuilding companies faced with a recession of markets may branch out into the production of caravans or hovercraft. The success of these innovations will depend on whether the companies concerned can command the managerial skills needed to direct new enterprises. This is particularly important if existing facilities are being used for some new purpose under the operation of the same personnel; but it also applies if diversification is being carried out by acquiring existing going concerns. A new company is not faced with the problem of reconciling its past inheritance with future opportunities, but it is not without its difficulties. Tradition may be no drag but its own experience is no guide.

Larger companies try to combine experience with innovation. One of the express functions of management is to seek new profitable opportunities, and new subsidiary companies, controlled by experienced managers, may be formed to exploit new ideas. Research and development may be given great emphasis with the intention of assuring the company's future by developing new products. Thus, some of the functions of the entrepreneur may be built into the company structure.

FACTORS CONTRIBUTING TO SUCCESS

The margin between success and failure in industry is narrow: it is unusual to make a profit of more than 10 per cent on the value of turnover. There is no safe margin in which the inefficient firm can operate; and the efficient firm, at any given time, cannot afford to be complacent if new products or new production or sales methods start to narrow profit margins.

The cost structure will vary from firm to firm even within the same industry; and when firms are located in different countries the differences may be considerable. A careful study of all the factors affecting costs is desirable before a decision is taken to start production. Location is one of these factors. In some circumstances it is important; it is impossible to mine coal where coal does not exist and difficult to grow bananas cheaply in this country. For industries processing large quantities of material transport cost may be significant (we discuss the factors relevant to the location of a strip mill in Chapter VI); but very few production activities are confined to a very limited choice of site such as the availability of some natural resource might imply. Other factors affecting costs may be more important, such as the cost or available supply of labour, for instance. There is more chance of getting labour in Northern Ireland than in the Midlands. But centres of population are both a source of labour and a potential market. When productive activities are not tied to one spot they tend to gravitate to centres of population where modern social organization is facilitated by the economies that result from large-scale organization. It is here that companies can cxpect to find the ancillary facilities that they and the people that work for them require. The precise location of a factory, so long as it is near to some centre of population, is often of little moment. But whenever it appears that location can affect costs by even 1 per cent it becomes a factor that must be taken into account. High costs, cheaper power, and handy source of raw materials from some other industry may all tip costs one way or the other.

There is a certain presumption that the successful company will often be large. There are many products that can be made economically or even best on a small scale, but often it is much cheaper to produce in large quantities. A jute mill can be small; but popular cars, many chemicals and even ships are produced much more cheaply in quantity than in small measure.

TAKING DECISIONS

We are not concerned to dwell in this chapter on the wider aspects of location, scale of operations, specialization or division of labour as they affect economic organization. What we wish to stress about them is that whenever a firm has a choice in these matters, it should attempt to decide between alternatives by calculation; it is not enough to list the factors that affect any given situation; it is also necessary to take the further step of assessing their quantitative importance.

It is sometimes thought that in business the 'hunch' or flair of particular individuals is more important than mundane analytical processes. In part the hunches of individuals are probably conclusions reached by analytical processes that are never written down and perhaps scarcely understood, but nevertheless very similar to the systematic analysis of business problems that we advocate in this book. Where it has been possible to compare the application of rule-of-thumb and analytical solutions to problems, the comparison is generally in favour of analysis.

A typical problem in business is that of attempting to establish the market potential that exists. If absolutely nothing can be discovered about sales potential, production in advance of sales is no more than a gamble. In many cases, however, the range of possibilities can be reduced. An understanding of the motives that make people buy, market surveys and a knowledge of the likely strategy of competitors can help to narrow the range of uncertainty about future sales. Thus, the collection and analysis of information can help the managerial decision and increase its reliability. Sometimes it is possible to solve a problem by experiment. An appraisal of market possibilities can be made by conducting, say, a limited sales campaign in one area and an appropriate strategy can be chosen for the country on the basis of the results observed, if necessary supplemented by further tests. In Chapter X we illustrate also how experiments can be conducted on paper to solve certain problems without the need of lengthy and perhaps inconclusive experiments on the ground. In these ways, appropriate analytical techniques can help to reduce some of the uncertainties in business decisions. But uncertainties remain. The further we look ahead the more difficult it becomes to prepare a reliable forecast. And it is not only in the long term that uncertainties enter into business calculations: the price that it is decided to charge for some product may often depend on the price that powerful competitors are likely to charge and this may be undetermined; and many other uncertainties arise and require appropriate decisions to be taken. Suppose the caterers for a cricket match have to choose between preparing tea for a large or a small number of persons when the number expected depends on the weather. The weather forecast may give some indication of what is likely to happen but if decisions have to be put into effect some time in advance the forecasts may not be sufficiently reliable. If it rained, the demand for refreshments would be small and the risk of wasted food considerable; it it kept fine, the demand for refreshments might be high and profits from catering large. If insurance is ruled out, the choice of strategy in such conditions may be largely a matter of personal preference. Some might prefer to play safe and cater for a minimum number and safe profits; others might prefer to take a chance and cater in the hope of fine weather and large profits, with, however, the prospect of substantial losses if the outcome were rain; still others might adopt a middle strategy which, having regard to the incidence of rain on previous occasions, would result on the average in maximum profits over a number of years.

Here again a survey of the facts and the alternatives would help in enabling a decision to be taken but the outcome would be uncertain resting on unknown factors that are not individually predictable. Because the outcome of all business decisions is uncertain in some measure, it is a good plan to make some provision for alternative outcomes; to keep arrangements flexible when this is possible; to spread risks in some measure; and to devise plans that do not hinge entirely on one set of possible circumstances.

This does not mean that all business decisions must be constantly reconsidered. Many of them may be of a nature that takes into account the effects of unforeseen changes. Controls that provide for the level of stocks to be related to production will automatically adjust stocks to varying rates of output. The appropriate action to be taken when sales increase may also be built into the standing orders under which the firm operates. Some problems may occur so repeatedly that the solution to them is known, even though the outcome is uncertain, and the course of action to be taken in response to them can be prescribed as a matter of routine. Problems that once taxed the imagination, experience and judgment of senior managers can be reduced by mathematical techniques to matters of routine decision. Once such techniques are prescribed the problems with which they were designed to deal pass largely out of the field of managerial decision, and even though they are of quite basic importance to the success of the business they can be related to the same class as minor decisions that can be left to subordinates and do not require consideration or authorization by the board of directors or the higher echelons of management.

A great many issues cannot be resolved in this way. New situations arise that cannot be covered by routine instructions and a fresh evaluation is needed. Basic studies must be started to establish the dimensions of the problem and see what elements of it can be decided by analysis; to determine the extent of uncertainties; and to decide the strategies that are necessary to deal with uncertain outcomes. The whole object of such basic studies is to reduce the area of uncertainty and guess-work in business decisions. Better and more complete knowledge skilfully analysed is one means of minimizing the risk of many decisions and by so doing introducing a greater element of certainty into business operations.

The board of directors will be asked to take a great many decisions during a year and many issues will come up for examination. Some of the work of the board will be routine consideration of regular matters. But from time to time it will be necessary to consider the outlook for the whole of the firm's operations and to consider its prospects. Such an examination may be confined to considering the likely outcome of operations as they are currently planned or it may be more radical, setting new objectives for the firm, and exploring future opportunities for the business. This might start with a review of sales prospects and the measures necessary to effect an improvement. A tentative decision might be taken to aim at greatly increased sales. But such decisions cannot be maintained irrespective of the conduct of the rest of the company's affairs. A decision to increase sales must be related to increased production possibilities, financial requirements and cost functions. The process of decision can start with the consideration of any aspect of a firm's operations but it must complete the process by considering them all and their interrelations. It is not just a question of co-ordinating activities, but of co-ordinating the plan itself and testing its validity.

THE PLAN OF THE BOOK

In the following chapters we look at the various factors that are relevant to this integrated view of a firm's operations. We discuss the various issues from the point of view of an economist concerned to relate the means at a firm's disposal to the objectives it has set itself and the policies that it can follow to achieve these objectives. We are concerned with business policy, not with the execution of this policy, which requires consideration from a different point of view. Although we have stressed the need for different facets of business policy to be properly integrated, it is seldom possible to consider a complicated problem without breaking it down into its component parts. Clear thinking requires that the main elements of a problem are given individual consideration. Only after this has been done is it possible to consider the problem as a whole and provide a properly integrated solution.

In the rest of this part of the book we consider some major elements in business decisions. In Chapter II we consider the main factors that affect the demand for a product and examine the influence of price and sales promotion on the volume of business done. In Chapter III we consider the nature of the production process, some of the practical issues involved in it, and productivity and costs. Chapter IV takes up the related but wider issue of price determination and effects a reconciliation between the views of economists and business practice. The nature of profits is examined in Chapter V and discussed in relation to the use of profits to expand the business in this chapter and in discussion of the investment decision and the financial decision in Chapter VI and VII.

The aim of the last three chapters is to suggest ways in which the principles discussed earlier can be given quantitative content. The level of discussion is elementary, concerned more with demonstrating that policies can be based on available figures than with attempting to place the tools to do this in the reader's hand. The handling of figures needs some mathematical techniques and very often considerable experience and it is not possible to impart these in a short introductory study. Chapter VIII considers what is meant by control, and goes on to explain how planning can be used to make control effective; Chapter IX explains how forecasts can be made, discusses the errors to which they are liable and gives some examples of good and bad forecasting results. When decisions have to be taken about the future, action has to be based on some view of what may happen, and it is important to try to make forecasts as reliable as is consistent with the expense of increasing their accuracy. Forecasts or assumptions about the course of future events that prove to be badly out are costly because they result in bad decisions. Chapter X rounds off the picture by illustrating how mathematical techniques can be used to throw light on a number of business decisions and to improve the quality of decision taking.

Chapter II

DEMAND AND MARKETS

It is a truism that one of a businessman's first decisions is that which he makes about the market for his product—few would manufacture a product unless they assumed (if no more) that there was a demand for it—but frequently the decision to produce is taken without forming any proper or sensible assumption about demand and markets, let alone undertaking any analysis of them. Economic theory can illuminate several of the major practical problems connected with markets.

There are four significant managerial aspects of demand; first is the analysis and forecasting of demand; second is the effect which demand may have on the organization and activities of the firm; third is the influencing of demand (or the ways in which demand may be affected by the actions of the businessman); fourth is marketing, or the positive approach to the meeting or satisfaction of demand. The first and second may be called the passive managerial aspects of demand because they represent factors which influence the firm; and the third and fourth the active aspects because they represent factors which the firm itself can influence.

The object of this chapter is to look at demand in general, to analyse the factors affecting demand, and the impact of demand and markets on the behaviour of the firm; and to proceed from this to an examination of the ways in which demand may be assessed, influenced, and eventually met.

1. DEMAND

Forecasting, which is examined in some detail in Chapter IX implies first of all some knowledge of the factors likely to affect demand in any given situation: theory, or application of principles, must precede any practical analysis of a situation if the analysis is to be of any value. In a general way many of these factors are fairly obvious: incomes and tastes of buyers, prices, the availability of substitutes, credit facilities, advertising —all of these clearly have some influence on demand, and even an intuitive 'hunch' about the market for a product contains an implicit consideration of these factors. It is worth while to identify them and look at them in more detail.

THE DETERMINANTS OF DEMAND

In practice demand is determined simultaneously by a whole complex of variables, and it is frequently not realistic to consider any one in isolation; but it is convenient for purposes of analysis to simplify the problem by considering each main factor in isolation, assuming that the others remain constant. At the back of many complaints about the lack of realism of economics is either a failure to realize that this assumption is being made (often implicitly), or an argument that such assumptions *in themselves* invalidate the analysis. In fact such assumptions are only made in order that the economist may concentrate on one factor at a time and become clear in his mind about the effect of this factor in isolation (which is exactly what the physicist or chemist does): from there on there is no logical difficulty (though there are frequently several practical difficulties) in generalizing the arguments to include more variables than one; and, indeed, most demand forecasts, whether verbally or numerically expressed, do take account of several variables, even though in practice the significant variables may prove to be few. An example, quoted in the discussion of forecasting, is the forecast of the demand for motor vehicles,[1] which is closely related to disposable income and stock of cars.

Prices and the Demand Curve

In a discussion of factors affecting demand, the price of a commodity is usually the first to come to mind. The simplest expression of a demand relationship is the *Demand Curve*, which demonstrates the relation between the price of a commodity and the quantity of it bought; and is really only a simple graph derived from a demand schedule, as in Fig. 2.1 and Table 2.1. On the vertical axis is shown the price of the commodity, and on the horizontal axis the quantities of the commodity bought at the various prices.

[1] See Chapter IX. The effects of changes in price and hire purchase regulations were also analysed, but 'neither of these factors contributed significantly to (the) explanation'. 'Prospects for the British Car Industry', *National Institute Economic Review* (September, 1961).

TABLE 2.1

DEMAND SCHEDULE FOR TEA*

Price per lb (*pence*)	*Quantity consumed* (*000 cwt*)
20	4000
21	3865
22	3775
23	3700
24	3650
25	3600
26	3550
27	3510
28	3475
29	3438
30	3405
31	3380
32	3356
33	3332
34	3315
35	3300

* This demand schedule covers approximately the same range of prices and quantities consumed as those in an empirical study of demand discussed later (R. Stone, *The Measurement of Consumers' Expenditure and Behaviour in the United Kingdom, 1920–1938* (Cambridge University Press, 1954)). This lends verisimilitude to the data, but it must be stressed that the observations themselves are not those of Stone's study.

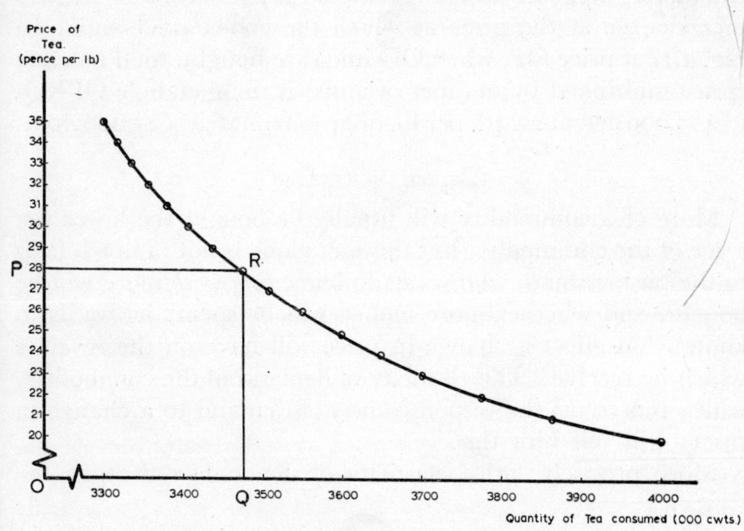

Figure 2·1. Demand Curve for Tea.

Typically the demand curve slopes downwards to the right, indicating that the lower the price the more of a commodity is bought; and this accords fairly well with general experience. There are cases, as of luxury, or 'conspicuous consumption' goods, where demand falls as prices fall, and other unusual cases,[2] but these are exceptions and are easily accounted for; in general the downward sloping demand curve is accepted as portraying reality for most practical purposes, and is the form normally used as a tool of analysis. A demand curve can, of course, be almost any shape, from a straight line to the most complicated of irregular curves, but whatever the shape it is a picture of the relationship between the price of and demand for the commodity and as such it serves a useful purpose.

By demand economists always mean effective demand, or demand backed by the ability to pay as distinct from a vague desire to possess a commodity. The demand curve therefore represents the curve of *average revenue* per unit sold by the producers of the commodity; and the price paid per unit of the commodity is the revenue received per unit of the commodity. In this sort of demand diagram the total revenue (or total consumers' outlay) from the purchase of a number of units of a commodity appears as the rectangle subtended under the demand curve at the price at which the goods are bought. In Fig. 2.1, at price OP, when OQ units are bought, total revenue (price multiplied by number of units) is the rectangle OPRQ. (3,475,000 cwt at 2s. 4d. per lb, or approximately £45,400,000).

Elasticity of Demand

More of a commodity will usually be bought the lower the price of the commodity, but this fact alone is not of much help to the businessman, who wants to know *how much* more will be bought, and whether more money will be spent: he wants to know what effect a change in price will have on the revenue which he receives. The elasticity of demand of the commodity, which represents the responsiveness of demand to a change in price, will tell him this.

More precisely, price elasticity of demand[3] represents the

[2] See p. 35.

[3] This concept—usually referred to as 'point' elasticity of demand—applies only to small changes round a defined point on the demand curve, although the point may be located anywhere on the curve.

proportionate change in demand resulting from a small change in price, and is measured by the formula:

$$\text{elasticity of demand} = \frac{\text{relative change in quantity purchased}}{\text{corresponding relative change in price}}$$

$$\text{or, symbolically: } e = \frac{\frac{dq}{q}}{\frac{dp}{p}} = \frac{dp.p}{dp.q}$$

where q = quantity purchased
p = price of commodity
dq = small change in quantity purchased
dp = small change in price

The response of demand for a commodity to a change in the price of the commodity involves two steps. The first (the 'income effect') is due to what may be thought of as a change in the real income of the consumer: if money income remains constant and the price of a commodity is reduced, the real income or purchasing power of the consumer is thereby increased, because his money goes further. The income effect may be positive or negative: if negative, demand for a commodity falls as its price rises; if it is positive the demand for a commodity will increase as the price of it rises. A positive 'income effect' may occur in the case of so-called 'inferior' goods: a large proportion of the income of peasants in the Far East is spent on rice, which is cheap and filling, and there is little left for other foodstuffs; if the price of rice increases the peasant may become so poor that he cannot afford any of the other foods and will buy even more rice simply in order to fill his stomach. The second step (the 'substitution effect') is due to the substitution which takes places between one commodity and other commodities when the price of the first commodity changes; this is always negative and a fall in the relative price of a commodity leads to an increase in the demand for it. Normally the substitution effect dominates and the demand for a commodity increases as its price falls.

Thus the numerical value of price elasticity of demand is usually negative; but it is fairly common practice to ignore the sign and to speak in terms of positive values.

Five interesting cases of elasticity may be distinguished: the first two are limiting cases, which it would be difficult to imagine in real life; the third is also rather unlikely, but conceivable, the fourth and fifth are typical of the whole range of possibilities within these limits.

1. *Completely inelastic demand* ($e = 0$)

This is the case where, regardless of changes in price, there is no change in quantity demanded and consumed, and total revenue changes solely in accordance with and in direct proportion to price. A completely inelastic demand curve may be represented diagrammatically as a vertical straight line, as DDi in Fig. 2.2a. This is a case which is most unlikely to be found in practice, but it is possible to conceive of a case in a very primitive society with one staple food (e.g. rice or bread), where over a very wide range of prices the demand for the staple food remained constant.

2. *Completely elastic demand* ($e = \infty$)

A completely elastic demand, represented diagrammatically by a horizontal straight line as DDi in Fig. 2.2b, is the case where any increase in price, however small, causes demand for the product to cease entirely. Although this is unlikely in practice for any commodity in total, many firms are in practice faced with something like a perfectly elastic demand for their product: they produce goods in the knowledge that there is in the market a ruling price for their product which may be fixed by custom, competition or possibly even by government regulation, to which they must conform if they are to sell anything. This may well occur in the case of easily standardized agricultural goods, such as eggs or milk, and in real life the producers of such goods are frequently faced with a completely elastic demand. If they raise their price above the ruling price, no one will buy from them and demand for their product ceases entirely; if they reduce their price they will attract the whole of the demand to them (though they would be unable to satisfy it).

3. *Unitary elasticity of demand* ($e = 1$) (or $e = -1$)[4]

An elasticity of demand equal to unity is most easily conceived as the case where, for any change in price, total revenue

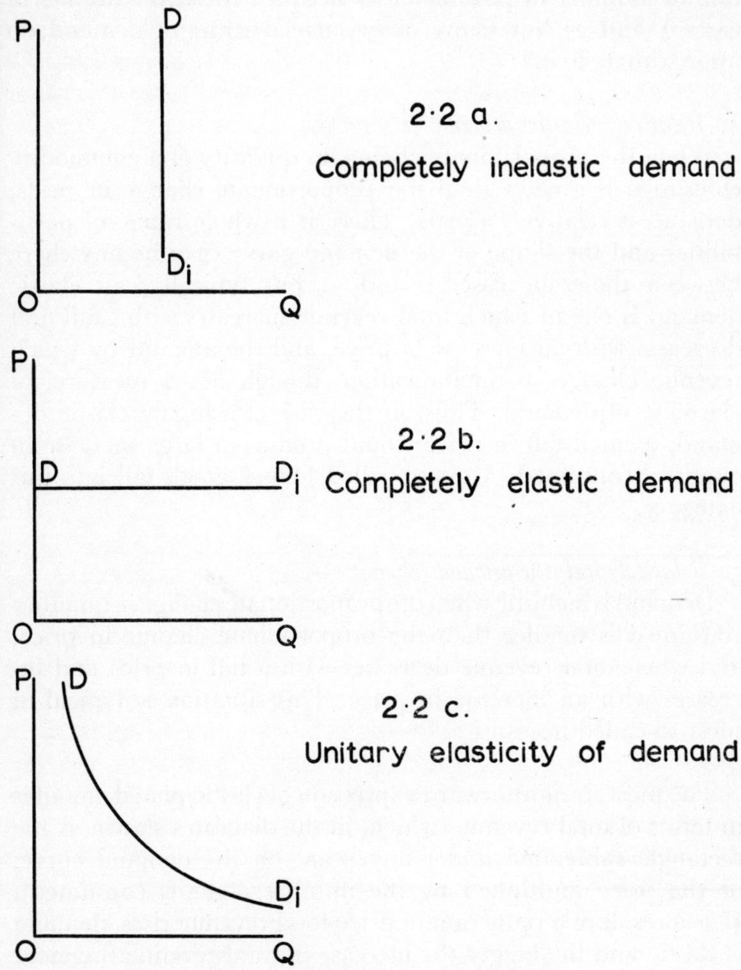

Fig. 2·2. Cases of Elasticity of Demand.

remains constant and demand changes absolutely in proportion to the change in price. This may be represented diagrammatically, as in Fig. 2.2c, as a rectangular hyperbola—a curve in

[4] See p. 36.

which the rectangle subtended under the curve is of constant area. To meet this precise case in real life, though perfectly possible, is improbable, because it represents merely one of an infinite number of possible cases between the two extremes of cases 1 and 2; but many observed elasticities of demand do approximate to it.[5]

4. *Relatively elastic demand* ($e > 1 < \infty$)

When the proportionate change in quantity of a commodity consumed is greater than the proportionate change in price, demand is relatively elastic. There is a whole range of possibilities and the shape of the demand curve may be anywhere between those for cases 2 and 3; but typically, an elastic demand is one in which total revenue increases with a fall and decreases with an increase in price, and the amount by which revenue changes is an indication, though not a measure, of elasticity of demand. Thus, in the case of a highly elastic demand, a small fall in price would produce a large increase in quantity consumed. Most so-called luxury goods fall into this category.

5. *Relatively inelastic demand* ($e > 0 < 1$)

Demand is inelastic when the proportionate change in quantity consumed is smaller than the proportionate change in price, and when total revenue decreases with a fall in price and increases with an increase in price. This situation is typical of most so-called necessities.

The most straightforward expression of elasticity of demand is in terms of total revenue (which, in the diagrams shown, is the rectangle subtended under any point on the demand curve, or the price multiplied by the number of units consumed). If as a result of a reduction in price total revenue rises, demand is elastic and the bigger the increase in total revenue the more elastic is demand; if total revenue falls demand is inelastic. In practice this may, of course, be difficult to determine, because some other factors may also affect demand at the same time as the price change; but it is the change in total revenue which interests the businessman.

[5] See Table 2.4.

The Importance of Elasticity of Demand

The examples given above are all simplified,[6] but are useful in that they indicate what economists mean when they talk about elasticity of demand. All businessmen would be expected to know something about the likely effect of price changes on the demand for their product, even though they would rarely express their knowledge in terms of elasticity of demand; but it is noticeable to the outside observer that several business decisions (particularly about the price of products) seem to ignore the elasticity of demand for the product. Chapter IV treats the theory of pricing policy in much more detail than is appropriate here, but in general it is quite clear that prices are not determined exclusively by either demand or costs; yet many changes in price appear to be made with purely cost considerations in view. When costs are rising, it is tempting to try to pass on the cost increases by increasing price to the consumer, and if demand for the product is relatively inelastic, this measure may well succeed; but when, as for example in the case of rail transport, there are many substitutes and the demand is relatively elastic, increasing prices may well lead to a reduction of total revenue rather than an increase, and increasing prices may well be the wrong answer. Similarly many businessmen are surprised by the apparent lack of success of price reductions, which may well indicate an inelastic demand for the product.

It is not necessary to labour this point further; most businessmen intuitively know something about the elasticity of demand for the goods which they make, and base their pricing policy on some notion of elasticity. Several do not, of course, behave in this way, and make the wrong decisions, and the remedy for them is obvious; but what is important is not so much to know

[6] Strictly it is not permissible to speak of the demand for any product as elastic or inelastic in total: at very low prices the demand for most products, even for luxury goods, is inelastic; at very high prices the demand for most goods, including necessities, is elastic. Formally elasticity of demand is different at each part of the demand curve: the only case in which elasticity of demand is constant at all parts of the curve is that where the curve is a hyperbola, the simplest case of this being the rectangular hyperbola, where $e = 1$.

The most that can usually be said of the demand for a commodity is that its demand is elastic or inelastic at prices around those which have been general in the market; but since it is in this range of prices that most decisions will be made, and very large price variations are not common features of business policy it is usually sufficiently accurate for practical purposes to talk of elasticity of demand without specifying the price range to which the statement refers.

vaguely that demand for a product is elastic, as to try to form as precise an idea as possible of the *degree* of elasticity of demand. The concept of elasticity of demand is useful because it is a convenient shorthand way of expressing the effects of price changes on the demand for a commodity and as such is relevant to price fixing.

Estimation of the demand curve and measurement of elasticity of demand are by no means easy, but as will be seen they are possible;[7] and the more that the businessman knows about the elasticity of demand for his products, the easier it is for him to make decisions about pricing and other aspects of policy.

But prices are not the only things which affect demand. The demand curve is an apparently simple device, and price elasticity of demand is an indispensable concept; but a great deal underlies both of them. When other things change and the other things being equal (or *ceteris paribus*) assumption no longer holds, the demand curve may change, either in shape or location (the latter being known as a shift in the demand curve) and the entrepreneur is faced with a new situation. This is because other determinants of demand are having their effect; this may be due either to the actions of the firm itself (as in the case of advertising) or to outside causes (such as changes in tastes, incomes of consumers, etc.). It is frequently convenient in practice merely to take note of the fact that such changes have occurred and that a new demand curve now faces the businessman; but we really need to know rather more about these other determinants, and, indeed, intelligent demand forecasting requires that we do so in order that policy may be adjusted to the new situation.

Incomes and Income Elasticity of Demand

Demand for a commodity is also affected by the incomes of the people likely to buy it.[8] At times of general prosperity, when incomes are high and unemployment is low, the demand for such commodities as motor cars[9] is likely to be high, but to fall off rapidly, regardless of price changes, when incomes fall. In the case of such commodities, it is frequently the case that

[7] See p. 45-50.
[8] See also discussion of 'income' effect of change in price, p. 35.
[9] See Chapter IX, p. 277.

income elasticity of demand, which represents the *responsiveness of demand to changes in income* is more important than price elasticity. There have been several examples of this in Great Britain since the war—mostly in the field of consumer durable goods—and with some products (refrigerators and second-hand cars are good examples), even when prices have been falling rapidly demand has continued to fall away. These examples have usually occurred in times of restraint, credit squeezes and other periods when the Government has been trying to reduce the level of activity and demand; indeed, one of the objects of such credit restraint is to reduce the size of disposable incomes and hence to reduce the demand for commodities which have a high income elasticity of demand. In general, goods which are looked on as luxuries tend to have a high income elasticity of demand, and the purchase of these goods is readily postponable when disposable incomes falls. There have been several interesting examples of the effect of income elasticity of demand for British exports: when there have been recessions in the United States, and when incomes were low, the demand for British exports in the U.S.A. has fallen off; and in general the demand for many British exports (motor vehicles, whisky, capital goods, etc.) is income elastic, and the volume of British exports depends very much on prosperity overseas.

Income elasticity of demand is frequently more important than price elasticity of demand in determining the volume of goods sold. The relationship between demand and income variations is not always straightforward: much will depend on the suddenness or permanence of a change in income, and there is frequently a lag between changes in income and changes in demand; it takes time to plan changes, some commitments, such as hire purchase repayments, may remain fixed, and old consumption habits tend to die hard, particularly if a change in income is only expected to be temporary.

Substitutes and Cross Elasticity of Demand

The existence of substitutes is another important factor affecting demand, and in fact price elasticity of demand may be looked on to some extent as an indication of the existence or otherwise of satisfactory substitutes for the commodity.

If satisfactory substitutes exist, and price is raised, demand will be transferred to the substitutes: and commodities with many substitutes are usually found to have a rather high price elasticity of demand. Thus the demand for margarine depends very much on the price of butter, for which margarine is a close substitute in many uses; the demand for chocolates as a whole may be rather inelastic, but the demand for a particular brand may be very elastic simply because there are several close substitutes. The substitutes need not be obvious: for example, gardening may well be a substitute for the ownership of a motor car, and the demand for more cars may, within certain limits, be affected by the availability of houses with gardens; but most substitutes are more easily recognized than that, and the substitutes with which many business decisions are concerned are the products of competitors. Cross elasticity of demand is a useful measure of the relationship between the demands for two commodities, or their substitutability, and may be defined as:

$$\text{Cross elasticity of demand} = \frac{\text{relative change in quantity of X}}{\text{relative change in price of Y}}$$

where X and Y are commodities, and where the price of commodity X is kept constant.

A similar concept is that of 'share elasticity'[10] or 'market share' elasticity of demand, which relates an individual firm's share of the total market sales of a commodity to the difference between its prices and general market prices. Sales of detergent X, for example, are likely to fall if the price of detergent Y in the same market falls. Other factors affecting demand, such as incomes, advertising, tastes, etc., may also have their relevant 'share' elasticities.

Since the businessman is not merely concerned with total market demand for his product, but also with how much *he* can expect to sell, the relationships between the demand for his product and that for its substitutes is clearly of some importance to him. An interesting example of the importance of substitution

[10] See, for example, Joel Dean, *Managerial Economics* (Prentice Hall, 1957). The only real difference between the two concepts is that cross elasticity refers to the response of total demand (or absolute sales) to a change in the price of a substitute whereas share elasticity refers to the response of one firm's share of the market.

is the market for fuels in the United Kingdom (see Table 2.2): the total demand for coal has been decreasing since 1951, but to compensate for the drastic fall in its direct use there has been an increasing consumption of coal in the generation of electricity. At the same time, however, consumption of oil has almost trebled during the period, and is being increasingly used in the generation of electricity and gas manufacture (both formerly the province of coal). Consumption of nuclear and hydro electricity and natural gas has increased, fairly slowly during the 1950s, but this trend can be expected to accelerate.

TABLE 2.2

INLAND FUEL CONSUMPTION ANALYSED BY TYPE OF FUEL

	Million tons of coal equivalent	
	1951	*1961*
Coal and coal-derived fuels		
Coal (direct use)	118.3	84.4
Coke and breeze	30.1	29.4
Electricity	36.5	56.2
Gas	18.7	16.6
Other fuels	2.5	3.2
Total coal	206.2	190.0
Oil and oil-derived fuels		
Oil (direct use)	23.8	59.6
Electricity	0.1	9.3
Gas	0.9	2.0
Total oil	24.8	70.9
Nuclear and hydro-electricity and colliery methane	1.0	3.5
TOTAL	232.0	264.3

Source: *Economic Trends* (August 1962), Table 2, p. iii (published for the Central Statistical Office by H.M.S.O.).

In general, the demand relationship between two commodities may be of two kinds: competing or complementary. If the demand for two commodities is competing, which is to say they are substitutes (e.g. lamb and beef), if one (lamb) falls in price, this will lead to a decrease in the demand or a fall or shift to the left in the demand curve for the other (beef); and, in general, demand for any commodity will move in the same direction as the price of its substitutes. Complementary goods, such as motor cars and petrol, are in the opposite relationship—

if the demand for one falls, so will the demand for the other; and if the price of motor cars rises there will be a reduction in the demand for petrol. In general, the demand for a commodity moves in the opposite direction to the price of its complementary goods.

Tastes and Preferences

One of the fundamental determinants of demand for most non-necessary goods is the taste or preference of the consumer. There are certain basic needs, such as a certain calorie intake of food, some warmth, some clothing, some shelter, but there are several ways of satisfying these needs, and given his income the consumer's preferences or tastes frequently determine in what form he will buy the goods to meet these needs. These tastes are usually shaped by the kind of society in which we live, and in which part of that society: housing 'needs', for example, depend very much on professional and 'class' status, clothing needs usually far exceed the minimum necessary for warmth. One of the tasks of market research must be to find out something about this society and the effects which it has on demand. Further, the businessman can influence tastes and preferences, mainly by advertising, and in the second part of this chapter we look more closely at ways in which tastes and demand may be affected by the actions of the businessman.

Some Empirical Findings

To sum up the discussion so far, the main factors likely to influence demand in a given situation are: the price of the commodity, the price of its substitutes, the price of complementary goods, the incomes of consumers, and the tastes and preferences of consumers; and demand will change as one or any combination of these factors changes or is expected to change.[11]

[11] Theoretical economists have evolved neat ways of expressing the logic underlying demand theory, by the use of 'indifference curve' analysis and 'revealed preference' analysis. This sort of analysis conveniently summarizes the fact that, with a limited income and known prices, a consumer's demand is limited: he must, therefore, make a choice and he will have a system of preferences between commodities (these may be subconscious and not formalized in any way). He may substitute one commodity for another (if he is indifferent between them) and what he is in effect doing is maximizing the satisfaction which he receives from the expenditure of his income. All of the factors influencing demand can be consistently analysed by the use of this sort of technique; but the analysis is more of theoretical than practical interest and has been omitted from the present discussion. The interested reader will find this sort of analysis conveniently summarized in W. J. Baumol, *Economic Theory and Operations Analysis* (Prentice Hall, 1961) Chapter VIII.

This discussion is of much more than theoretical interest. One of the main practical interests of the businessman is the forecasting of the demand for his product, and good forecasts demand sound analysis of the factors underlying demand. Crude rules-of-thumb may appear satisfactory, and may be the only data available for quick decisions in many circumstances, particularly where many factors may be assumed (usually implicitly) to remain unchanged. An illustration[12] points the moral: the demand for electricity in Britain tends to be closely associated with population and as population increases the demand for electricity increases, but the main factors affecting the demand for electricity are probably consumers' incomes, the level of activity of the economy as a whole (and particularly those industries which are large users of electricity), the price of electricity, the price of substitutes, and the tastes of consumers (which may depend on incomes). If these factors remain in some unchanged relation to population, it will be possible to predict the demand for electricity by relating it to published projections of the trend of population, and this may well work and give a similar answer to a more sophisticated prediction based on analysis of the other factors. But if another factor changes (if, for example, in a slump incomes and activity fall, or if the price of gas falls considerably) a prediction based on population trends may go sadly astray while a prediction based on analysis of the other factors may be more accurate. It would certainly stand a better *chance* of being more accurate.

Valuable research has been done in recent years, in two main directions. Forecasts have been made of the demand for individual commodities,[13] and academic economists have also analysed many of the basic relationships affecting demand.

The most comprehensive survey in Britain was undertaken by the Department of Applied Economics of Cambridge University.[14] For a whole range of commodities (broadly food, drink, tobacco and fuels) it was possible to calculate three categories of elasticity of demand: income elasticity of demand; price elasticity of demand (or, more accurately, the substitution effect of a change in price[15]); and two main cross-elasticities

[12] This is a hypothetical case. [13] See Chapter IX.

[14] See R. Stone, *Measurement of Consumers Expenditure and Behaviour in the United Kingdom*, 1920–1938 (Cambridge University Press, 1954).

[15] See p. 35.

of demand (elasticity with respect to the price of certain related commodities, and with respect to all other prices). Table 2.3 gives an isolated example chosen at random.

Significant relationships were obtained from individual foods or food groups, which are summarized in Table 2.4.

TABLE 2.3

SOME CALCULATIONS OF THE ELASTICITY OF DEMAND FOR BUTTER, 1921–38

Income elasticity	0.37
Own price elasticity	−0.43
Substitution Elasticity with respect to:	
Flour price	−0.23
Margarine price	0.10
Cakes and biscuits price	0.59
Carcass meat price	0.56
All other prices	−0.58
Residual trend coefficient	0.04

Notes: This table gives the results of only one out of a number of sets of calculations made. On the calculations as a whole the author comments:

'A small but positive income elasticity is found. The own-price (substitution) elasticity is of a similar absolute magnitude and is significant, as also is the considerable upward trend. The use of butter in home cake making is reflected in the relationship of supplementarity with flour and of substitution with cakes and biscuits. Both coefficients are significant. A significant relationship of substitution with carcass meat is also found. There is evidence of a relationship of substitution with margarine, but the elasticity is small and it is not significant. This result is not surprising in view of the size of the substitution elasticity with respect to butter in the analysis of margarine and the smallness of the expenditure on margarine relative to that on butter.'

Source: Stone, op. cit., p. 334 and Table 106.

An older study[16] of the price elasticity of demand for agricultural products in the U.S.A. between 1915 and 1929 yielded the following measurements: sugar, 0.31; corn, 0.49; cotton, 0.12; hay, 0.43; wheat, 0.08; potatoes, 0.31; oats, 0.56; barley, 0.39; rye, 2.44; buckwheat, 0.99.

Another interesting study was recently made of the factors affecting the ownership of durable goods (specifically motor cars, television sets, washing machines, and refrigerators) in the United Kingdom.[17] Three non-economic factors were

[16] See H. Schultz, *Theory and Measurement of Demand* (University of Chicago Press, 1938), especially Table 49.

[17] J. S. Cramer, *The Ownership of Major Consumer Durables*, University of Cambridge Department of Applied Economics, Monograph No. 7 (Cambridge University Press, 1962).

considered—size of household, age of head of household and habitat (rural or urban)—and these affected ownership in different degrees. Washing machine ownership is related to size of family, motor car ownership to age and habitat,

TABLE 2.4

DISTRIBUTION OF FOOD ELASTICITIES, 1920–38

	Frequency of elasticities with respect to		
Range of elasticity	*Income*	*Own price (substitution)*	*Other specific prices (substitution)*
−2 to −1½	—	2	1
−1½ to −1	—	5	4
−1 to −½	1	16	5
−½ to 0	4	10	7
0 to ½	10½	3	15½
½ to 1	12½	—	13½
1 to 1½	2	—	7
1½ to 2	2	—	5
2 to 2½	—	—	2
2½ to 3	—	—	1
3 to 3½	—	—	1
TOTAL	32	36	62

The author comments:

'This table shows that the income elasticities for foodstuffs are predominantly positive and largely concentrated in the range 0–1. Of the thirty-two income elasticities in the table only five are negative and twenty-three lie in the range 0–1. In the case of the own-price (substitution) elasticities three, which are not significant, are positive and the remaining thirty-three are negative as in theory they should be. Of these no less than twenty-six lie in the range −1 to 0. The cross (substitution) elasticities shown in the last column of the table are spread, as might be expected, over a wide range. Relationships of substitution are more frequently observed than relationships of complementarity, since there are forty-five positive as against seventeen negative values. No less than twenty-nine values are found in the range 0–1. Thus food demand responses appear to be predominantly inelastic. Elastic responses both positive and negative are found, but they are comparatively infrequent.'

Source: Stone, op. cit., pp. 339–40 and Table 108.

television to size of family and habitat, but refrigerator ownership is not influenced by any of these factors. Two economic factors were also considered—income and net worth (or capital)[18] —and were found to have an effect on ownership, conveniently summarized respectively as income elasticity of demand (as

[18] Defined as the difference between the assets of a household (liquid assets, securities, house and property, unincorporated business value, car and loans) and its liabilities (overdraft mortgage, hire purchase debt and personal debts). Ibid., pp. 20–1.

defined earlier) and net worth elasticity of demand (which measures the responsiveness of demand to a change in net worth). Table 2.5 shows these two elasticities.

TABLE 2.5

THE DEMAND FOR CONSUMER DURABLE GOODS

Ownership of	*Income Elasticity*	*Net worth Elasticity*
Refrigerators	0.96	0.93
Washing machines	0.74	0.54
Motor cars	0.69	0.86
Television sets	0.50	0.33

Source: Cramer, *The Ownership of Major Consumer Durables* (Cambridge University Press, 1962).

Such analyses as these are full of pitfalls and require the use of sophisticated statistical techniques if they are to overcome the difficulty that all other things cannot be held to have been constant during the period of the observations. Controlled experiment is not easy with economic variables.

Thus, to take a simple example which typifies a fairly common sort of error, one could take the data of Table 2.6 and plot it on a graph as in Fig. 2.3. It would be tempting to say, then, that the line of best fit (AB—fitted freehand) represented the demand curve for this commodity: it may *possibly* do so; but equally the series of points on the graph, being observations for different years, may each be on different demand curves (for example CD, EF, GH, etc.), which represent the different conditions of individual years and may reflect (for example) changes in incomes, tastes, increasing number of substitutes, etc., which have caused the curves to shift.

But controlled experiments have been carried out which have yielded excellent results. Perhaps the best known of these was a study[19] of the short-term relationship between prices and sales of certain staple products over a period of 2½ months in a large American store. The details of this study are not needed here, but what is interesting is that the author of the

[19] R. H. Whitman, 'Demand Functions for Merchandise at Retail', in *Studies in Mathematical Economics and Econometrics*, edited by O. Lange (University of Chicago Press, 1924), pp. 210, 214.

TABLE 2.6

ESTIMATED PRICES AND QUANTITIES CONSUMED OF TEA, UNITED KINGDOM, 1920–38

Year	*Estimated average price (d. per lb)*	*Estimated quantity purchased (000 cwt)*
1920	34.50	3297
1921	31.00	3455
1922	28.75	3467
1923	30.50	3406
1924	28.75	3531
1925	29.25	3560
1926	29.25	3599
1927	28.75	3661
1928	29.00	3727
1929	25.75	3761
1930	23.75	3922
1931	22.25	3963
1932	21.00	3968
1933	21.50	3887
1934	23.25	3844
1935	23.50	3942
1936	24.75	3913
1937	26.00	3880
1938	27.50	3855

Source: Stone, op. cit., p. 151, Table 49.

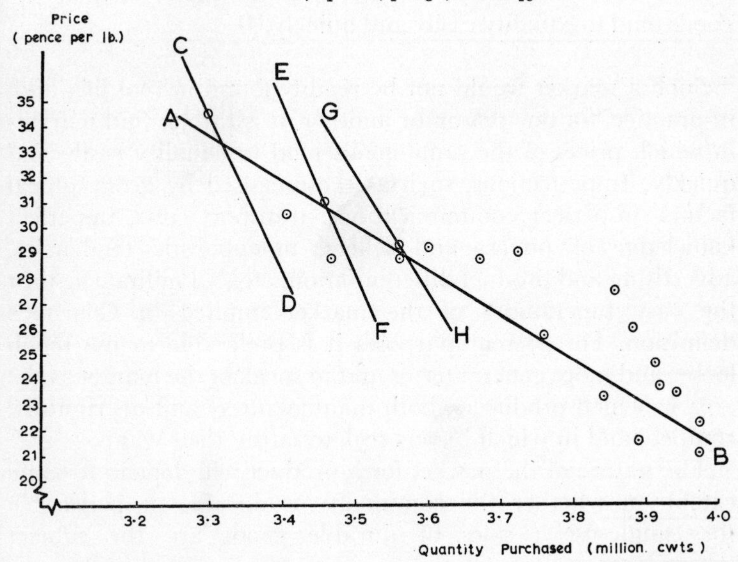

Figure 2·3.
Prices and Quantities Consumed of Tea. 1920 - 1938.

study was able to draw demand curves for the products; he chose demand equations representing curves of constant elasticity[20] which, when plotted on a graph with logarithmic scales on both axes, appear as straight lines.

II. MARKETS

It is time now to examine the more practical implications of demand, in the form of markets and what the businessman does about them. The marketing decision consists of the formulation of policy with the objective of selling the product. Successful policy depends on having the right information, analysing and interpreting it, and using this as a basis for courses of action.

For the rather specialized purposes of economic theory, economists have tended to adopt rigorous definitions of markets. For example:

> 'Economists understand by the term *Market*, not any particular market place in which things are bought and sold, but the whole of any region in which buyers and sellers are in such free intercourse with one another that the prices of the same goods tend to equality easily and quickly.'[21]

Such a market would not be readily found in real life, and, in practice, for one reason or another, it is rare to find markets in which prices of the same goods tend to equality easily and quickly. Imperfections, such as those caused by geographical factors, imperfect communications, transport costs, imperfect knowledge of buyers and sellers, monopolistic tendencies, advertising and product differentiation, etc., all militate against the easy functioning of the market implied in Cournot's definition. For present purposes it is preferable to use much looser and more general terms and to speak of the market as the area in which producers, both manufacturers and distributors, compete and in which buyers seek to satisfy their wants.

The nature of the market for a product will depend to some extent on whether the commodity is durable or perishable (or 'single-use'): sales of durable goods are the subject

[20] That is, hyperbolic demand functions, see footnote 6, p. 39.

[21] Cournot, *Recherches sur les Principes Mathematique de la Theorie des Richesses*, Chapter IV, quoted by Alfred Marshall, *Principles of Economics* (8th edn.) (Macmillan, 1920), p. 324.

of much more complex decisions by the buyer. The demand for most consumer durable goods is postponable and, in total, very volatile and dependent on fashion and changes in income.[22] Much of this sort of demand (particularly, for example, for motor cars) is a replacement demand, and the rate of replacement or depreciation depends on changes in fashion, the number of new models and so on. Technological change can produce sweeping changes in the demand for durables: the advent of the motor car fundamentally changed the whole demand for transport and transport facilities in all civilized countries, the invention of television had far-reaching effects on the demand for radio, cinemas, public houses and other forms of entertainment outside the home. And the demand for durable goods is very much a function of the credit facilities available. A high proportion of consumer durable goods are bought on hire purchase: it has been estimated that about 25 per cent of new cars and two-thirds of second-hand cars are bought on hire purchase; almost half of the sales of furniture and radio shops, and a quarter of the sales of cycle shops are on hire purchase terms.[23]

An analysis of the users of hire purchase provides a convenient illustration of some of the factors affecting the demand for this class of goods. Surveys carried out by the Oxford University Institute of Statistics provide some such information.[24] In 1953 22.5 per cent of all income units in a Savings Survey sample purchased durable goods costing £25 or more, and of these 43 per cent actually used hire purchase; in 1954 a quarter of all income units had hire purchase outstanding. The average amount of hire purchase outstanding was quite small (about £10 in 1955), but this amount has probably doubled since then. The middle-income ranges were the most frequent users of hire purchase—70 per cent of total hire purchase in the consumers' sector of the economy was held by people in the income range £400–£800 in 1953 (which probably corresponds roughly to the range £600–£1000 in the early 1960s), but such debt is becoming commoner in higher

[22] See pp. 40-41.

[23] The *Board of Trade Journal* publishes monthly statistics of hire purchase debt; the proportions quoted here are fairly typical of the 1950s and 1960s.

[24] K. H. Straw, 'Hire Purchase in the Consumer Sector', *The Bankers Magazine* (February and March, 1957).

income ranges (mainly for motor cars). Hire purchase is commonest in the age range 25–44 and is used most commonly by relatively young married couples with children. People living in rented accommodation accounted for over a quarter of the debt outstanding, but more and more people who are buying their houses on mortgage are contracting hire purchase debts. As would be expected, people with small liquid assets, bank deposits, savings certificates, etc., and with small wealth and capital were also the commonest users. Similar factors were found to be dominant in their influence on hire purchase in the U.S.A.'[25] but there nearly half of the total number of families owe money on hire purchase.

The importance of hire purchase is such that any changes in the regulations affecting hire purchase credit will radically affect the demand for consumer durable goods.[26] Similarly changes in the rates of purchase tax (or effectively in the selling price of the goods) will have a considerable effect, the extent of which will depend on the price elasticity of demand; and other credit restrictions (such as reduction of bank advances) will also have a large impact, acting as they do on the disposable incomes of consumers. The motor car industry is particularly sensitive to such changes in Government policy, but so, too, are the radio, electrical and furniture industries.

The distinction between derived and autonomous demand is of some importance, autonomous demand being demand for a commodity in its own right, derived demand being derived from the demand for something else (a large part of the demand for coal, for example, is derived from the demand for steel). Derived demand is usually more price inelastic than autonomous demand, partly because the cost of the producers' good usually only represents a small proportion of the price of the final product. The demand for steel for motor cars, which probably only accounts for about 10 per cent of the final cost of motor cars, would be little affected by, say, a 5 per cent increase in the price of steel, since this should only cause a 0.5 per cent increase in the cost of manufacturing motor cars.

[25] J. Lansing, S. Maynes and M. Kreinin, 'Factors Associated with the Use of Consumer Credit', *Federal Reserve Board Report on Consumer Instalment Credit* (Federal Reserve Board, Washington, D.C., 1957). See also *Federal Reserve Bulletin* (July, 1957).

[26] See F. R. Oliver, *The Control of Hire Purchase* (Allen & Unwin, 1961).

The distinction between derived and autonomous demand is often arbitrary—is the consumption of potato crisps partly derived from the consumption of beer?—but the assessment of demand in practice implies a recognition of the fact that it may be influenced by much more complex factors than are apparent at first sight.

There is also a distinction to be drawn between producers' and consumers' demand, though again, in practice, the distinction is not always easy to draw (is a salesman's car a producers' good or a consumers' good?) The demand for most producers' goods is derived from the demand for something else, and a demand forecast has to look more at the final product than the intermediate product. The demand for car headlamps and other motor vehicle accessories is obviously closely related to the demand for motor cars, and the manufacturer of components must look at the final demand when planning his production. It is often claimed that the demand for producers' goods is more rational that the demand for consumers' goods, since the motives for purchase are purely economic, products being bought for the profit prospects, not for themselves alone; and that the buyers are usually more expert. But it would not be difficult to make an impressive list of pieces of machinery which have been bought because of some fashion fad, some gimmick, 'keeping up with the Joneses', or high-pressure salesmanship (it is often argued that electronic computers come into this category); and although there is a lot of truth in this proposition it is by no means so self-evident as is frequently claimed. What is usually true, however, is that the demand for producers' goods (both for capital and current use) usually fluctuates more violently than the demand for consumers' goods[27]: this, again, is because such demand is derived from final demand and is subject to the lags between production and consumption.

The consumer has all sorts of motives for buying, and it is neither necessary nor desirable to list them all, but there is a distinction which is frequently made between so-called rational and irrational motives for choosing a particular product from the range available to the consumer. Rational motives might be defined as those which are influenced by the quality and

[27] See G. Haberler, *Prosperity and Depression*, p. 180, and W. Beveridge, *Full Employment in a Free Society* (Allen & Unwin, 1944) pp. 287–94.

price of the product and include considerations of durability, economy in operation, dependability of after-sales service, the desire to take advantage of low prices and so on (the so-called motives of 'economic man'). Irrational motives include 'keeping up with the Joneses', impulse buying, etc., and the term might even be stretched to include various emotional factors such as pride in appearance, fear of monotony and desire for individuality (the sort of motive which induces people to put fancy and operationally useless trimmings on their cars). These motives may well conflict, but the successful businessman is the one who best understands and caters for them: it is frequently argued that the market for consumer goods is much influenced by irrational motives.

Consumers also have their reasons, rational or irrational, for buying from particular suppliers: many housewives, for example, prefer to buy their groceries from the corner shop rather than from the supermarket where they may well be both cheaper and as conveniently bought, and they do so because they enjoy a chat with the local grocer or their neighbours. Buying *habits*, too, may influence demand: much buying of books, for example, is on impulse by people who happen to be in the shop, and the successful bookseller may well be the one who attracts the casual buyer by his display (successful marketing by the publisher may also involve choice of those sellers who cater for the impulse buyer). The railway bookstall, for example, caters almost entirely for the impulse and casual buyers, particularly for the lighter sorts of reading; the specialist, stock-holding bookseller caters for a different public but, like a supermarket, his sales may depend a great deal on having a wide variety of books on display to attract the casual purchaser.

These habits may change with time: the increase in the number of married women who go out to work has led to an increase in all types of buying by men, who now have to help with the shopping, and the best approach to selling to men is usually different from that needed for selling to women; urban and suburban populations have different buying habits from the population of villages, and the growth of the former group has brought about changes in marketing methods.

Structural or institutional factors may also have their effect. In Britain we have not yet approached the American level of supermarket selling, but the trend has been established,[28] and there are several differences between marketing *via* the small seller and the big supermarket. The lower costs of bulk distribution from the manufacturer or wholesaler to the supermarket are usually offset to a large extent by the demand of the latter for bigger discounts for bulk purchase, but these in turn are frequently compensated by bigger sales and economies of scale for the manufacturer. It has been estimated[29] that in the food trade it is possible for the supermarket to save one-third of the wage-bill of a counter grocery shop, and that it would be possible for supermarkets to do over two-thirds of a country's food trade. The small manufacturer, however, is frequently in a disadvantageous position in such circumstances since he has to accept the terms dictated by the big seller (who may be a monopsonist): several large chain stores in Britain owe their success in large part to the fact that they have been able to dictate terms to several manufacturers. It has been argued on the other hand, however, that 'Supermarkets, with their concentrated buying power, their competitive situations and their price flexibility, can be an important power on the side of the consumer, countervailing the power of the manufacturer, which is widely judged to be not only excessive but overweening ... they could do for the food shopper what Marks and Spencer have done for the clothes shopper'.[30] The attempts by groups of smaller retailers to achieve co-operatively what the supermarkets have achieved unilaterally in the purchasing field is another move in the direction of changing the structure of the retail trade.

Customs of the trade frequently determine the structure of markets, but these can be, and indeed often are, changed by a progressive approach to marketing.

To some extent also the nature of the marketing problem depends on the product itself; we have already noted the distinction between producers' and consumers' goods, but there is another distinction which cuts across these divisions. Some firms work entirely to specifications from other firms (who may be retailers or other manufacturers) and their marketing

[28] W. G. McLelland, 'Economics of The Supermarket', *Economic Journal* (March, 1962). There were eighty supermarkets in Britain in 1957, and 572 in 1961.
[29] Ibid. [30] Ibid.

problem is very largely a matter of securing a contract from customers; others concentrate on producing fairly standardized commodities (either for producers or consumers) which they then put on the market for sale after manufacture. In a report on the survey of small manufacturing firms carried out by the Oxford University Institute of Statistics, H. F. Lydall[31] commented on the differences between the two types of firm, which he called respectively *jobbers* and *marketers*, depending on whether they were predominantly engaged in the former or the latter activity. He found that, in the sample analysed, about half of the firms were jobbers, and half marketers; jobbers predominated in metal manufacture, engineering, wood products, and paper and printing; marketers predominated in bricks, concrete and glass, chemicals, textiles, clothing, and food and drink; there was also a tendency for the proportion of jobbers to be less amongst larger firms than smaller.

The nomenclature of the distinction is not particularly helpful in the present context, since it obscures the fact that both types of firms, in fact, have a marketing problem (a problem of getting their goods to buyers in the shape which they want); what does matter, however, is the timing of the marketing, and the effect which this has on the marketing decision. The jobber can to some extent adapt his productive process after he has received the order; the marketer has to find out about the market first (or take a guess); but all that this means is that the market analysis of the jobber is of a different nature from that of the marketer. One waits for the order before starting production, though he may stock up in anticipation of the renewal of an order; the other produces in advance of the order; but if the marketer finds out about his market first in an intelligent way there is little difference in the final analysis, since he knows what he has to make in much the same way as does the jobber, and, since he usually standardizes his product and production processes, he may have fewer production problems into the bargain. All that happens is that the proper assessment of demand replaces the firm order from someone else; and the function of market analysis is to minimize the difference between the two methods.

[31] H. F. Lydall, 'Aspects of Competition in Manufacturing Industry', *Bulletin of the Oxford University Institute of Statistics* (November, 1958).

The nature of the marketing problem also depends to some extent on the geographical distribution of markets and incomes. In Britain there is a tendency to concentrate intensive marketing in the large concentrations of population around London and in the Midlands (though the advent of television advertising has spread the net a little further.) Table 2.7 highlights the tendency for population to concentrate in these areas; one of the more frequently discussed problems of Britain in the present century (and particularly in the 1950s and 1960s) has been the

TABLE 2.7

GEOGRAPHICAL DISTRIBUTION OF POPULATION OF THE UNITED KINGDOM, 1911 AND 1955

	1911		*1955*	
Standard regions of England and Wales	*No. (000)*	*Per cent of total*	*No. (000)*	*Per cent of total*
Northern	2,815	6.7	3,160	6.2
East and West Ridings	3,564	8.5	4,114	8.1
North-Western	5,793	13.8	6,449	12.6
North-Midland	2,623	6.2	3,456	6.8
Midland	3,277	7.3	4,512	8.8
Eastern	2,106	5.0	3,316	6.5
London and South-Eastern	9,100	21.7	10,962	21.5
Southern	1,864	4.4	2,804	5.5
South-Western	2,507	6.0	3,073	6.0
Wales	2,421	5.6	2,603	5.1
Scotland	4,760	11.3	5,145	10.1
N. Ireland	1,251	3.0	1,397	2.7
TOTAL	42,082	100.0	50,968	100.0

Source: *Annual Abstract of Statistics, 1957*, p. 16, Table 14.

drift of population and industry to the Midlands and south-east of England. To some extent the table underestimates the shift in demand: since these are the prosperous areas of Britain, incomes and spending power are higher there than elsewhere.

Patterns of consumption also differ locally—haggis is rarely eaten and the kilt rarely worn outside Scotland, tripe and onions is still very much a north country dish—but these differences are tending to disappear in much the same way as dialects are tending to die out, largely because of the 'success' of mass media of communication.

And, of course, markets and consumers are never static. They may change because of changes in prosperity or incomes, or changes in tastes or preferences, or increasing competition: the coal industry, the cotton industry and the shipbuilding industry have all declined during the present century because of changes in the composition of demand; the motor industry, the electronics industry, chemicals and plastics have prospered. Or the changes may be more fundamental and due to changes in population, birth rates, marriage rates, age structure of the population, its geographical distribution and so on. Table 2.8 illustrates some of these changes: it shows that total population

TABLE 2.8

AGE AND SEX DISTRIBUTION OF POPULATION OF THE UNITED KINGDOM, 1901 AND 1955

	1901		*1955*	
	No. (000)	*Per cent of total*	*No. (000)*	*Per cent of total*
Male	18,492	48.4	24,523	48.2
Female	19,745	51.6	26,445	51.8
Age groups				
Under 5	4,382	11.5	3,851	7.5
5–9	4,105	10.7	4,283	8.4
10–19	7,762	20.3	6,816	13.4
20–29	6,981	18.2	6,654	13.1
30–39	5,328	13.9	7,171	14.1
40–49	4,002	10.5	7,508	14.7
50–59	2,801	7.3	6,408	12.6
60–69	1,808	4.8	4,618	9.0
70 and over	1,066	2.8	3,659	7.2
TOTAL	38,237	100.0	50,968	100.0

Source: *Annual Abstract of Statistics*, No. 94, 1957, Tables 6 and 7 (figures for 1955 are mid-year estimates)

in the United Kingdom has increased by approximately one-third since the beginning of the present century, the proportion of males and females remaining approximately the same; but the age distribution has changed considerably: 28.8 per cent of the population were over 50 years old in 1955, compared with 14.9 per cent in 1901; 29.3 per cent were under 20 in 1955, compared with 42.5 per cent in 1901. Marital conditions have changed as well: in 1901 there were about 11 million single males in the United Kingdom and 6½ million married males; in 1951 there were 11 million single males and over 12 million married ones.[32]

[32] *Annual Abstract of Statistics*, 1957, p. 14, Table 13.

In the foregoing pages we have discussed the nature of markets, their structure and factors influencing them. These represent the facts which face the marketer, whether he be manufacturer, wholesaler or retailer, and it is in relation to these facts that the businessman has to make his decisions about markets. What the businessman decides to do, and how he does it, are the subjects to which we now turn.

MARKETING

A lot of mystique attaches itself to the term *marketing*, and there are several text-books devoted exclusively to this aspect of business behaviour, but what these usually do is to spell out and describe in detail the principles and managerial aspects of demand referred to at the beginning of this chapter. Such exhaustive treatment is not possible in one chapter, but it is possible to isolate the significant principles of marketing. The details can be filled in from other sources: it is rather more helpful for present purposes to get away from the detail in order to see what marketing is about.

Marketing may be described as that part of business activity which is concerned with the assessment, manipulation and fulfilment of demand; it therefore includes all activities necessary to the end of putting goods in the hands of the consumer, and strictly excludes activities which involve a change in the goods themselves. Clearly, at some points the borderline between production and marketing must be indistinct: at what point does a change in design become a marketing rather than a production matter, for example? and the two functions do overlap (this usually results in arguments between the production and marketing sides of a firm).[33] In the final analysis both marketing and production are concerned with the meeting of demand; the difference between them is simply that they are specialized aspects of the process, and it is convenient to separate them for purposes of analysis.

[33] One of the major problems of many firms in real life is that of integration of the production and marketing functions, and frequently these two 'sides' of a firm pursue mutually inconsistent objectives to the detriment of the efficiency of the firm. For an example of such a process at work in a large British manufacturing company see James Bates and A. J. M. Sykes, 'Aspects of Managerial Efficiency', *Journal of Industrial Economics* (July 1962) and same authors 'A Study of Conflict Between Formal Company Policy and the Interests of Informal Groups'. *Sociological Review* (November, 1962).

It is often argued that marketing is unproductive and wasteful, since it adds nothing tangible to the product. It is true that much marketing activity is inefficient, that distribution is often conducted wastefully and that much of the effort and resources put into the manipulation of demand (detergent and cosmetic advertising are oft-quoted examples) could be put to better use; but this is also true of much manufacturing activity. In fact a certain amount of marketing activity is necessary to get the goods to consumers at all, and the creation of a market for goods is just as necessary as the production of them. Marketing adds value (or utility) to goods in the sense that it puts the goods where they are wanted when they are wanted;[34] and efficient marketing adds no more to the cost of goods than is necessary for the fulfilment of these functions.

It is not easy to get an accurate estimate of the total cost of marketing in a country. In Britain the *Census of Distribution* provides information about the cost of retailing and wholesaling; but there is little adequate information about a large part of the marketing process, which is undertaken by the manufacturers in the form of advertising, market research, payment of sales staff and so on.

An estimate was made in the U.S.A.[35] in 1948. In mining, quarrying, agriculture, manufacturing and construction the value added by production was 37.7 per cent of sales, value added by marketing was 8.9 per cent of sales. For the American economy as a whole (including retailing, wholesaling and transport) value added by production was 16.4 per cent of sales, value added by marketing was 15.2 per cent of sales. The marketing process as a whole accounted for about half the total value added.

For Britain information is available about value added by wholesale and retail trades and is summarized in Table 2.9 In retailing, the gross margin (or value added), was 22.2 per cent of total receipts, in wholesaling it was between 12 and 13 per cent of total receipts. These gross margins differ considerably from trade to trade and by size of firm; 'bread and flour

[34] This is analogous to the addition of value in the production process (see Chapter III, p. 94) and Chapter V.

[35] P. D. Converse, H. W. Huegy and R. V. Mitchell, *Elements of Marketing* (6th edn.) (Pitman, 1958). The percentages are worked out from data in Appendix A (p. 742).

confectioners with baking', with working proprietors and sales of over £100,000 had gross margins of 49.5 per cent of total sales; tobacconists had gross margins of only 9.2 per cent of sales; the former have a large manufacturing element in their sales, the latter are largely stockholders. Gross margins for the main retail and wholesale groups are summarized in Table 2.10.[36]

TABLE 2.9

THE STRUCTURE AND COSTS OF RETAIL AND WHOLESALE DISTRIBUTION IN THE UNITED KINGDOM, 1950

	Retail (£ million)	*Wholesale (£ million)*
Costs, etc.		
(1) Total receipts	4,941	9,444
(2) Purchases	3,918	8,295
(3) Increase in stocks	73	−20
(4) Cost of goods ((2) less (3))	3,844	8,315
(5) Gross margin, or value added ((1) less (4))	1,097	1,129
(6) Wages and salaries	(434)	(300)
Number of organizations and persons employed		
Number of organizations	404,845	43,533
Persons engaged	2,386,443	798,582
Working proprietors	555,650	43,169
Paid employees	1,830,793	755,413

Source: *Census of Distribution, 1950*, Vol. II, Tables 27 and 28; Vol. III, Tables 13 and 15.

There are approximately half a million retail and wholesale outlets in Britain, employing between them over 3 million people, 20 per cent of whom are working proprietors. Grocery and the food trades account for about a third of total retail sales and 47 per cent of the number of retail organizations. The biggest gross margins are in the service trades, in which purchases are a relatively small proportion of total costs, and

[36] The *Census of Distribution*, from which this information is taken, analyses the retailing and wholesaling trades in considerable detail, giving among other information size and ownership patterns in individual trades, and dispersions of gross margins around the mean. It is a mine of useful information about wholesale and retail outlets.

wages and salaries are high; but even in the retail trades gross margins range from 12 per cent in confectionery trades to 30 per cent in bookselling and the jewellery, leather and sports goods trades. Wholesale margins are lower on average than retail margins, ranging from 3 per cent in tobacco to 28 per cent in furniture; this is largely due to the fact that purchases are a

TABLE 2.10

GROSS MARGINS AS PERCENTAGE OF TOTAL RECEIPTS IN RETAILING AND WHOLESALE TRADES IN UNITED KINGDOM, 1950

Trade	*Gross margin* %	*Total sales (£ million)*	*Number of organizations*
(A) RETAIL TRADE			
All trades	22.2	4,941	404,845
Grocery trades	15.3	890	98,459
Other food retailers	23.8	777	92,466
Confectioners, tobacconists, newsagents	12.9	451	57,971
Clothing	24.8	830	63,267
Hardware	27.3	214	23,108
Booksellers, stationers	30.0	71	7,548
Chemists, photographic goods	31.2	150	11,597
Furniture	27.5	237	12,087
Jewellery, leather and sports goods	30.3	78	11,362
Coal, builders' materials, etc.	20.9	116	11,193
Other non-food retailers	37.0	49	9,348
Motor vehicles, cycles, etc.	18.1	209	8,670
SERVICE TRADES			
Catering	42.0	192	39,957
Canteens	x	110	17,157
Hairdressers	69.8	34	28,754
Funeral furnishers	58.6	10	2,779
Portrait photographers	71.5	4	2,044
Repairers	56.3	24	20,858
Motor vehicle repairers, garages, etc.	23.0	342	17,225

high proportion of total costs and value added by processing is small. In wholesaling there is not the same concentration of sales and organizations in the grocery and food trades.

Marketing Practices and Policies

Marketing is also part of the competitive process, and to the economist the many marketing policies which are possible are in fact simply forms of competition. Marketing policies and practices must therefore be aimed at the fulfilment of three of the functions of marketing discussed earlier—the assessment, meeting and manipulating of demand—and must all be judged by their efficiency.

TABLE 2.10 (*cont.*)

Trade	*Gross margin* %	*Total receipts* (*£ million*)	*Number of organizations*
(B) WHOLESALE TRADE			
Wholesalers with stocks (*total*)	12.8	3,192	24,080
Agricultural products	11.5	222	1,442
Builders' materials, hardware	19.4	192	1,877
Coal	8.9	118	268
Metals, metal products	14.7	551	98
Timber	18.2	90	666
Scrap and waste materials	20.2	55	1,092
Other industrial materials	9.2	184	955
Machinery, vehicles	21.7	157	1,608
Electrical goods	17.9	72	655
Groceries, confectionery, drinks	8.4	661	2,884
Other food	13.7	170	1,945
Clothing, footwear, textiles	14.3	457	3,846
Chemicals, oils, drugs	16.0	82	663
Furniture, musical instruments	28.1	13	275
Glass, china, earthenware	23.8	13	296
Paper, stationery, books	17.5	119	1,158
Petroleum products	12.5	40	79
Tobacco	3.0	256	1,110
Other manufactured goods	19.3	67	1,098
Secondhand goods	16.6	20	461
General	14.7	108	1,151
Wholesalers, other than those with stocks	12.0	1,934	9,242
Export merchants	9.0	807	1,499
Import merchants	8.8	750	1,734
Invoicing agents	7.8	252	2,330
Non-invoicing agents	22.4	110	3,059
Government departments	7.4	1,717	38
Marketing boards	11.2	454	161
Purchasing branches of overseas firms	35.8	18	153
Wholesaler-producers	25.8	198	1,064
Warehousing	99.9*	13	173

Note: x signifies not ascertained.

* 'The purchase and sales of goods on own account is a subsidiary activity of organizations classified under 'warehousing'. The gross margin of warehousing organizations normally consists of receipts from the provision of warehousing and storage services for other traders ... Gross margin and Receipts are therefore nearly identical.'

Source: *Census of Distribution, 1950*, Vol. II, Table 28; Vol. III, Tables 13 and 17.

Each of the practices and policies is a separate study in itself, and it is not possible to cover the fields in any detail;

they are outlined here as policy possibilities and are examined purely from the point of view of their impact on policy, their effectiveness as policy weapons, their economic content and their relevance to business decisions.

Market research

Assessment is the job of market research and demand forecasts, and marketing decisions depend on the availability of adequate information and its interpretation. Market research is quite simply the scientific assessment of demand and is closely analogous to the intelligence services of the armed forces.

The major uses of market research are:[37] to tell management of the position of the firm in its industry and its share of the market; to provide information about present and possible future trends of the industry; to help in the development and introduction of new products and the improvement of old products; and to provide for the appraisal and improvement of the effectiveness of sales management.

Market research is a tool of management, but it cannot by itself solve marketing or other problems. What it can do is narrow the range of uncertainty and help to make decision making more intelligent and less of a guess. Sales managers may have hunches, they may be good, they may be bad (and if they are, they may be expensive). Market research reduces the chance of bad hunches turning out to be expensive. The production manager needs market research just as much as anyone else in the firm, for without it he cannot intelligently plan his production in advance.

But it remains true that the ultimate value of market research depends on how the results are used. Market research is not a method of formulating decisions, but of providing a guide towards this; and the evaluation of results and the formation of policy is still in the last analysis the job of the manager.

Having decided to embark on market research, management still has to decide on how to do it, and there are several possibilities. Some firms employ outside agencies, some do their own, but most do a bit of both. Whether or not to perform a particular piece of market research oneself is a straightforward

[37] See R. D. Crisp, *Company Practices in Marketing Research* (American Management Association, New York, 1953) pp. 28–9.

economic decision (similar to the decision to manufacture or sub-contract)[38] and depends very much on the scale of operation of the company. The costs of the market research must be weighed against the returns expected from it: almost all market research expenditure is overhead cost, and whether or not to use a particular method depends on whether the firm can work on a large enough scale to justify the expenditure involved. Small firms can rarely afford the specialized staff for field research, and indeed most big firms, too, prefer to have such work done outside by specialized agencies, of which there are several. The cost of field research, surveys, etc., is rather high, and this sort of work involves a great deal of specialized knowledge and planning which is rarely possible even in very large firms. And even firms which have their own market research departments frequently buy regular, specialized services, such as the products of Retail Audits,[39] in addition to their own work. But most firms, as will be seen, can do a great deal of intelligent market research on their own, at relatively little expense.

But however the research is done, few firms can afford to be without some market research,[40] carried out independently of the Sales Department. In a firm manufacturing electrical components, the production and sales side of the firm had for several years worked on the assumption that theirs was a seasonal trade (largely because everyone said so). A statistician was engaged by the company, and, in order to determine the magnitude of the seasonal fluctuations, he did some research into the sales of the firm over a period of years: there was no seasonal pattern whatever. In the same firm, the Production Departments had relied for several years on the sales forecasts provided by the Sales Department (though with some adjustments in the light of past experience of these forecasts); but these were becoming increasingly unreliable, and, since the scale of operation

[38] See Chapter III, pp. 119-120.

[39] See p. 67.

[40] A study of the preparation of sales forecasts by 297 American companies examined the principal factors considered in the preparation of the forecasts. The most important factors, listed in order of importance, were: (1) past sales trend of firm; (2) sales department estimates; (3) judgment and hunch; (4) general economic indicators; (5) economic data on own industry; (6) salesmen's field reports; (7) new product plans; (8) competitors' activity; (9) production capacity; (10) market surveys; (11) promotion plans; (12) other sources. *Sales Forecasting, Uses, Techniques and Trends*, American Management Association, Special Report, No. 16.

of the company was increasing and more accurate forecasts were needed, the statistician was asked to make a demand forecast. This was used, and turned out to be much more accurate and usable, and has since superseded the forecasts of the Sales Department. All of this was done internally by one man, at very little cost to the company.

Possibilities in the field of market research can be enumerated briefly. Even the vaguest hunches can be improved by a quick look at some of the mass of published information now available: the *Monthly Digest of Statistics*, the *Trade and Navigation Accounts*, the *Board of Trade Journal*, the *Census of Production and Distribution*, the *National Income Blue Book*, the various publications of trade associations,[41] and several other sources quickly yield useful quantitative information to the intelligent searcher. Even in its raw form such information is useful, but its utility can be increased enormously by intelligent statistical analysis.

In the field of capital goods, for example, there are several series of statistics which provide good indicators of demand. Every 4 months the Federation of British Industries conducts a survey of the intentions (in the form of authorizations) of manufacturers to spend money on capital equipment and buildings; the Board of Trade also publishes tables showing quarterly estimates of planned industrial building; the Royal Institute of British Architects also surveys and publishes details of new commissions of private architects; and a new index (the Cubitt Index)[42] of construction activity provides a guide to about half of total investment in the economy. There is also a large variety of published information in trade journals, the financial press, company reports and several other sources.

Similarly, still within the firm, the analysis of the firm's own sales patterns can give very useful clues to markets; it is frequently possible to find out with little trouble the patterns of distribution (does the firm sell, for example, mainly to small corner shops or to large chain stores?), and from this to deduce an intelligent sales policy. Masses of such information comes into most firms daily and is frequently ignored, or treated unsystematically.

Even so, there are usually important gaps in the information

[41] See also Chapter IX.

[42] Published quarterly by Holland & Hannen & Cubitts Ltd.

required for policy making,[43] and there are many forms of market research which the typical firm cannot conduct for itself, for which it needs to employ a specialized agency. External market research is usually carried out on a basis of sample surveys, either by interviewers, through the mail, on the telephone (a method rarely employed in Britain, where telephone ownership is not widespread), by consumer panels and so on.

Such surveys cover a wide field and there is a range of alternatives: they may concentrate on past sales, on the buying intensions of consumers, or they may approach the problem from a psychological standpoint.

Surveys of past sales are useful, partly because they give an indication of the firm's share of the market, and partly because the proper statistical analysis of past trends is a particularly effective way of forecasting.[44]

Ascertainment of a firm's share of the market is an indispensable function of market research, and it can often best be carried out by an external agency which can, as part of its normal activities and at small extra cost, collect a great deal of the available information about the market, much of which is inaccessible to the firm without considerable expense. One such method is the Retail Audit, effectively developed by the A. C. Neilsen Co., which consists of regular periodic visits to a selected sample of retail shops, during which checks are made of stocks and purchases of the commodities under review, enabling sales of brands to be computed. Another method is the Consumer Panel, members of which keep diaries of products purchased. The information which can be obtained from Consumer Panels[45] is extensive: it includes the extent of the market, market structure (geographical distribution, habitat, household composition, etc.); and from this data it is possible to make studies of consumer buying habits, such as frequency of purchases, quantities bought, brand loyalty, seasonal pattern, patterns of distribution and types of outlet; and they may also help in the assessment of the effectiveness of advertising.

[43] One danger of relying on internal market research is that the department may merely tell management what it wants to hear rather than the facts of the situation.

[44] See Chapter IX.

[45] See *The Consumer Panel* (Technical Leaflet of the Belgian Distribution Committee, Brussels) summarized in *Digests of Marketing and Distribution Publications* (O.E.E.C.), No. 5, 1961.

Some useful information about share of the market may also be obtained without the use of an external agency. In some industries members report their sales to a trade association or similar body, which publishes for members a total figure. The growth in the number of trade associations which publish such information does mean that much of this type of market research is possible within the firm at relatively small cost.[46]

Whatever the method, however, the firm can compare its own sales with totals for the trade and so ascertain its share of the market.

Surveys of consumer buying intentions are useful, within broad limits, as guides to market expansion, and they may help to narrow the range of error of forecasts. In the U.S.A. such surveys are carried out for a fairly wide range of goods and are published quarterly in the *Federal Reserve Bulletin*; in Britain, with the exception of a small range of capital goods, such surveys are usually available only from specialized agencies. A danger of such surveys is that people do not always act in accordance with their expressed intentions, however honest they may try to be (there is a similar difficulty with public opinion polls, which are a relatively unsophisticated form of this type of survey). But experience allows intentions to be checked against realizations, and some correction of estimates is possible to allow for this sort of difficulty.

Motivational research is another possibility. This has been defined as '... a phase of marketing research which attempts to answer the question "Why?" ... [and which] seeks to relate behaviour to underlying processes, such as people's desires, emotions and intentions'.[47] The rationale of motivational research is that if one knows why people buy things, one can not only predict how they will behave in given conditions, but one can also decide on ways on which they can be influenced, which form of advertising or other promotional method to use. Its main usefulness to date has been in the second sphere, and much advertising, many styling 'gimmicks' and so on owe their existence to motivational research.

Whatever the type of market research used, if it is compe-

[46] The Society of Motor Manufacturers and Traders, for example, regularly publishes analyses of sales and stocks of all types of motor vehicles.

[47] G. H. Smith, *Motivation Research in Advertising and Marketing* (McGraw Hill, 1954), p. 3.

tently carried out, it can provide useful information for decision making. The more and the better the information which a firm has about the market and the demand for its products, the better it is able to formulate marketing, production and financial policy.

Despite advances since the Second World War, market research is surprisingly little used in Britain. According to a survey[48] carried out in 1960, external expenditure (outside the firm) on market research was about £7 million, total expenditure about £18 million (less than 0.1 per cent of total industrial turnover).

Market research for capital goods in particular is a sadly neglected field. In the B.I.M. survey twenty-nine out of thirty-six manufacturers of industrial products possessed market research departments (and spent less than £600,000), compared with twenty-five out of twenty-six manufacturers of consumer goods, who spent more than £1,500,000. This is rather surprising in view of the fact that the markct for capital goods is generally much more sensitive to trade fluctuations than the market for consumer goods and that, since buyers are few and orders usually relatively large, a mistake can be even more expensive than in the consumer goods field. Market research for capital goods is usually aimed at end products, since the demand for capital goods is a derived demand, and this does tend to make the research more difficult. Some capital goods, of which steel is a good example, are the raw materials of a wide variety of finished products, so that the problem is one of building a complex model of a very large part of the economy (though experience may suggest that certain key indicators may be sufficient for planning and predictive purposes in many circumstances).

Changes in tastes, incomes, substitutes, etc., are often sudden, and frequently when it is found out that such changes have taken place it is too late to have much effect on goods in the pipeline and for which production plans and investment decisions have been made. The invention of a commercial process of manufacture for seamless nylon stockings (which are not prone to 'laddering') brought severe competition in the

[48] *A Survey of Marketing Research in Great Britain* (British Institute of Management, 1962).

American industry to get the new product on to the market first: several new processes and patents are involved, all expensive. A review of the market reported: 'The seamless fad itself had already caught the manufacturers flat footed and with them the manufacturers of stocking-making machinery. But by this spring (1962) some fifteen makers of seamless machinery were competing. If now the lock-stitched seamless and ladderless stocking makes the new machinery obsolete, there will be carnage in the stocking industry.'[49]

The analysis of distribution costs is another important field of market research. Not only does the entrepreneur want to know how much his distribution is costing him in total, he also wants to be able to allocate his costs to products, areas, salesmen, customers and so on. By so doing he can decide, for example, whether concentration on a few outlets would yield better results than a wide spread of sales; and sales control is just as important an aspect of business as cost control. It is by no means uncommon to find, particularly in the capital goods industries, that products are sold at a loss to some customers when the full analysis of distribution costs and profits is made out. This may well be desirable in certain cases, for prestige reasons or for future relations, but these are exceptional cases, and in general it is preferable to avoid losses on individual products wherever possible.

An Example of Market Research in Practice[50]

The Edison Group, which produces most of the electric power used in Northern Italy, carried out a survey of domestic refrigerators.

The survey was in two phases. The first, in May and June of 1957, was devoted to ascertaining the distribution of refrigerators in the areas served by the Group, and the effect of four major factors: (1) area (divided into The Riviera, the plains, hills, mountains, urban centres); (2) demographic size of the areas; (3) number of family members and (4) occupation of the family's wage earner. A 5 per cent sample was drawn from the total of 1.9 million customers for house lighting.

[49] *The Economist* (June 2nd, 1962), p. 897.

[50] Thea Gelsomini, 'Market Research on Domestic Refrigerators among Customers of the Edison Industrial Group', *Studio di Mercato* (Rome, April 1960).

The second phase, from January to April 1958, consisted of analyses of owners and non-owners of refrigerators in an attempt to identify the characteristics of the present and potential market.

The results of the first phase showed that: (1) only 11.8 per cent of customers had a refrigerator; (2) the market was concentrated in Milan and Genoa (41 per cent of the refrigerator owners, 20 per cent of customers); (3) ownership is directly connected with standard of living (71.6 per cent of professional families had refrigerators compared with 1.2 per cent of rural families); (4) ownership was also connected with size of family.

The results of the second phase were divided into two groups. Among refrigerator owners: (1) 88 per cent of refrigerators were of the compressor type, 49 per cent had a capacity of 100–150 litres, 26 per cent had a capacity of 150–200 litres; (2) 64 per cent of refrigerators were less than 3 years old, 78 per cent less than 5 years old; (3) 61 per cent had been purchased from shops, 14 per cent from manufacturers; (4) the advertising media most frequently remembered were magazine advertisements and television; (5) 70 per cent of owners used the refrigerator throughout the year; (6) 70 per cent thought that meat, dairy products and vegetables are best suited to refrigerators; (7) for 44.9 per cent the major advantage of refrigerator ownership was preservation of foodstuffs, for 13.6 per cent it was the saving of shopping time which was thought to be most important; (8) only 19.6 per cent found inconveniences in the use of refrigerators; (9) the automatic light and inner door shelves were thought to be useful, the locking key was little used; (10) only 9 per cent planned to replace the refrigerator within 2 years.

Among non-owners: (1) 55 per cent had food preservation problems; (2) 26.5 per cent intended to buy a refrigerator within 2 years (95 per cent of these preferred the compressor type, 82 per cent the ordinary model, 76 per cent a 100–175 litre capacity, 94 per cent a white refrigerator; (3) the probable sales channels would be household appliance stores (53 per cent), manufacturers (15 per cent), electric companies (11 per cent); (4) the basic sales appeals of a refrigerator were a well-known brand (21 per cent) and a guaranteed motor (17 per cent); (5) as regards questions of the usefulness of accessories and best advertising media, the answers were the same as those of the non-owners.

The Manipulation of Demand

We now turn to the second managerial aspect of demand mentioned in the second paragraph of this chapter: the influencing or manipulation of demand. There are three broad ways in which management may attempt this: by advertising (and its corollary of product differentiation); by product development and design (under which head we can also subsume the third, passive managerial aspect, the effect which demand may have on the activities of the firm); and price policy. In formal terms, the first two of these policies attempt to bring about a shift in the demand curve, or to substitute a new demand curve for the existing one; the third policy attempts to move the producer and consumer further to the right on the existing demand curve.

Advertising

The principal function of advertising is to bring about a change in the tastes and preferences of the consumer and hence to bring about an expansion of the market; but it has other useful roles as a marketing tool. Advertising can be used to prepare the market and help in the introduction of new products, and similarly it prepares the way for, and to some extent eases, the task of the sales force; and, by making it easier for dealers to sell it helps in the acquisition of 'dealer outlets'. It is sometimes claimed that advertising performs a useful service in the provision of information to the public. This is not a primary aim, and in any case the information provided is selective and not of much direct help to the public in choosing between products, but at least advertising does tell the public what products are available.

That much advertising is irresponsible and even mischievous is undeniable, and management has something of a social responsibility to minimize these undesirable aspects, but it is not the task of this book to pronounce on these aspects so much as to evaluate the usefulness of advertising as an aid to marketing, and a way of improving the overall efficiency of the firm.

One big advantage of advertising is its relatively low cost per contact: one newspaper advertisement frequently places the product before the eyes of many more prospective buyers than the equivalent expenditure on salesmen. But it is usually only a preliminary part of the operation of selling, and its weakness lies in the fact that advertising rarely closes a sale (though mail-order selling relies almost entirely on advertisements—plus in most cases the offer of credit facilities).

An interesting example of the effectiveness of advertising is in the sales of washing machines on the British market.[51] The most successful sales records in the years 1960–62 were of companies selling direct to the public: low price was the main reason for their success (they were selling at between a half and two-thirds of the price of machines sold through the electrical goods trade), but advertising was also responsible. The technique used by one firm (Rolls Razor) was to advertise in the national press, wait for reply coupons, next send out brochures and follow this with a salesman's visit. The head of the firm claimed that sales were almost directly related to advertising.

The effectiveness of, opportunities for and methods of advertising clearly depend on the nature of the business and the market. Firms selling mainly 'within the trade' clearly have to restrict their advertising largely to trade journals and catalogues, and a nationwide television advertising campaign would be inappropriate. A manufacturer of a new brand of cigarettes, or motor car, however, operating in a field where competition is intense and the market conditioned to advertising would have little prospect of success without large expenditure on advertising in mass media.

It is possible to create demands where none previously existed, and to arouse latent demands, by advertising; and similarly 'psychological obsolescence' can be brought about by advertising.[52] Much of this sort of advertising is socially undesirable and economically wasteful, but some of it is reasonable and acceptable and achieves the aim of expanding sales and efficiency.

[51] *The Economist* (June 2nd, 1962) p. 919.

[52] Vance Packard's book, *The Hidden Persuaders* (Penguin), is an entertaining though eclectic, description of some of the less favourable features of advertising.

It is important to recognize that advertising has its limitations, and some businessmen expect far too much of it. Expensive advertising cannot compensate for poor quality, poor service, excessively high price, poorly selected channels of distribution; and it is rarely effective if only used for a short period. It is but one tool of marketing, and it cannot do the job alone.

A recent study[53] enumerated a series of conditions favourable to advertising:

1. The product should be identifiable (by means of a brand).
2. It should be possible to differentiate the product.[54]
3. The consumer should be able to judge, or notice, the characteristics of the product.
4. It should be possible to give the product 'subjective' values, which should be of some importance to the consumer.
5. The product should be readily available on the market.
6. The product should be bought regularly.
7. The consumer should be able to choose the product without the help of the retailer (it should, in the jargon of the trade, be of the 'self-selection' type).
8. There should be a trend of increasing demand for the product group as a whole.
9. The product should be acceptable to the consumer (it is pointed out that too novel products often create unfavourable reactions among consumers).
10. The product should have a certain share (undefined in the report) of the market.

The survey selects certain goods as suitable for advertising: cosmetics, branded foods, some consumer durable goods (television sets, washing machines); and others as unsuitable: most producers' goods (bought by professional buyers to certain specifications), and such consumer goods as those for which individual fitting is required (shoes, some types of clothing, etc.).

The requirements of successful advertising similarly are

[53] Bo Wickström, *About Measures to Measure the Effectiveness of Advertising* (European Productivity Agency, Organization for European Economic Co-operation, 1961).

[54] See p. 79.

fairly readily summarized: They are: the *definition of the objectives* (at whom it is to be directed, how much to spend, on which products, at what time, how much the firm wants to sell, etc.); *determination of the direction of advertising* (which must clearly be towards the main existing and potential markets); *the choice of media* (which will depend partly on the market aimed at, partly on the circulation and 'contact potential' of the media, partly on cost: the main categories are television, the press, catalogues and display, but there are scores of alternatives and possibilities in practice); *and the nature of the advertisements*, the arguments or appeals to be used, etc.

Advertising is similar to market research in that most advertising campaigns beyond simple use of trade journals and classified advertisements in the press can be carried out more efficiently by specialized agencies, which have expert knowledge, contacts, and specialized services (which may be too expensive for the individual firm because they depend on large-scale operation for their most efficient use). Like market research, advertising is largely an overhead expense, and specialized firms can often do the job more cheaply and efficiently.[55]

Whatever the method used, however, close contact is necessary between producer and advertiser throughout a campaign: it is possible for the aims of advertising and production to conflict in much the same way as any marketing process may conflict with production. It is possible for an advertising campaign to be too successful and for the firm to lack the productive capacity needed to meet the demands placed on it. In the early 1950s a large British manufacturer of cosmetic and allied products undertook a large-scale advertising and marketing campaign, and found that its production and distribution facilities were unable to cope with the success of the campaign. Such a selling campaign is probably worse for the firm than none at all, but it can usually be avoided by intelligent planning.

The cost of advertising and the advertising appropriation or budget must clearly depend on the nature of the product and market. The budgeting process is simple in principle—the advertising appropriation should be related to the estimated

[55] This is closely analogous to the vertical integration decision discussed in Chapter III.

volume of sales in the period of the campaign—and the total cost must clearly depend on the expected return. In highly competitive fields, where real distinctions between products are small, advertising usually represents a high proportion of total costs: such fields are medicines (37 per cent), cosmetics (34 per cent), shampoos (50 per cent), toothpaste (28 per cent) and some foods.[56]

The Government, in its role as consumer of some heavily advertised products, occasionally shows concern at the high cost. In August 1962 the Public Accounts Committee criticized the excessive sales activity of drug firms, and quoted figures which showed that on sales of £67 million in 1961, advertising expenditure amounted to £6.5 million (almost 10 per cent), and the cost of representatives calling on doctors for about £3 million.

Intelligent advertising has one remaining fundamental requirement—testing. In the economist's terms, it is necessary for the firm to know whether, and by how much, the advertising campaign has had a significant effect on the demand curve, and whether it has justified its real cost (which may be higher than the appropriation). Pre-testing is one way, attractive because it can prevent wasteful expenditure in advance; but it suffers from the disadvantage that, being on a 'pilot' scale, it does not always accurately reproduce the conditions under which the actual campaign will be carried on (this is a disadvantage of all pilot testing, but there is one further factor which is specific to advertising—the effect is cumulative, and the existence of the campaign itself influences the circumstances of the campaign). Post-testing may be carried out by consumer juries or similar devices, but the ultimate test is whether the campaign affected sales. Sales are, of course, affected by influences other than advertising, and in addition the effect may not be immediately apparent since it is likely to be cumulative, but statistical and econometric techniques have improved so much in recent years that useful testing is now possible.

A convenient summary of methods of testing is given in Table 2.11. There are several ways of measuring the potential audience of an advertising campaign and the various media; ranging from Television Audience Measurement to surveys of

[56] See Packard, *The Hidden Persuaders*.

readership of newspapers and journals, all of which are fairly readily available; but these are not sufficient alone. The firm needs to know more than the size of its audience: it wants

TABLE 2.11

MEASURES OF THE EFFECTIVENESS OF ADVERTISING

Method of Measurement	*Timing* (*A*)	*Effects on* (*B*) *Decisions*	(*C*) *Consumers*
INTERVIEW METHODS			
(1) *Judgment*			
(*a*) Expert	Before		Information
(*b*) Consumer	Before	4	Influence
(2) *Indirect methods*			
(*a*) Product, brand image (*b*) Attitude	Before or after	2, 4	Influence
(3) *Memory methods*			
(*a*) Brand awareness	After	1	Information
(*b*) Audience, readership value	After	2, 3, 4	Information
OBSERVATION METHODS			
(4) Purchase studies	After	1, 3, 4	Behaviour
EXPERIMENTAL METHODS, ETC.			
(5) Time series analysis	After	1	Behaviour
(6) District analysis	After	1, 2	Behaviour
(7) Campaign analysis	Before or after	1, 2, 3, 4	Behaviour
(8) Coupon analysis (D)	Before or after	2, 3, 4	Behaviour
(9) Retail index studies	After	1, 2	Behaviour
(10) Consumer index studies	After	1, 2	Behaviour

Notes: (A) Time of measurement in relation to actual advertising campaign.
(B) Effect within the company on:
(1) Advertising versus other marketing activities.
(2) The allocation of advertising between media.
(3) The allocation of advertising within media.
(4) The qualitative design of advertising.
(C) The effect of advertising on the consumer:
Information—the transmittal of information to the consumer.
Influence—influence on consumers' scales of values.
Behaviour—influence on consumer behaviour.
(D) The analysis of the effect of 'coupon' schemes (e.g. for soaps, detergents, etc.) on sales.

Source: Adapted from Wickström, op. cit., p. 63.

to know whether the advertising is effective or not; it can find this out indirectly by asking consumers, or directly by assessing the increase in sales; and in the end it wants to know whether advertising has increased the profitability of the firm.

In 1956 the U.S. Department of Agriculture[57] made a study of a promotion campaign aimed at increasing the consumption of lamb carried out in Cleveland, Ohio, in July and August 1956. Advertising was carried out mainly through newspapers and radio plus some display material for shops and visits to retailers, and cost about $20,000.

Analysis yielded the following regression equation.

$$x_1 = -37.2 - 7.1x_2 + 3.4x_3 + 8.7x_4 + 9.4x_5 + 7.4x_6$$

Where

x_1 = estimated sales of lamb per month in 000 lb (712.2)
x_2 = weighted retail price of lamb in cents (68.1)
x_3 = weighted retail price of other meat, etc., in cents (63.1)
x_4 = total consumer income in Cleveland in $m (27.4)
x_5 = regular advertising for lamb in per cent of total advertising (4.2)
x_6 = seasonal index per cent (100)

(Figures in parenthesis indicate mean values for the preceding 40 months)

Using this equation predictions of actual sales were made for July, August, September and October. In July actual sales were somewhat below predicted sales (but within the range of error); in August sales were 14 per cent higher than expected; in September (after the campaign finished) sales were again below the expected value. The study showed that in the short run advertising and other methods had an effect, and that it was possible to sell a surplus of lamb with the aid of a short, intensive campaign, but to do so was expensive (the cost was 20 cents per lb, the average price of lamb was 17 cents during the period).

Whilst it is true that successful advertising campaigns can be conducted for homogeneous products, these are usually carried out in terms of the whole market and by co-operative endeavour: examples are the Drinka Pinta Milka Day campaign, advertising by the Egg Marketing Board, by other national boards and some trade associations. Detergent and soap manufacturers claim that what they try to sell through their campaigns is the

[57] *Promotion of Lamb, Results of a Campaign in Cleveland, Ohio, U.S.* (Department of Agriculture, Washington, D.C., 1958).

'concept of cleanliness', oil manufacturers sell the concept of oil, cosmetic manufacturers sell 'charm' and so on; and it is claimed that by increasing the total market for these 'commodities', all manufacturers gain. There may be some truth in these claims, but generally the aim is more competitive, and individual manufacturers try at least to maintain their share of the market, or, better, to increase it by advertising.

Most advertising is competitive, and the competition takes place between firms in the same, or closely related industries. And in these circumstances some differences, real or imaginary, between the products of the firms, are an essential pre-requisite of the advertising campaign.

The economist calls this product differentiation; along with this it is convenient to discuss some of the more practical aspects of product development and design, brand policy, etc., and to examine the real as well as the imaginary differences between products, and the business operations which underly these approaches to markcting.

Product Differentiation and Development

'A general class of product is differentiated if any significant basis arises for distinguishing the goods (or services) of one seller from those of another. Such a basis may be real or fancied, so long as it is of any importance whatever to buyers, and leads to a preference for one variety of the product over another.'[58]

Classic examples of product differentiation are motor vehicles, detergents, cosmetics, petrol and petroleum products, breakfast foods, confectionery and so on.

A study of product differentiation in the United States classified a sample of industries according to the basis of differentiation as follows:[59]

(1) Advertising; (2) product quality; (3) product design; (4) consumer service; (5) controlled distributive outlets.

The industries were ranked as:

(*a*) *Those with 'great' differentiation:*

Cigarettes (1); distilled liquor (1, 2); automobiles (3, 4, 5);

[58] E. Chamberlin, *The Theory of Monopolistic Competition* (Harvard U.P., 1935).

[59] The data is adapted from Joe S. Bain, *Industrial Organization* (Wiley & Sons, 1959), pp. 222–3. The basis of differentiation is in parenthesis after each industry.

heavy farm machinery and tractors (3, 4, 5); high-quality fountain pens (1, 3); typewriters (1, 3, 4).

(*b*) *Those with 'moderate' differentiation:*

Petroleum refining (1, 4, 5); rubber tyres (1, 3, 4, 5); high-quality men's shoes (1, 5); tin cans (4, 3); flour (1, 4).

(*c*) *Those with 'slight' differentiation:*

Steel (4); meat packing (1, 2); low-priced fountain pens (1, 3); low-priced men's shoes (1, 5); and

(*d*) *Those with 'negligible' product differentiation:*

Copper; cement; rayon yarn and fibre; tinned fruits and vegetables; flour (commercial); fresh meats.

Products may be differentiated in a variety of ways—by exclusive patent features and trade marks—brand policy, packaging, design, or by advertising—and it is possible to extend the notion to include such factors as reputation (of manufacturer or distributor), location of distribution (e.g. in a 'high class' district) and a whole host of intangible and personal factors which may bind a consumer to a seller. This wider definition really covers the whole field of marketing, but it is possible to pick on certain factors connected exclusively with the product itself, which are usually referred to under the heading of product development and design.

Product Development is a positive managerial function, and may be defined as the effort to improve or add to the variety of the products of the firm. All too frequently this function is only performed haphazardly or indeed accidentally; but conscious and intelligent effort is necessary if the function is to be performed adequately. During this century the haphazard approach of leaving this to free-lance inventors and brainwaves has given way, at least in the bigger firms and the newer and more progressive industries, to systematic programmes of research and development. The returns from comparatively small expenditure on research and development may be large and striking; as a proportion of total costs this sort of expenditure is usually small. Research and development is still very much a matter of chance: major discoveries are often made in small sheds in back yards at relatively small expense, but steady if unspectacular developments stream constantly from the systematic expenditure of large corporations on this important aspect of their activities, and the National Research Development Corporation makes a substantial contribution on the national scale.[60] Research can be directed to any of a number of ends; apart from the reduction of production costs and genuine improvements of the product, it can be aimed at the development of new lines, new uses for by-products or the improvement of sales appeal.

Other methods of product development are less direct, and the aim may be achieved *inter alia* by integration with other firms, manufacturing different ranges of products, by reorganization of the production on marketing sides of the company in order to increase its own range of products, or through market research aimed at finding out what people want. But whatever the methods the aims are the same, and the directions of development of most products follow well-defined patterns, which include the addition of refinements in operation or style and design, the improvement and standardization of quality, the provision of services, use of new materials and methods and packaging. Most mass-consumer goods on the market these days have been the subject of product development, which has come to be one of the major methods of marketing—motor cars, detergents, electrical goods, furniture—the list is endless.

It is only in recent years that design has come to be accepted as of fundamental importance in the selling of a product. In Britain we still tend to lag in improvements of design—the Scandinavians are far ahead in the design of furniture, household goods and buildings; for many years the European manufacturers of motor vehicles were more prepared to experiment with the technological aspects of design—but there is a growing realization of the need for good designs, and in particular of the need to adapt designs to the market. Continental and African motorists still deplore the failure of the British manufacturers to produce suspension units suitable for their rougher roads, to produce draught-proofed and adequately heated cars. Even so there is a growing realization of the importance of design, for functional as well as aesthetic reasons: some of it comes about at the initiative of consumers, but the good design policy is that which anticipates or forms the consumers' preferences.

[60] See K. Grossfield, 'Inventions as Business', *Economic Journal* (March 1962).

Another aspect of product development is what is generally called *Brand Policy*. The importance of brands lies in the fact that the success of marketing policies depends very much on the identification by the consumer of certain standards of quality with a particular product or source of supply. The building up of a 'brand image' underlies much effort in sales promotion and product development: it has led to advertising wars between rival manufacturers but, outside the rather weird world of detergents, aspirin and cosmetics it has brought benefits. Brand policy really implies some acceptance of responsibility for standards and service, and this is part of the price paid for the gains from brand policy. The advantages of branding by manufacturers are many: it simplifies and aids advertising and other methods of sales promotion; if successful it encourages later repeat sales; a sound brand image helps with the introduction of new items; and branding is some protection against competition. In addition many wholesalers and retailers prefer to handle branded goods. Some goods do not lend themselves to branding, but most do; and branding, like the advertising which usually goes with it, can be carried to excess and result in social waste.

It is possible to make too many claims for brand policy, and many firms are obsessively concerned with 'brand images' and brand loyalty, which they may not be able to demonstrate. Brand awareness does tend to be closely associated with recent advertising campaigns, and housewives buying toothpaste and detergents frequently tend to buy that brand which has been most recently advertised on television. It is frequently claimed that motor cars have a brand image to which patrons tend to be loyal through the years, and the brand policy of the British Motor Corporation, with its range of Austins, Morris, Wolseleys, Rileys, and M.G.s which differ in little but trimmings, appears to be based on some such concept.

Some interesting results of brand awareness for men's and women's wear came from an investigation made in 1954–55 by the Swedish Institute for Marketing and Management Research.[61] 1813 consumers were the basis of the study, 1170 of whom were men; observations and interviews were made in fifty-eight shops in twelve Swedish cities. Table 2.12 shows that

[61] Quoted by Wickström, op. cit., p. 23.

between a third and a quarter of those interviewed could mention no brand for different types of garments.

So-called *Packaging Policy* is really only a further development of brand policy, aimed broadly at making the product more immediately attractive to the consumer. A certain minimum of packaging is necessary for the protection of the product, or for hygienic reasons and general cleanliness; but beyond this it is doubtful whether heavy expenditure on packaging fulfils its purpose of attracting the purchaser. Much

TABLE 2.12

AWARENESS OF BRANDS

Type of garment	*Knows one or more brands* %	*Knows no brand* %	*Total* %
Men			
Suit	58	42	100
Jacket	75	25	100
Trousers	68	32	100
Heavy coat	55	45	100
Light coat	27	73	100
Suit	51	49	100
Women			
Dress	67	33	100
Suit	45	55	100
Heavy coat	60	40	100
Light coat	70	30	100

Source: Wickström, op. cit., p. 23.

packaging policy would not stand up to rigorous *costs versus returns* analysis. As a method of competition it is merely an extension of product differentiation, and it is open to the same snags and advantages.

The Marketing Process and the Selection of Channels of Distribution

Many firms have no consciously formulated policy about channels of distribution. For some firms—'jobbers'[62] are a good example—this may not matter, but in general, as in all aspects of business behaviour, some policy is desirable. Standardized procedures save time and trouble and make control, prediction

[62] See p. 56.

and evaluation of success much easier; co-ordination within the firm is easier; and the firm's channels of distribution themselves find advantages in standardized policies. A possible danger is that competitors, too, will find prediction easier, but reasonable flexibility reduces the risk of this. Whatever policy is chosen it is an elementary principle of marketing policy that channels should be subject to frequent review and reappraisal.

A range of alternatives is possible. The simplest channel of distribution is from producer direct to consumer; goods may pass through middlemen (wholesalers, retailers, agents), and the commonest arrangement for consumer goods is a chain of producer, wholesaler, retailer, and consumer. Generally the less complex the links the better, and, since price mark-ups are charged at every stage, the lower the price to the consumer;[63] but the solution to any particular problem is rarely as simple as that. Wholesalers may be necessary because the cost to the manufacturer of providing specialized storage facilities at widely dispersed points may be excessive (much depends on the scale of operation of the firm); and the wholesaler provides useful services to the retailer by maintaining large and usually varied stocks from which choice is possible. There are very few consumer goods which can be sold direct to the consumer without a retailer. The growth of discount houses in the U.S.A. (and more recently in the U.K.), with their own warehousing, transport and retailing facilities, or special bulk agreements with suppliers has tended to reduce the number of links in some circumstances and the growth of large retail chains and supermarkets, which can often afford their own warehousing, operates in the same direction; but customs of the trade, and restrictive practices of one kind or another, tend to restrict possibilities in this direction. On the whole middlemen do perform a useful function (for which they receive a reward in the form of a profit) by making the goods available at the right time and place: but that the system is open to abuse is undeniable. It is hard to justify, for example, charging the consumer 1s. for a lettuce when the grower probably received less than 1d. Inefficiency of channels of distribution is often the reason and it is in the interests of all that this should be removed.

[63] As in the case of washing machines (see p. 73).

The policy chosen depends partly on the nature of the product, partly on the nature of the market, partly on the existing structure of distribution (though, unless there are established restrictive practices it is usually either possible to change the structure or to use other methods); and partly on the sort of consumer at whom the product is aimed. A first step in the selection of outlets is inevitably the question—what exactly does the firm want of the outlet? (which products to sell there, which consumers to aim at, etc.); but the final selection of the channel will depend on the sales expected from the use of the channel balanced against the costs of using it: research, which may well be based on past sales or Retail Audits, will usually give the necessary information. Frequently the most costly methods are those which involve selling direct to final buyers (as with most capital goods and such consumer goods as encyclopaedias), largely because individual or personal selling is usually required, but clearly there are cases (such as the direct sale of market produce) where this may be cheaper. But frequently middlemen do in fact reduce costs by providing specialized services at lower costs than are possible for the producer himself.

Co-operation with the distributor is part of marketing policy. It may be necessary to supply display material, to guarantee rapid delivery, to provide financial aid in the form of extended credit, to be prepared to offer after-sales service and so on. The co-operation may be mutual, and the distributor may be prepared to offer long-term contracts and special facilities. In this field much again depends on the customs of the trade, particularly in the case of credit and discounts.

The sole agency is one such form of co-operation, which has mutual benefits. These accrue to the retailer in the form of a certain degree of local monopoly, advertising carried out by the producer, elimination of duplicate brands and lower stock costs. The producer gains by having a semi-guaranteed and regular outlet, he can concentrate his promotional effort, and he benefits from the fact that the distributor can carry complete stocks of his range of goods and provide after-sales service and repairs. For some goods, particularly those bought on impulse, sole agencies offer fewer advantages. One of the arguments in favour of sole agencies—that they help in resale price maintenance and price stability—is likely to be of decreasing force in the U.K. in future.

Another aspect of the marketing process is the decision about number of outlets: complete coverage may be desirable, as in the case of detergents and many foodstuffs; but selective distribution through a limited number of outlets is often preferable, as in the case of products sold largely to a few income groups or specialized sectors of the economy, where large-scale distribution would be wasteful. In general, expensive durable goods such as refrigerators and motor cars, which usually have to be maintained in fairly large stocks at the outlet, with relatively infrequent turnover, are best distributed selectively; single-use mass-demand goods, most foodstuffs, groceries, cosmetics, detergents, etc. (usually manufactured on a large scale), are best distributed through as many outlets as possible. With selective distribution more care is necessary in selecting outlets for their sales potential, with large-scale distribution such care is neither possible nor in most cases necessary. Multiple-outlet selling also frequently involves selling through varied channels: many goods, for example, are sold by grocers, chemists, confectioners and multiple stores, and have to be distributed through the appropriate wholesale channels for each type of shop.

Recent developments in markets have complicated these decisions. The growth of the supermarket, large chain stores and other organizations with near monopolistic powers have tended to take the marketing initiative away from the producer and to give it to the distributor. There have been big changes in both the scale and technology of distribution. In the U.K., Marks & Spencer are renowned for the fact that they employ their power over manufacturers in the interests of securing cheap goods of consistent quality for the consumer. The economic principles underlying such situations are quite clear: the balance of power depends on the relative share (of output or market respectively) of the manufacturer and distributor. The power of Marks & Spencer depends largely on the fact that they buy from many dispersed and independent producers; the power of the British Match Corporation and the British Oxygen Company is due to their domination of the sources of supply. The large distributor is tending to win this battle at present, and is also tending to present virtually unassailable competitive power to the small distributors (who are being forced to band together to achieve some of the economies of scale and bargaining power of the large concerns, and even then may run up against restrictive practices legislation).

Manufacturers are therefore having to think much more deeply about marketing policy than in the past: choice of distribution channels is narrower and distributors have more power; and in some fields effective marketing in the future may well demand the choice of one of (or a combination of) three factors: larger shares in the market (*via* integration or spontaneous growth),[64] co-operation with other producers, or the ownership of the manufacturers' own channels of distribution. Other policies are still possible: advertising and product development; wider spread of outlets (books, for example, are now sold in shops which would never have considered such merchandise 30 years ago); the spread of the book-club idea to gramophone records, reproductions of paintings, wines, travel and even some foodstuffs are an indication of these new approaches to marketing.

Recent changes in markets have not changed the situation fundamentally, they have merely underlined the need for intelligent policies and decision.

An interesting example of the choice of a channel of distribution is provided by the Olivetti Company[65] in the case of its portable typewriter 'Lettera 22'.

Traditionally in Italy the distribution pattern for office machinery was one of direct sales through branch offices and sole concessionaires. This was justifiable for several reasons: the market was concentrated (mainly industrialists and commercial undertakings); most office machinery sales are made by personal salesmen; it is necessary to provide technical assistance and repairs, which are best operated under the direct control of the manufacturer; and the system allowed direct contact between producer and market.

But in 1950 the company introduced a new portable typewriter, and was faced with the question whether the existing

[64] See Chapter III.

[65] U. Galassi, 'The Case of the Portable Typewriter "Lettera 22" ' published in *Marketing by Manufacturers* (Organization for European Economic Co-operation, 1957).

policy was adequate or whether some new sales policy would have to be adopted. The company believed that it would be possible to create a large market for portable typewriters in private households (it was also hoped that this would be good advertisement for the bigger machines, and would help their sales in offices).

In order to achieve this result, certain conditions had to be fulfilled; sales price had to be rigidly controlled, and kept below the monthly salary of a clerk; advertising was needed to stress the usefulness of typewriters; a wider knowledge of typewriters should be fostered; and lastly, distribution arrangements should be tightened up in such a way as to bring the machine to the notice and within the reach of passers-by.

The company conducted an experiment in Trieste and Milan with retailers of household electrical equipment with encouraging results: sales were mainly made to clerks, artisans, students and women; and sales of the company's own branches were not affected. Electrical goods shops were chosen because they are numerous; even in small towns, they have good display windows, they have regular customers, with high purchasing power, and they are organized for hire purchase sales.

There were objections from concessionaires and from office machinery dealers, but the company managed to overcome these.

In view of the experience of the experiment, the policy of sales through these outlets was adopted, and was bolstered by other measures such as advertising, the formation of typing schools and so on.

In 5 years the volume of sales of this model was increased to a figure four times higher than that of its predecessor.

Sales Management and Personal Selling

The term 'Sales Management' means different things in different firms. In some firms the sales manager or director is responsible for all aspects of marketing; in others (the majority) he is merely responsible for the management of the sales force; in others he may be the man responsible for personal selling, or for price policy, or for any other aspects of marketing. It is defensible (if not completely logical) to think of sales management as the function of organizing the sales force and personal selling, and that is the sense in which the term will be used in this chapter.

Supervision of sales personnel is largely an administrative task whose economic significance rests on the efficiency with which it is carried out. Very briefly, the manager will want to know how well his men are doing their work, their problems, and what assistance is necessary; and this means that he must have the necessary information. Much of this comes from proper records in his own department; some comes (occasionally in the form of rebukes) from other departments. Volume of sales is not necessarily the best measure of performance, since this will depend on the size and complexity of the sales area, the number of calls and the number of other tasks which the salesman has to perform: against these the personal selling ability of the salesman may have little chance. And 'super-salesmen', though frequently successful in the short run, often antagonize customers and work against the long-term interests of the firm. Experience and research (market research, time studies, etc.) can usually help management to set and maintain reasonable performance standards.

Personal selling—the job done by the sales force of both manufacturers and distributors—is the oldest marketing method, and still in many circumstances the most effective. The term embraces over-the-counter selling, house-to-house selling, the calls of salesmen on wholesalers and retailers, specialist salesmen, executives calling on important customers, and pervades the whole market complex. More often than not it is the method used to close the sale. Effective personal selling, though it is frequently left to inferior personnel, depends on a knowledge of the market and the products, on locating the buyers, on making the sale and on the maintenance of good will. A whole industry has grown up based on the training of salesmen, and training courses of this sort usually ring the changes on a few basic ways of being a good salesman (finding out the customer's needs, presenting goods as effectively as possible, meeting objections, and ways of closing the sale); but always with the proviso that it rarely pays to upset the customer, effective personal selling depends much more on the representative just being there than on tactics or gimmicks. Contact above anything else is the essence of salesmanship.

Personal selling usually has a high cost per contact, but it is also, as a rule, more effective than other methods. How many salesmen to use and where to concentrate them is an integral part of the whole marketing decision, and has to be seen as part of the 'promotional mix';[66] but the personal salesman remains a key part of the marketing process.

Pricing Policy

The question of pricing has a chapter to itself, but, since pricing policy is clearly one important form of marketing policy and competition, some of the practical aspects are considered here. Given that in the long run no firm is going to charge a price which will not cover total costs with a margin for profit, there is plenty of room for manœuvre in price policy.

It is not always possible for the firm to charge a price which meets these requirements, and the firm, having made the product, or being committed to do so, has to charge what the market will bear. When the firm is faced with a ruling price in the market (as is frequently the case with agricultural goods), the decision is a relatively simple one of whether or not to manufacture at that price, or whether it is possible to sell at a lower price (and whether this is worth while, as it rarely is if the producer has only a small share of the market). Even this decision is fairly complicated for the producer who already has a plant in operation: if he can cover direct costs and make some contribution to overheads he will, for a time at least, continue to produce and sell at the ruling price in the hope that things will improve; but below a break-even point, or after a period of time, he may be forced to cut his losses and sell his plant for what it will fetch.

But given these basic considerations, other considerations of demand and tactics still apply.

One of the basic factors affecting pricing policy is elasticity of demand, and the producer needs to have some idea of expected responses to the prices which he intends to charge. Share of the market and production capacity may determine whether or not an attempt to attract extra buyers by a price reduction would be an intelligent policy or not. The danger of retaliation by competitors always underlies such decisions.

[66] The combination of marketing methods used by the firm.

Pricing too high on the other hand simply attracts competitors who see the potential gains for themselves.

The price of an individual item sold by a firm depends on overall price policy. Commonly in retailing, but also in manufacturing, certain items (loss leaders) are sold at low prices in order to attract customers who may buy other products; or certain lines may be sold at a small profit or loss to a potentially valuable customer in order to create or maintain good will. Such policies are open to the danger that the loss leader only will be sold, but the tactic frequently works.

Tactical considerations may also dictate the use of discriminatory price policy: discriminating between classes of consumers (e.g. medical and public supply of certain gases); between geographical regions, granting discounts for bulk purchases, or graded price schemes (such as operate for gas and electricity). Discounts usually depend on the practice of the trade, and there is still scope for flexibility.

In some fields pricing policy depends on the price leader. One large firm may be able so to dominate the market that it can set prices which the rest follow. But it is rare for such leadership to be absolute. Often the leadership is confined to a fall in price, when other firms have to follow suit or lose sales, but if the leader puts up the price the others simply take competitive advantage and keep their prices down. And the leadership may be restricted to certain price ranges. Tactical considerations will still influence price leaders: they are usually interested in price stability and the avoidance of price wars; and even in circumstances where they might raise prices as a result of temporary shortages, they may refrain from doing so on the grounds of good will and public relations and reaping long-run benefits which would outweigh short-term gains.

Finally, since price policy is a form of competition, the impact on competitors and their possible consequences of action always have to be borne in mind. Pure monopoly is rare, and even the monopolist does not have a completely free hand in determining his price.

CONCLUSIONS

Drawing together the many threads of this chapter, it is possible to sum up the main elements of the marketing decisions.

Four main managerial aspects of demand were outlined at

the beginning of the chapter. These are clearly interdependent, but functionally they may be looked on as distinct, and the classification provides a framework for the examination of market decisions. Two of these aspects were designated passive, two active, but in all four cases positive policy decisions are involved: all form part of the process of competition in the market.

The first aspect is analysis and forecasting. This is the function of market research into consumption and distribution, and includes an examination of competitors and methods of competition. Such research may be carried out both internally and externally, and necessitates not only a decision about the type of research, but also the evaluation of results as a basis for policy. The second passive aspect, the effect which demand may have on the organization and activities of the firm is partly a production problem and partly an administrative problem. It concerns the fields of production development and design, organization of the marketing department, adaptation of the productive process to meet the conditions of the market, and policy with regard to stocks.

The influencing of demand, the first active aspect, is also partly a matter of product differentiation, development and design, but it also embraces advertising, pricing policy and the various methods of sales promotion. The fourth aspect, which clearly overlaps with the third, is the positive approach to meeting demand, or marketing. This includes the choice of channels of distribution, problems of transport and storage, of finance, the provision of services before and after sale, and co-operation with distributors.

Policy decisions are necessary about all of these, and the decisions have to be made in the light of the firm's assessment of the factors affecting markets. This includes consideration of factors within the firm itself, general considerations affecting the market, and specific consideration of consumers and distributors.

Within the firm itself, marketing is only one aspect of general policy and must be adapted to overall policy. But certain factors bear more directly than others on the marketing decision and these can be isolated. Policy is affected by production capacity; its flexibility and projected changes; the production time lag (which determines the length of forecast necessary); research; development and design; the storability of the product; the number of suppliers and the flexibility of supplies.

In the market in general, the main points to consider are: the size and structure of the market; transport facilities; distance from the main parts of the market and main centres of demand; credit possibilities, the seasonality of demand, the number of competitors, their share of the market, and the forms of competition; the number and type of substitutes; prices; prospects for various types of sales promotion; and the relative powers of producers and distributors.

Coming to the consumer, the main factors affecting policy are: the number of consumers and the number of economic units (such as households); their incomes, tastes and preferences; their demand patterns; their consumption capacity over a period of time; the storage capacity of the household or other unit; and the time lag of consumption (the increasing number of refrigerators and freezers, for example, tends to impose new time patterns on consumption).

The main considerations relating to distributors are: the structure of distribution and the variety of channels; the number of distributors and their power; the ability of distributors to handle products; the attitudes of distributors; warehousing facilities; the customs and the traditions of trade; trade association policies; discount and credit possibilities; the possibilities of mutual co-operation; and the costs of distribution.

The reconciliation of all of these factors and individual decisions forms the marketing policy of the firm. The 'promotional mix' (the best combination of various methods of sales promotion—mainly, but not entirely, a question of advertising and personal selling) and the final combination of policies clearly depends on an assessment of the balance of advantage to be gained within the limits of the sales budget. Logically the problems are not terribly difficult, consisting of a series of least cost and maximum 'output' (= sales) combinations: in practice they are more difficult because many of the facts are not known (intelligent research can reduce the number of unknowns); and in the last resort the marketing policies of the firms must depend on judgment, backed by economic insight.

It is all very complex, but if marketing is to be anything more than an incoherent jumble of *ad hoc* decisions and expedients, it is all very necessary.

Chapter III

PRODUCTION AND COSTS

Production is the organized activity of transforming resources into finished products in the form of goods and services; and the objective of production is to satisfy the demand for such transformed resources. Coal and iron in their natural state in the ground are of little use to anyone until they are mined and worked on to produce steel for motor vehicles, bridges, ships and other goods.

To be more specific, the productive process consists of taking materials,[1] and adding value to them by the application of factors of production in the form of labour, machinery and all of the other services of modern industrial organization. The addition of value means that goods are sufficiently different at the end of the productive process to justify charging a higher price for them; and the rewards of production go to those factors (including capital and management) which add the value. Any activity which results in such added value constitutes production and, whilst we tend to think in ordinary life of production as being confined to manufacturing, strictly speaking the processes of marketing and transport are just as much a part of production.

For practical purposes, however, it is usually convenient to think of production in terms of the two main categories of manufacturing and distribution.

Thus, the *net output* of an enterprise consists of the *value added* to materials by the processes of production; or, looking at it from the point of view of rewards to the factors which make up the productive process, it constitutes a fund from which charges are met, in the form of wages and salaries, rents, taxes, depreciation, advertising, etc.[2]

The composition of costs and net output differs considerably

[1] Which are usually the products of some other processes—coal, for example, is the finished product of coal mining and a raw material of steel making, steel is a raw material for many other processes.

[2] See an example in Chapter V.

from industry to industry and, even within the same industry and among firms with essentially similar processes, differences between firms may be great. Apart from the obvious physical and technical characteristics which differentiate firms from each other there are also differences in the efficiency of utilization of factors and processes which affect cost structures.

The main items of expenditure in most businesses are materials; the main costs of *production* proper (or net output) are

TABLE 3.1

PRODUCTION AND COSTS IN BRITISH MANUFACTURING INDUSTRY, 1958

Industry	Sales	Cost of materials and fuel	Net output	Wages and salaries	No. of establishments
	£ million	Per cent of sales		Per cent of net output	
Food, drink and tobacco	4,263.6	68.9	21.4	40.0	9,233
Chemicals and allied industries	2,309.7	65.6	31.8	39.5	3,566
Metal manufacture	2,318.6	66.7	30.0	55.5	2,876
Engineering and electrical goods	3,470.3	47.6	50.1	60.7	14,992
Shipbuilding, etc.	496.0	43.7	45.7	76.5	1,255
Vehicles	2,233.0	59.9	36.7	65.1	2,289
Metal goods	1,183.6	59.8	37.2	58.1	10,588
Textiles	1,882.6	61.2	32.6	61.2	8,461
Leather	138.0	64.8	31.4	63.6	1,945
Clothing	749.8	54.2	40.9	66.3	9,592
Bricks, cement, etc.	591.7	43.4	50.2	58.9	2,252
Timber and furniture	510.9	55.2	41.6	66.3	9,976
Paper and printing	1,255.7	45.1	45.8	58.4	9,371
Other manufacturing	543.1	55.9	41.8	58.7	3,389
ALL MANUFACTURING INDUSTRY	21,947.0	59.1	35.8	56.7	92,785
Mining	931.5	25.1	78.0	77.9	3,372
Construction	2,779.4	37.8	44.8	70.8	95,629
Gas, electricity and water	1,172.2	41.8	32.7	39.1	1,903
ALL INDUSTRIES	26,830.0	55.2	39.0	58.8	193,689

Source: *Census of Production for 1958*, Part 133 (Summary tables) (H.M.S.O., 1962).

wages and salaries. These are shown for the main manufacturing industry groups in the U.K. in Table 3.1, which in some degree illustrates the diversity of conditions. Wages are a relatively small proportion of net output in the 'food, drink and tobacco' group, a large part of net output being accounted for by advertising, selling expenses and depreciation; but even within this group of trades wages vary from less than 20 per cent of net output in 'spirit distilling and compounding' to over 70 per cent in the sugar industry; and the cost of materials ranges from 27.8 per cent of total sales in spirit distilling to over 100 per cent (in other words a loss was made) in milk products. At the opposite end of the scale wages in mining and shipbuilding account for nearly 80 per cent of net output; but whereas materials are a relatively small proportion of sales in mining (25 per cent) they are over 40 per cent in shipbuilding.

The *Census of Production*, from which this summary table is taken, tells us a little about the costs of the productive processes, but not much about the processes themselves. These clearly differ a great deal from trade to trade: some industries, such as light engineering, require a great deal of intricate and relatively expensive machinery; others such as shipbuilding, require heavy and expensive machinery; some industries need a lot of skilled workers to operate their machines, others, like the motor industry, with a lot of automatic processes, require a great deal of unskilled and semi-skilled labour but a large expenditure item over the years is in respect of machinery. The clothing industry is different from all of these industries: it requires little machinery, most of it relatively inexpensive, a large amount of semi-skilled labour; and premises in the industry are usually small and an insignificant item in costs. In this industry the main costs are materials and labour.

If this diversity of conditions is taken to its extreme, every firm is different, but fortunately there are some basic principles which are of some help to the economist and the businessman in sorting out the meaning and efficiency of the productive process in general terms without the need to consider each individual technique. In one sense the techniques themselves do not matter: what matters is the most efficient use of them, and this is both a technical and an economic problem.

PRODUCTION AND BUSINESS DECISIONS

In order to carry out the productive process costs are incurred in payment for factors of production and resources, and as a result the businessman has to solve two main problems. The first is to find the combinations and types of factors which will produce his output at least cost; the second is to find the most profitable or economical output at which to produce, and the proportions in which he will produce the components of his output. To put it at its simplest, he has to think in terms of costs and scale of production.

In the short run the production problem is to make the best use of available productive facilities: there is usually a variety of ways in which they can be employed profitably.

The cost of using given capital equipment to manufacture some product is measured largely in terms of the contribution which it could make to revenue if it were employed in producing some other product.[3] Thus, in a jute mill the cost of using machinery to spin yarn for carpet backing is to be measured in terms of the returns to be obtained from spinning yarn for the production of sacking. But these in turn have to be related to the availability of looms suitable for the weaving of the respective products. How the optimum use of machinery can be determined is discussed in Chapter X.

As time goes on there may be various opportunities of modifying capital equipment: this may range from the addition of comparatively small pieces of capital equipment to help balance productive facilities, to a far-reaching and fundamental change in productive methods.

It is unusual to find that there is only one method of producing goods or services. In the production of electricity, for example, generators may be driven by steam turbines, diesel engines or water power. The proportions of capital and running costs involved in the use of each of these methods differ appreciably: the construction of a dam usually involves large capital expenditure, but once it is completed the cost of keeping the turbines in operation is small. The capital cost of generating electricity by steam turbines on the other hand is much less, and the operating costs, in the form of fuel, much higher than for hydro-electricity.

The choice between these alternative methods of generation will depend on the precise circumstances encountered, but if interest rates are high and the cost of fuel needed for steam turbines low, the choice will be tilted against hydro-electricity and in favour of conventional stations.

Similarly, it is possible to construct roads using either modern

[3] This is the rationale of the economist's definition of costs as alternatives foregone, or opportunity costs.

machinery and limited numbers of men or by primitive methods involving the employment of large numbers of men. In underdeveloped countries, where wages are low and the cost of road-making machinery relatively high, the choice generally lies in favour of an intensive use of man-power.

Thus, the choice of productive methods is always affected by relative prices of factors of production or inputs.

COSTS AND RETURNS

Underlying these observations are the Laws of Return, which depend on the facts (*a*) that factors of production are not perfect substitutes for each other; machinery cannot be substituted for labour indefinitely, grades of labour are not completely interchangeable and so on; and (*b*) that it becomes progressively more difficult to substitute one factor for another the further the process has already gone. The *Law of Diminishing Returns* (or Variable Proportions) is simply a statement about the returns which accrue to a factor of production, and says that, in a combination of factors of production, if the employment of one (the variable) factor is increased whilst the others are held constant, the additional units of the variable factor will, after a certain point in production, yield a smaller return than the preceding ones (this is conveniently summarized by saying that marginal returns will diminish). The total product of the group of factors will continue to increase, but at a decreasing rate in proportion to the increase in the variable factor; the reason being that the additional units of the variable factor, not being perfect substitutes for the fixed factor, cannot make up for the fact that fixed factors are not being increased. The law operates, *not* because less efficient factors are being employed, but because identical factors are being employed less efficiently: and this is so *not* because entrepreneurs make mistakes, but because in these circumstances no other result is possible.

The law may best be illustrated by a simple hypothetical example (see Table 3.2). In the example all of the factors save one (labour) remain constant, labour input is increased in units (column 1). The total product increases, but after the sixth man is employed, the average product falls (i.e. average returns start to diminish); after the fourth man, marginal returns[4] (i.e. the additional return to each further unit of labour) start to diminish. For a while the marginal product of labour increases because it is possible to make better use of the fixed factors of production; but this is no longer possible once four men are employed and thereafter the marginal product falls and continues to fall. Following the change in marginal product the average product of labour at first increases but with the addition of the seventh man it too starts to fall.

TABLE 3.2

ILLUSTRATION OF THE LAW OF VARIABLE PROPORTIONS

Units of labour (man hours)	*Total product (gallons of paint)*	*Average product of labour (gallons per man hour)*	*Marginal product of labour (gallons per man hour)*
0	0	0	0
1	10	10	10
2	26	13	16
3	46	15.3	20
4	76	19.0	30
5	100	20.0	24
6	120	20.0	20
7	134	19.1	14
8	148	18.5	14
9	162	18.0	14
10	174	17.4	12

Several proofs and demonstrations of this law have been put forward,[5] but stated in this form the law is merely a statement of a physical fact: as each man is added he has less and less of the fixed factor to work with and cannot himself do the work of the other factors: therefore, his product will be less than that of earlier men.

Formulation of the Law of Diminishing Returns in terms of units of output is helpful in elementary exposition, but it is more convenient to discuss the application of the law to business situations in terms of costs which, being payments to the factors whose returns are measured, are merely the inverse of returns. Thus Increasing Costs mean the same thing as Decreasing Returns, Decreasing Costs mean the same thing as Increasing

[4] Returns are not the same things as profits: returns are measures of output or product; profit is the surplus of revenue over cost.

[5] See G. J. Stigler, *Theory of Price* (Macmillan).

Returns; and the Law of Diminishing Returns may be restated as a statement of the tendency for average and marginal costs to increase beyond a certain level of output. Corresponding to fixed and variable factors respectively are the fixed (or overhead) and variable costs which are the rewards of the factors to which they are paid.

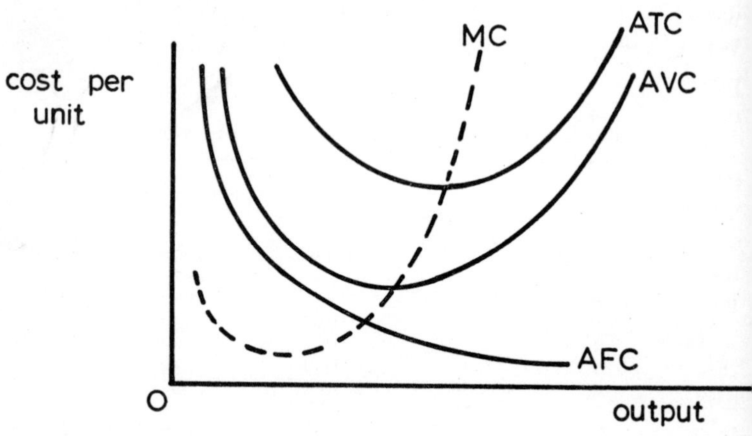

Average Fixed, Variable and Total Cost

Figure 3·1.

It is usual to define fixed costs (sometimes called supplementary costs or overhead costs) as those costs which do not vary with output, and variable costs (or prime costs) as those which do; fixed costs therefore fall per unit of output as output expands, average variable costs tend, according to the law of diminishing returns to fall initially and then to increase as output increases. At any level of output, therefore, average cost is made up of two parts—average fixed cost and average variable cost. A typical situation is shown in Fig. 3.1, which shows average fixed costs declining with output,[6] average variable cost first falling and then rising, and average total cost doing likewise. The interesting thing is that there is a point of minimum average cost, at which the firm will be working at its best

[6] The average fixed cost curve is always a rectangular hyperbola.

(or optimum) level of output, and where average costs are at their lowest because this is where the variable factors are used most efficiently (as a result of the operation of the Law of Diminishing Returns). Variable cost per unit of input (e.g. per man hour) is constant, but per unit of output or product, it first decreases and then increases. And even if the fixed factor were free (and fixed cost therefore zero) this would still happen. Where average total cost of a product is at its minimum production is being carried on at maximum efficiency, and this is the optimum scale of production.

This is the simplest possible case of a cost curve, and there are several complications which must be admitted in real life (to which we shall return later), but the basic principles are as outlined here. The notion of average total cost reaching a minimum as a result of the operation of the Law of Diminishing Returns is fundamental to cost theory.

These fixed and variable costs are close to, but not precisely the same as what are usually known in business as indirect and direct costs respectively: the direct costs being wages of what are often called 'productive workers' (those whose contribution to output can be measured); indirect costs being all of the so-called 'overheads' of the business, including rent, rates, salaries of management and clerical staff and wages of 'indirect' or 'non-productive' workers (such as labourers, maintenance engineers and all whose performance or contribution to output cannot be measured or attributed directly to them). Perhaps one of the most useful operating bases of distinction is still contained in the traditional definition of the economist: variable costs are those which can be avoided if production ceases entirely, whilst fixed or overhead costs cannot; but this definition is not quite appropriate to the practical distinction between direct and indirect costs in that several indirect costs (such as labourers' wages) are avoidable by stopping production (in business these are often called 'semi-variable' costs; the economist would treat them as variable).

Another concept of the economist which needs to be introduced here is that of *marginal cost*,[7] which is the addition to total cost of producing one more unit of output. Whenever

[7] The economist's concept of marginal cost is not the same as that of the accountant—the distinction is discussed later.

average total costs are falling, marginal cost is lower than average cost (in other words it costs less to produce one more unit than it has done to produce all units to that point); when average cost is rising, marginal cost is higher than average cost because it is costing more to produce each extra unit than the average cost of all units to that point. It follows from this that when average cost is at a minimum (that is to say it is neither rising nor falling) it must equal marginal cost.

The cost curves outlined here are short-term cost curves, usually defined by the economist as the curves relevant in a time period when it is not possible to alter plant or methods of production. This time period differs considerably from industry to industry and depends on the techniques and methods of production: in the rubber plantation industry, where it takes several years for a tree to come into full production the production period is long (this is true of most agricultural products and of many of the products of heavy manufacturing industry); in the clothing industry the period is relatively short. In the long run, of course, all costs are variable costs, since there is time for everything to be altered; but it is convenient to define fixed costs as those which refer to factors which cannot, within a defined period, be altered, and variable costs as those which can be so altered. In the short period the businessman similarly cannot normally alter many of his salaries, interest charges, etc., and these are also fixed costs. In practice it is not always easy to separate these, however, and the more complex is the production process and the more items of equipment there are at different stages of their lives and with different lengths of life, the more difficult the problem becomes. On the whole it is usually unrealistic to think of the cost of machinery as being entirely a fixed cost: depreciation through wear and tear is avoidable through stopping production, but obsolescence is a fixed cost. Accountants and economists usually do treat machinery as a fixed factor depreciated through time rather than use, but the justification for this practice is convenience rather than logic.

Returns to Scale

In the long period, when plant can be altered, the situation is rather different. A series of average cost curves, each appropriate to a similar amount of the fixed factor(s) may be drawn, and the new long-run average cost curve may be defined as the lowest possible average cost of producing a given output when the businessman has time to make the necessary adjustments to his plant. The shape of the long-run average cost curve depends on the application of what are known as *Returns to Scale of Plant*. This is slightly more complex and realistic than the Law of Diminishing Returns, but it may be stated in fairly simple terms for three main cases: *constant returns to scale of plant*, under which, when all of the factors are increased in proportion, the product, too, is increased in proportion (this results in constant long-run average cost); *increasing returns to scale of plant*, when long-run average cost falls; and *decreasing returns*, when long-run average cost rises. Increasing and decreasing returns to scale are usually portrayed as different stages of the growth of the same firm, which is then assumed to operate at its optimum at the point of minimum long-run average cost.

Constant returns to scale are likely to occur in cases where it is possible to duplicate all services for each short-run cost curve (or to share out equally between all plants any fixed services which may belong to the firm as a whole), so that from the *production* point of view, ignoring the problems of selling larger outputs and leaving aside questions of maximizing total profits, the businessman is indifferent to the scale of his output, because each plant is as efficient as the rest.

The main reason usually given for the fact that constant returns to scale are not to be expected in real life is the fact that certain productive services are indivisible and come in fairly large discrete units.

A machine may be able to turn out, say, 1000 parts per day, and, if it is to be used efficiently, the other factors (labour and materials) will be so employed that the machine is utilized to that capacity. If output is to be increased by the use of the same methods of production, it is only economical to do so if a further 1000 parts are required—if only 500 parts are required there is underemployment of the fixed factor (the machine) and decreasing returns to scale are the consequence. Much machinery in use nowadays is of this type: it is expensive to produce, and a machine with an output of 1000 units may be no cheaper than one capable of producing a hundred times as much (small machines usually are more expensive in relation to their output).

In terms of the hypothesis of constant returns to scale, it is not always possible to increase all productive services in a given proportion. It is often argued that the most important of these indivisible services is management, which sets a limit to the size and rate of growth of the firm: this is a point to which we shall return later in our discussion of the scale of production.

The distinction between short- and long-period cost is important in another context. Since, in the short run, fixed costs are irrevocable, they can, in certain circumstances, be ignored. In a period of falling prices and declining activity the price which can be obtained in the market may fall below the minimum level of average cost, but it may still be worthwhile to continue in operation so long as revenue is sufficient to cover variable costs and some small contribution is made to fixed cost; at any price which does not cover variable cost it is preferable to shut down. In the long run, however, the fixed-cost commitment is no longer irrevocable and the firm is no longer in a position where it is preferable to produce at a loss rather than not to produce at all. Again, in real life, where fixed assets are wearing out at different intervals, the period long enough to satisfy these conditions may be so long that it is never reached.

In the short run it is also possible to neglect other items of cost which need to be met in the long term if the firm is to continue in operation. A rush order may be met by running machinery without proper maintenance, and this may not matter much in the short run (provided that it is not done too often); but in the long run to do so may be very costly. Running of machinery beyond its proper speeds comes into the same category. The efficient firm may temporarily behave in this way without impairing its efficiency, but the less efficient firm may well fail to take account of short-run neglect of costs such as overtime pay, excessive use of machinery and so on (some firms even neglect to take account of wear and tear).[8]

Although this distinction between short- and long-period

[8] Wiles in *Price, Cost and Output* (Blackwell, 1962) in this context distinguishes between what he calls *Immediate* and *Ultimate* costs, the latter being those which must eventually be met.

costs is important, it is not always so clear cut in practice as in theory. The typical firm incurs costs over a wide variety of periods, and the distinction between the long and short period often has to be arbitrary. A realistic approach is to assume that there are certain factors which a firm possesses at any one time, which cannot easily be reproduced and which are in a very real way fixed resources: these set an upper limit to the amount of such resources available for use in the short period. But within these limits the amounts used can be fairly freely varied over time, and hence the proportion in which they are combined with variable factors can also be altered.

Cost Curves in Practice

These, in rough outline, are the terms in which economics text-books usually discuss costs, and they provide convenient theoretical abstractions which serve the very useful purpose of isolating some of the important factors affecting the cost structure of the business. Things in real life are rarely as simple as this.

The first thing to note is that the cost curves as they are conventionally drawn do not really refer to the business unit at all, but to a technical process (or 'product line'); and a firm may be made up of a whole group of such product lines. Thus the economies of scale which are derived from producing at a larger rather than a smaller output, and of producing at minimum average cost, refer to the product line only and are usually distinguished from other economies, being referred to as 'technical' economies of scale. This problem is discussed in more detail under the heading 'The Scale of Production' later in this chapter.

The elegant simplicity of the conventional cost curve has led many economists to doubt its validity in real life, and, partly in an attempt to quantify cost data for research purposes, partly in the solution of practical problems, several quantitative estimates have been made. Many of the best known of these are presented, along with some of his own original estimates, in a research monograph by J. Johnston.[9] The general burden of these is that, although the initial stage of decreasing costs (or increasing returns) is very similar to that depicted in theory,

[9] J. Johnston, *Statistical Cost Analysis* (McGraw Hill, 1960).

once a stage of slowly decreasing, or constant, average costs is reached, cost curves show no inclination to turn upwards, and the typical short-run cost curves are of the shape shown in Fig. 3.2.

It is possible to argue against this that the reason why the curve never turns up again is that firms realize that they are in this position, and that to produce more in this situation would

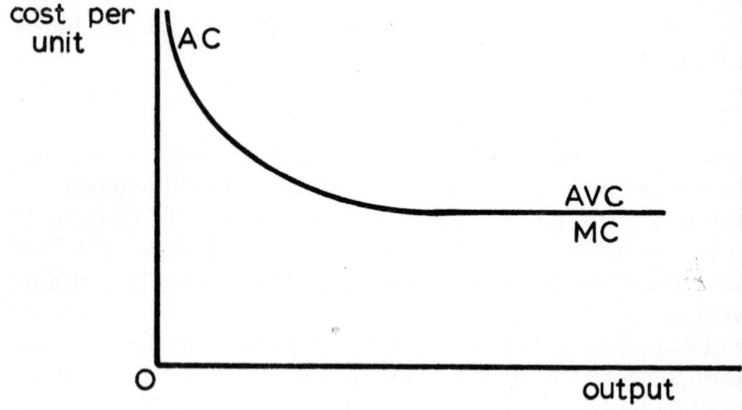

Figure 3·2.

lead to decreasing returns (that is to say, they operate, as the theory says, at minimum average cost). But many of the studies imply more than this, and go on to say that there is a wide range over which average cost remains constant and at a minimum: in other words, there is no unique optimum position of minimum average cost, but a flat bottomed L-shaped long-run average cost curve.

The implications of this are important. It means that in a situation where average cost is constant over large ranges of output, marginal cost is the same as variable cost (because each increment of cost is the same as the preceding one), and is itself constant over these large ranges: this has important implications for price theory (see Chapter VI). It also means that many of the traditional arguments about diseconomies of scale[10] are of less force than has been held.

THE SCALE OF PRODUCTION

The reasons for this are to be found in a closer examination of the causes of economies of scale. A distinction may be drawn between technical and managerial economies of scale: technical economies refer to the plant, or product line, managerial economies refer to the business unit.

Technical economies of scale are those which result from the operation of the Law of Variable Proportions. To some extent these are simple arithmetical economies due to the presence of fixed costs (which fall per unit of output as output increases), and even with constant average variable costs, average total cost is bound to fall (though there may come a point where the rate of decline approaches zero). But such economies are also due to the *indivisibility* of factors of production: many industrial processes need expensive equipment which, if it is to justify its cost, should be used to full capacity, and all related operations must be so arranged that it is in fact so used. For example, if three main processes of production are required to manufacture a given product, it is possible to find out for each process the average output per process: thus, there may be a purely hand process which produces 60 units per hour per man (this may be, for example the delivery of bought-out billets of steel to the second process); a second semi-automatic process of, say, rough machining, may be able to produce 400 units per machine hour; a third, purely automatic process, may produce finished goods from the roughly machined billets at the rate of 1000 units per machine hour. The most efficient use of the whole combined process will require that the machines operating the last two parts of the process should be fully utilized: this can only be done if an output equivalent to the Least Common Multiple of all of the processes (6000 units per hour) is achieved, requiring the use of 100 men in the first operation, fifteen machines (with their operators) in the second operation, and six of the last type

[10] Johnston sums up the new arguments: 'The empirical results on long-run costs seem to us to confirm the widespread existence of economies of scale. The evidence on diseconomies is much less certain for, while there is in some studies a suggestion of an upturn at the top end of the size scale, it is usually small in magnitude and well within the range of variation displayed by the data' (op. cit., p. 193).

of machine. Such an output is necessary because the machine for the last process cannot be divided to produce small enough units of output to allow the use of smaller quantities of the other factors.

As technology advances and as there is more and more plant of this type in use, so economies of scale tend to become an increasingly important feature of the economic scene, and the size of plants tends to grow. In the steel industry, for example, the most efficient size of blast furnace is very large and to some extent dictates the size of steel works; in the motor industry[11] and others the growing use of expensive automatic machinery tends to set minimum size limits. Most modern industry is based on the large plant.

At the technical, or plant, level there are several other economies. Modern techniques have resulted in an increase in the number of specific or single-use machines and processes, designed to perform one operation more efficiently than by any other means: these are frequently expensive and the small manufacturer cannot afford to use them, and although they are not necessarily large machines, there is a tendency for machines with large outputs to be more efficient. Small manufacturers often do not know of the best types of machinery and cannot afford to take big risks or make experiments.

There are also what are sometimes referred to as 'economies of skill', or of specialization and the division of labour, which result from the fact that it is possible with large-scale production to assign each individual to the tasks for which he is best fitted and in which he can indeed increase in efficiency by concentration on and repetition of the tasks.

At the plant level, too, there may be economies in the use of materials and utilization of by-products; the size of minimum stock requirements tends to fall as the scale of production increases; and it is often cheaper to buy and sell in large quantities than small, because up to a point it is administratively no more difficult to deal with large than small quantities.

Technical economies of scale provide an adequate explanation of the importance of large-scale operation at the plant, or product-line level; but they are not sufficient alone to explain

[11] For a lucid discussion of economies of scale in the motor industry, see G. Maxey and A. Silberston, *The Motor Industry* (George Allen & Unwin, 1959).

the growth of business units, which may have several plants, each achieving its own technical or productive optimum. There are other economies of scale, which we have labelled *managerial*, which may refer to whole series of plants and may indeed require a group of optimum plants and product lines if maximum efficiency is to be achieved.

The market may well set the limit to the scale at which a firm may operate: if a market is small, or highly specialized, like the market for 'quality' motor cars, the technical economies of scale may not be realizable, because a firm could not sell an output which could achieve such economies. The application of this principle is more widespread than is sometimes realized: an interesting current example of this limit is in the British motor car industry in which it is argued that significant economies of scale may still be achieved at levels of output which cannot be achieved in the British market. One of the arguments often put forward in favour of Britain's entry into the European Common Market was that such entry would give British manufacturers duty-free access to one of the biggest and fastest-growing mass markets in the world, which would enable the more efficient firms and industries to reap greater economies of scale and growth (the less efficient would not survive).

At the upper limit, of course, the necessary market size for the achievement of economies of scale may be so large that it cannot be realized in practice, and the firm may never be able to operate at the optimum. It is sometimes argued, for example, that the long run average cost curve of the railway industry continues to decline for so long that minimum long-run average cost could never be achieved because there would never be a big enough demand for the services of railways. The statistical cost studies mentioned earlier indicate that this is a state of affairs which may be more common in manufacturing industry than is generally supposed. This, of course, provides a built-in incentive to growth which is greater, the more technical economies of scale can be achieved.

The large operating size required by this market limitation may mean that a monopoly is the most efficient form of organization, because the market can only support more than one firm if all firms act in collusion and share the market at agreed prices. But a monopoly brings its own disadvantages, the most important of which is probably the danger of Government intervention to protect the interest of the consumer, who stands to suffer from monopolistic exploitation. Fear of this may itself prevent a firm from growing to such a size, though it has rarely done so in practice.

On the other hand it is possible to create new markets by means of mass production and the lower prices which result. In the early days of the motor car[12] it was widely believed that motor cars were a commodity which, by virtue of their cost, could only sell to a limited market (this appears to have been based largely on a false analogy with the days of coaches, which could only be sold to a small and relatively wealthy section of the community). Henry Ford saw the fallacy and mass-produced a cheap car which could be sold to a much wider group: in so doing he revolutionized the industry and created a new market. Mass production and low prices have repeated the trick so often and in so many different fields that it is no longer possible to accept without reservations and closer examination the old dictum that the market always limits the scale of operation: perhaps in the final analysis the market *is* the limiting factor, but it is doubtful in many cases whether the limit has any practical significance.

There may also be economies in the marketing process itself:[13] it is often as cheap to sell a hundred units as it is to sell one unit, and the larger the scale of marketing the more economies there are. Advertising provides the classic example: it rarely pays to have a widespread and expensive marketing campaign for small-scale products, unless they are the 'prestige' products of a larger group.

Financial factors may also be important. As is demonstrated in Chapter VII the large firm has advantages over the small firm in this field: it has access to capital markets and usually has substantial resources of its own, whilst the small firm frequently finds that, partly for institutional reasons, it cannot raise all the funds which it may need. Once a firm has succeeded in growing beyond a certain point (which is frequently though not invariably associated with its becoming a public company) these particular difficulties become less important, but it may still find it difficult to obtain further funds. The reason for this

[12] See the Introduction. [13] See Chapter II.

is usually that it is the most successful, or potentially most successful, firms which find it easiest to raise money, and frequently it is the big firm which is also the most successful. With the exception of the particular set of difficulties facing the small firm which are usually discussed under the heading of the Macmillan Gap,[14] it is usually true that the financial factors affecting scale of production are to a large extent reflections of the other factors; and if all else is efficient, finance is not usually a limiting factor on the firm. There are, in fact, those who argue that the Macmillan Gap is a good thing in that it prevents funds from being channelled into occupations in which funds and the inputs which will be bought with the funds would be used at less than their maximum efficiency. This superficially attractive argument does, however, ignore the fact that, there are some occupations which can only be carried out on a small scale, and that many small firms are small merely because they are at an early stage of their growth and may require funds in order to grow.

Management is frequently cited as one of the main factors limiting the size of business units in that it is an indivisible and not easily reproduced factor of production subject to diminishing returns and, if what is known as the 'managerial optimum' is exceeded, managerial efficiency declines and increasing costs set in.

About the first stage of this process—the period of increasing returns to management—there is not much controversy. There are economies of scale in management as with most other factors and the larger the firm is the more it is able to employ specialists; in the small firm, for example, one man may be in charge of production, sales and finance, in the larger firm specialists can be appointed under one head man.[15] Improvements in management techniques and the development of more systematic management in recent years have proceeded *pari passu* with improvements in other techniques, and in particular the realization of the importance of delegation has meant that managerial economies of this sort are easier to achieve. Delega-

[14] See Chapter VII.

[15] 'For any given degree of specialization, further economies may often be obtained by the spreading of managerial overhead cost, thus reducing average cost as output increases.' E. T. Penrose, *The Theory of the Growth of the Firm* (Blackwell, 1959).

tion is a form of specialization: it enables the head of a firm or department to pass on a great deal of routine and other work to subordinates whilst he concentrates on his own job of *managing* the whole firm or department; and in turn his subordinates can delegate functions to their staff and so on.

Delegation is probably the key to managerial efficiency[16] and it explains why management in practice does not become progressively less efficient as firms grow. The school of thought which cites management as the limiting factor on size depends on an assumption that management efficiency is given and remains constant. In fact, however, it does not and management tends to become more efficient the bigger the firm becomes. There are managerial problems of size[17] but these are usually outweighed by the economies.

Sargant Florence[18] puts the case cogently:

'Business enterprise today is a corporate manifestation and its capacity to cope with large outputs is not fixed but expands with its structure.'

and

'most of those who have made a special study of organization differ from the economists. They come to the conclusion that no limit is set to the size of organization, if correct principles are adopted to enable a single leader to delegate control.'

The case against managerial diseconomies does depend, however, on management being employed efficiently and adapting itself to changing economic circumstances; and in real life one of the major problems of a business is to make sure that the whole management structure is efficient. Frequently it is not, and in such cases, bad management has set a limit. Management is probably the least homogeneous of factors of production. At the highest levels of entrepreneurship we find men like Lord Nuffield and Henry Ford,[19] but few achieve such

[16] See Bates and Sykes, 'Aspects of Managerial Efficiency', *Journal of Industrial Economics* (July, 1962).

[17] The problem of excessive centralization of control in the nationalized industries is an example. It is interesting, however, that one of the findings of the Fleck Committee was that the organization of the National Coal Board was in fact excessively *de*centralized.

[18] P. Sargant Florence, *The Logic of British and American Industry* (Routledge & Kegan Paul, 1953).

[19] Besides their entrepreneurial foresight such men also possess the ability to manage their firms efficiently and to choose the best men for various jobs. A

heights and most managements operate at much lower levels; and among the less distinguished the inability of much management to operate at higher outputs does restrict growth. Many firms remain small simply because their owners cannot or will not find and trust subordinates or partners with whom to share functions.

Without enterprising and efficient management a firm is unlikely to achieve its most efficient scale of operation. Management may not be the limiting factor in that it *can* be adapted to any size and rate of growth, but efficient management is a necessary condition of growth.[20] Good management will ensure that the productive, marketing and financial sides of the firm are efficient, poor management will not.

There are also what are frequently called economies of *risk-bearing*. Large firms are usually (though not necessarily) less exposed to risk than small ones, because they can spread their risks: to the small manufacturer the breakdown of one machine or the accidental poor quality of a production batch may be a hazard which he cannot predict with certainty, but which may cause him a great deal of harm; the large concern on the other hand knows that a certain proportion of breakdown failures and low-quality batches are to be expected, and the probability of these can usually be predicted and allowed for; and in any case, even if unpredictable, the loss of (say) 1 per cent of one's output is much less serious than the loss of 50 per cent or more. The risks of failure are small with large firms. The costs of total failure are, however, much greater and, whilst large firms can spread similar risks in this way, they are still vulnerable to the risks of depression and loss of markets.

Firms may seek to spread their risks in other ways by diversification, a practice which has become increasingly common in the last generation or so. A common objective of diversification is to ensure that a firm does not 'put all of its eggs in one basket': an age-old example is mixed farming, and in the sphere of manufacturing industry there are numerous examples of firms which produce a whole range of products which may have no

[20] See Penrose, op. cit., *passim.*

distinction is often drawn between enterprise (which conceives plans) and management (which executes them) but in practice the one depends very much on the other.

apparent similarity of market condition or production method. Vickers Ltd, for example, make aircraft, ships, armaments, food processing plant, rubber, plastics, paint, instruments and a wide range of other products. Markets, too, may be diversified, even when firms produce only one product: the sale of fuels, for example, is for a variety of purposes—heating, lighting, power for vehicles, industrial and domestic use and so on—and this again is a way of spreading risk.

But risk-spreading is not the only motive for diversification.[21] Often new lines of activity may be suggested by research or technological change, which show a firm the way to make better use of its materials and processes, by-products or marketing facilities. A highly diversified output may, for example, be produced from one basic set of productive processes or materials: the chemical industry is like this and Imperial Chemical Industries have products ranging through paints, man-made fibres and explosives in addition to the chemicals themselves. Similarly, a whole range of goods which may be marketed through similar channels may be produced: Unilever supply a large range of manufactures which are supplied through the retail grocery trade—margarine, soap, vegetable oils, frozen foods, fish, etc.—some of these come from common raw materials, many do not. Sometimes the diversification occurs because of a firm's attempts at vertical integration (discussed shortly); sometimes a firm may reach its market limit in one line of production and can only expand by diversifying its output.

Most big firms are diversified in some way. About two-thirds of all firms with over 500 employees operating in the United Kingdom have more than one plant.[22] Not all are diversified—Imperial Tobacco, for example, one of the biggest firms in Britain, is almost entirely specialized in tobacco products (though it does also have some substantial interests in the paper industry)—but a high proportion are. An inquiry by the National Institute of Economic and Social Research[23]

[21] For a fuller discussion of the economics of diversification, see Penrose, op. cit., and Lloyd R. Amey. 'Is Business Diversification Desirable?', *District Bank Review* (June 1960).

[22] *Census of Production.*

[23] See *Company Income and Finance* (National Institute of Economic and Social Research, 1956), p. 68.

showed that in the chemical industry only 79 per cent of persons employed by chemical companies were actually working in the chemical industry; in the metal goods industry, iron, steel and shipbuilding the proportion was 81 per cent; whilst in clothing and footwear and in paper and printing the proportion was 97 per cent.

To some extent the risk-bearing economies associated with diversification tend to conflict with technical and managerial economies of scale, since diversification usually involves the presence of a proportionately larger number of specific fixed factors (equipment used in the manufacture and processing of plastics, for example, is not usually suitable for use in the explosives industry) and in any case the different operations are usually carried out in separate, specialized plants. Increasing specialization is also called for in management. On the whole the attempt of a firm to achieve economies both of scale and of risk-bearing usually points to bigger and bigger business units. Small firms may diversify their output from common processes —this is true of parts of the light engineering industry; mixed farming usually results in small farms with non-specialized labour and, again, the use of an adaptable common factor (land); but these are special cases and more usually diversified firms are large.

External Economies

The economies of scale which we have been discussing so far are internal to the firm in the sense that they arise from the activities of the firm itself and are independent of the actions of other firms. There may also be some external economies, shared by a number of firms, which arise when the scale of production of an industry (or group of industries) increases; in other words, they arise because of outside influences and occur when an increase in the scale of production of other firms brings benefits to a firm. The main external economies arise from the common use and provision of certain services and factors of production: for example, in most industries there are trade associations which provide information and other services to members, and the identity of interests among firms in an industry makes it worth while to issue trade publications and information. The concentration of firms in a neighbourhood brings a series of mutual advantages in, for example, the growth of a pool of specialized workers, transport and ancillary trades. Clydeside, with its shipbuilding and engineering, the Birmingham area with its multiplicity of engineering trades and skills are both areas in which firms derive substantial external economies. A major disadvantage of such a process is, of course, that if there is depression in one of the major industries it soon spreads to all of the others, and this is a serious contingent diseconomy. There may be other diseconomies—the most popular example is that of several firms pumping oil from the same pool, a situation in which the more one firm gets the less is available for others—but such external diseconomies are frequently avoidable.

Principles of Large-scale Production

Sargant Florence[24] presents the case for economies of scale in three basic principles, which may be summed up:

(i) *The Principle of Bulk Transactions* states the case that the costs of dealing in large quantities are usually not proportionately greater than the costs of dealing in small quantities.

(ii) *The Principle of Massed Reserves* is based on the statistical theory of large numbers, which may be simply stated as the fact that the greater the number of individual items involved the more likely is it that deviations will cancel themselves out and leave the average achieved results nearer to the expected results (this principle is the basis of risk-bearing economies).

(iii) *The Principle of Multiples* is an expression of the economies of specialization and large-scale production. In order for specialists to be used efficiently they must be used to their full capacity (in other words they are indivisible); and the more specialization is needed the larger becomes the size of firm required to make the most efficient use of them (the optimum size).

The Growth of Firms

A distinction may be drawn, after Mrs Penrose[25] between economies of scale and economies of growth, and it is arguable

[24] P. Sargant Florence, op. cit., pp. 49–60.
[25] Penrose, op. cit., *passim.*

that there is a limit to the *rate* at which a firm can grow without loss of efficiency, even though there may be significant economies at the size to which it wishes to expand. Mrs Penrose's own words[26] put it best:

'Economies of growth are the internal economies available to an individual firm which make expansion profitable in certain directions ... At any time the availability of such economies is the result of the process ... by which unused productive services are continually created within the firm. They may or may not be also economies of size.'

The distinction is less obscure than it may seem. For any given scale of operations a firm possesses resources appropriate to that scale of output and to the type of products made by the firm. The fact that many such resources are indivisible means that a firm has an incentive to use them as profitably as possible, and the existence of indivisible resources provides a built-in incentive to growth. Such economies may exist for all sizes of firm and they need not be purely technical; the owner of a business may feel that he is not using his abilities to fullest advantage at a particular size and may wish to expand to utilize his own services to the full; the minimum amount of finance which it is worth while to procure may induce a firm to expand in order to use it; the necessity to advertise may dictate a larger scale of operation to absorb the extra overheads involved; and in order to take advantage of opportunities for research and development, and the technological change which stems from them, firms seek to expand still further.[27]

The limit to a rate of growth at any one time may well depend on such factors; the rate of growth of a market may be limited, or the market may be resistant to sales pressures; a firm may wish to make sure of its reserves and its general financial position before it expands; it takes time to instal new plant; but Mrs Penrose's argument is that the limit to the process is

[26] Ibid., p. 99.

[27] This produces what may be called the dilemma of growth: '... competition is the essence of the struggle among the large firms that induces and almost forces the extensive research and innovation in which they engage and provides the justification for the whole system; at the same time the large firms expect rewards for their efforts, but this expectation is held precisely because competition can be restrained' (Penrose, op. cit., p. 264).

set by the ability of management to sustain the growth. It takes time for a firm to develop a new administrative structure appropriate to its new size, and this limits the rate at which a firm can grow if it wishes to maintain its efficiency. But the efficient firm with good management will evolve a new structure in time. The firm with bad management will not, and in this sense management is a limiting factor on growth, but it is not an inevitable limit and indeed it is quite likely that in the long run there is no natural limit to the size of business units.[28]

The straightforward desire for monopoly is, of course, another reason why firms grow: not merely or even mainly in order to charge excessive prices and reap excessive profits, but also in order to remove possible wasteful and unnecessary competition (and so to protect the firm), and because there may in fact be room for only one firm if an industry is to operate without surplus capacity. These are what might be called the 'economies' motives for size which may produce monopoly and in certain cases there are sound economic reasons for growth to monopoly size. But whatever the reasons, and however good they may seem, there is always a danger that a monopoly which grows up for sound economic reasons may be perpetuated for wrong reasons and may result in the long run in exploitation.

The Direction of Growth

Growth is not a homogeneous process, and firms may grow in any of several directions and by a variety of methods. They may, for example, grow spontaneously or by combination: spontaneous or autonomous growth occurs when a firm grows by adding to its own resources by capital expenditure on plant, equipment, etc. (the rationale of this sort of expansion has been one of the main concerns of this chapter so far); growth by combination occurs when several business units combine, voluntarily or involuntarily, by formal mergers. Autonomous growth adds to the total productive capacity of an industry, unless by virtue of growth one firm achieves a superior competitive position and drives out other firms; growth by mergers

[28] Even Adam Smith's limit of the market is, as we have seen, not inevitable; markets can expand, both spontaneously and under the influence of advertising, etc., and even if the market limit for one product is eventually reached, the firm can diversify.

merely involves a change in ownership and control. Most firms in practice expand in both ways.

Whichever method a firm uses, it usually results in some change in the scope of its activities by adding to (or occasionally subtracting from) the number and variety of its products and processes. The term *integration* is usually employed to designate the bringing of a group of activities under one single control.

Two main types and a number of subsidiary types of integration may be distinguished. Horizontal integration, which is the extension of the scale of production of similar products by combination or by plant extension, leaves the range of a firm's activities largely unchanged. Such integration was common in the coal and the cotton industries between the wars, in the steel industry, and nowadays is very noticeable in the aircraft industry. Such growth may be motivated by the search for increased technical efficiency and large-scale production, or by the desire for monopoly, and it is the commonest form of integration in practice.

Vertical integration consists of an increase in the number of consecutive processes which are undertaken by one firm. Textile firms, for example, may undertake both spinning and weaving, iron and steel firms might (before nationalization in Britain) have their own coal mines, iron mines, furnaces and so on through the whole productive process; motor car firms possess their own foundries. Such integration may be backward (towards the raw material and ancillary goods) in which case the motive is usually to secure supplies; or forward (in the direction of the market), in which case the motive is usually to secure outlets for a firm's products. The main economy to be expected from vertical integration is that processes may be linked together and so phased that continuous production of the right things is possible throughout the process, with insurance against the failure of supplies. Attractive though this form of integration may appear at first sight, however, it is less common than may be expected: partly because to some extent it works against the advantages of specialization and large-scale production and is limited by a lack of knowledge of the techniques of earlier or later stages of production (this may, of course, be overcome by hiring the right people when such integration is planned). In the past this form of integration has often been tried and abandoned—one of the most frequently cited cases is of Ford's purchase of rubber plantations—and the abandonment has usually been because independent specialist firms could do the job more efficiently, because they had the specialized skills and, probably more important, by working for a large number of customers, could achieve economies of scale beyond those possible for the large combine. On a relatively small scale vertical integration is common (many firms have their own transport, for example) but in general, the case for vertical integration is much less clear than for horizontal integration: in the last resort its effectiveness depends on whether a firm can operate on a large enough scale and with the necessary technical efficiency to achieve an optimum at each stage of production.[29]

Other forms of integration are possible. Lateral integration (which is similar to, but to be distinguished from horizontal) is fairly common, and consists of the combination of processes which may not be related directly to the same productive process. It occurs when a firm extends the list of its products: British Railways owns hotels to cater for passengers, aeroplane firms may manufacture motor cars, road and rail transport may combine to reduce risk and competition; firms may diversify for any of the reasons discussed under that heading. What Sargant Florence calls diagonal integration may be sought, and consists of 'the provision within one organization of auxilliary goods and services required for the several main processes or lines of organization'[30] (such as the provision of a firm's own power or repair services).

Integration is based, in one way or another, on either the materials which the firm uses, on its products, or on its processes and services, or on all three major ingredients of the productive process. What matters to the economist is that integration should increase the efficiency of production or distribution.

[29] What is often called the 'make or buy' decision—whether a firm should buy its components out or make them itself—is a decision about vertical integration. The fact that so many firms, even large ones like the motor car manufacturers, decide in favour of buying rather than making, illustrates that the case for vertical integration is by no means straightforward or uncomplicated and needs to be proved positively.

[30] P. Sargant Florence, op. cit., p. 45.

Methods of Growth

As we have seen, whatever the direction of growth, a variety of methods is possible. We need not concern ourselves further at this point with autonomous growth (though we shall return to the investment decision, which underlies this form of growth, in Chapter VI); but we must examine briefly the various ways in which growth by combination may take place.

Cartels, trade associations, restrictive practices, market-sharing agreements, collective resale price maintenance (now illegal in Britain) are all ways in which firms may combine, but they need not concern us here because strictly they are not methods of growth but ways of restricting competition or of achieving a growth in the size (and power) of the marketing unit. As well as these looser agreements, mergers too may be motivated by the desire to reduce competition, but they are also a way by which the firm can achieve integration and growth.

Mergers may be brought about in a variety of ways, but two main methods are important for this discussion: amalgamation (often through the formation of holding companies, etc.) or a merger between 'equals' is one way; the other is by acquisition of a controlling interest in one firm by another (this may be in the form of a take-over or voluntary sale by one firm); the essence of the distinction is that the latter method involves the absorption of one party by another, the former does not. Both forms, however, result in formerly separate units of control becoming one, and they are usually aimed at securing economies of scale.

One advantage of combination with other firms, particularly important when a business is diversifying its operations, is that existing firms frequently have specialized staff, equipment and expertise which the business would have to develop for itself, possibly at great expense and over a long period of time if it attempted to grow by extension of its own plant. On the other hand, buying up another firm as a going concern may involve the purchase of 'goodwill' (which is usually supposed to represent the difference between the value of a firm's assets as a going concern and its value as individual pieces of equipment and buildings); and this may well cost more than the alternative of autonomous development.

Take-over bids are a form of merger by acquisition which have attracted a great deal of attention since the Second World War, but they are by no means a new phenomenon. In general, any change in the control of a company by acquisition of its shares is technically a take-over: a distinction may, however, be drawn between cases where there is a willing buyer and a willing seller and cases where the seller is unwilling, or may not even know of the bid until it is too late to do anything about it. It is the second type of bid which usually makes the headlines. Although some take-over bids are undoubtedly the work of financiers manipulating the market for their own ends, it is probably true that most are the work of businessmen seeking to expand and strengthen their firms (and sometimes to diversify), to increase the scope for profitable operation, and sometimes to suppress competition.

Two main motives for take-overs may be distinguished. The first is the straightforward expansion motive which we have already discussed; the second is what we may call the 'bargain' motive, which induces a businessman to buy up a company for what he thinks is a bargain price. The taker-over may see, for example, that a company's assets are undervalued, or that excess profits have been retained in the past so that shares may be undervalued. There have been extreme cases where ultra-cautious firms, or firms which believe in financing all of their own development without going outside the firm, have acquired excessive liquid assets in the form of securities and cash (which, being the property of the company, are taken over when the firm changes ownership). When such firms have been bought out by the medium of share purchases, the purchase price of the firm has sometimes turned out to be less than the value of the liquid assets. Such extremes are rare, but cases of similar cash 'gifts' to take-over specialists are by no means uncommon.

Spectacular as these cases are, however, they are by no means the most important. Much more frequently a businessman sees that another firm has valuable assets which could yield big profits if efficiently managed: property take-overs are usually motivated by the desire of the bidders to acquire sites of high development value which is at present put to less profitable use; land used for public houses, for example, may be put to more profitable use as shoe shops, supermarkets and so on. Since the end of the war there have been big structural changes in British industry, which have had two main effects: on the one hand some industries have declined, either relatively or absolutely, and their assets have been used less profitably than they might otherwise; and in addition even within industries the differences between the most efficient and the least efficient firms have become more obvious (this is always likely to be the case in a period of change, because some adapt themselves more readily than others). More efficient firms have taken over less efficient; growing industries have taken over the assets of declining or less profitable industries.

It is even argued that, by improving the allocation and distribution of resources in this way, take-over bidders perform a useful social service via the price mechanism. The claim may not be universally valid, but at least it is true that many take-overs are from legitimate business motives. Capital gains are often made as a result of the process, and these are frequently criticized, but against this it must be argued that a bidder will only offer more than the market value of securities if they have been undervalued in the past, for instance because of bad management, bad dividend policies, etc., and in fact there have been several cases in which bidders have withdrawn when market prices have gone too high. It is also argued that any capital gains which may accrue merely compensate for years of underpayment of dividends and low capital values; an argument which would be more convincing if such gains went to the people who had held these securities through the bad period, whereas the gains frequently go to speculators or other people who have bought the shares just in time for the take-over gains to be made.[31]

Like every other form of business activity the take-over may be abused (and it is arguable that there is a case for legislation), but they are merely one form of merger, and one of the many ways in which a firm may grow in order to achieve the various technical and other economies of scale with which we have been concerned in this chapter.

[31] See George Bull and Anthony Vice, *Bid for Power* (Elek, 3rd edn., 1961) and Paul Ferris, *The City* (Gollancz, 1960). These two books give entertaining, if superficial, accounts of some take-over bids in practice.

During the present century the tendency in Britain, as in all of the industrialized countries of the world, has been towards a growth in the size of business units. Before the First World War industry in the United Kingdom was dominated by the small, highly individualistic business unit, with unincorporated businesses and small private companies predominating. There were, of course, some large corporations, and many of our present-day giants were beginning to grow even then, but the large concerns were not yet of dominant importance. There were mergers and other monopolistic agreements, too, but again these were on such a relatively small scale in proportion to the total number of firms that they did not invalidate the general principle that British industry was operating with small-scale units. Many of the seeds of growth had been sown, but in the particular type of competitive world of the nineteenth century, small-scale operation paid.

Between the wars, in the depressed state of British industry, the climate of operation changed, and there was some acceleration in the tendency towards growth in the size of units: this was due partly to mergers, often of a defensive character, which were common in such industries as coal and steel; and partly to a growing realization of the importance of operating at the optimum size. The call for 'rationalization' of production in bigger units was familiar in the 1930s, particularly in the heavy industries.[32] Since 1939 this tendency towards increasing size of business units has continued.

Small firms have by no means lost their importance, however, and well over 80 per cent of manufacturing establishments in Britain employ fewer than 100 work-people. They account, however, for only 17 per cent of total sales and just over 20 per cent of total employment.

The size structure of manufacturing establishments in Britain in 1958 is shown in Table 3.3: the table does not provide an accurate picture of the size of business units, since it refers to establishments (defined as the whole of the premises under

[32] In 1926 the Report of the Royal Commission on the Coal Mining Industry, Cmd. 2600 (The Samuel Commission), stressed that one of the things wrong with the industry was its organization in excessively small units of production; a point which was stressed again almost 20 years later in the Reid Report (Report of the Technical Advisory Committee to the Ministry of Fuel and Power, 1945, Cmd. 6610.)

the same ownership or management at a particular address; or approximately the plant); and a business unit may consist of several such establishments or plants. In terms of sales and

TABLE 3.3

SIZE OF MANUFACTURING ESTABLISHMENTS IN GREAT BRITAIN, JANUARY 1956

	Total	Number of employees					
		11–24	24–99	100–149	500–999	1000–1999	2000 or more
Number of establishments							
Mining products, etc.	2,611	585	1,330	601	65	20	10
Chemicals, etc.	2,239	528	923	607	111	42	28
Metal manufacture	1,915	314	751	581	148	68	53
Engineering, shipbuilding and electrical goods	8,886	2,210	3,772	2,089	436	248	131
Vehicles	5,672	2,099	2,522	716	140	96	99
Precision instruments	5,708	1,665	2,742	1,091	154	44	12
Textiles	6,210	1,002	2,770	2,197	183	43	15
Leather	930	316	466	143	5	—	—
Clothing	6,254	1,823	3,156	1,154	99	20	2
Food, drink, tobacco	6,070	1,990	2,670	1,182	133	70	25
Paper and printing	4,334	1,273	1,995	899	113	39	15
Wood, cork, etc.	5,484	1,704	2,733	918	80	32	17
TOTAL	56,313	15,509	25,830	12,178	1,667	722	407
Number of employees (thousands)							
Mining products, etc.	304	10	66	126	44	30	28
Chemicals, etc.	436	9	48	130	78	60	111
Metal manufacture	552	5	39	135	102	94	177
Engineering, shipbuilding and electrical goods	1,856	39	189	457	306	351	514
Vehicles	1,034	36	117	147	100	141	493
Precision instruments	580	29	135	220	106	58	32
Textiles	862	18	149	464	121	60	50
Leather	56	6	23	24	3	—	—
Clothing	517	32	157	226	67	27	8
Food, drink, tobacco	704	34	130	248	94	99	99
Paper and printing	481	22	97	187	79	51	45
Wood, cork, etc.	506	30	135	179	51	41	70
TOTAL	7,888	270	1,285	2,543	1,151	1,012	1,627

Source: *Annual Abstract of Statistics*, No. 94 (1957), Table 150, p. 129.
Note: A further 68,050 manufacturing establishments employed fewer than ten people.

employment, establishments with over 1000 employees are predominant, and large business units are even more important.

An inquiry by the National Institute of Economic and Social

Research[33] throws further light on the importance of large companies: 3000 or so quoted public companies out of a total of 276,269 with share capital accounted in 1953 for 46 per cent of total paid-up capital, 56 per cent of company profits and (in manufacturing industry only) for 46 per cent of total employment. Even within this group, 512 companies with net assets of over £2.5 million each predominated, and these 512 companies[34] earn almost half of the profits and are responsible for about half of the capital expenditure of private industry.

An alternative approach is to measure the concentration of ownership of industry, which gives some idea of the importance of the largest business units of all. There are several measures of concentration, some more sophisticated than others, but perhaps the easiest to comprehend is the one used in the *Census of Production*. This is a ratio expressing the employment of the three largest business units in a particular trade as a percentage of the total employment in that trade: this is known as the Concentration Ratio. In manufacturing industry as a whole in Britain this ratio averaged 26 per cent in 1935 and 29 per cent in 1951.[35]

Evely and Little distinguish between three categories of concentration, shown in Table 3.4. The greatest volume of employment in British industry is in those industries and trades in which the three largest business units account for less than a third of total employment. They also point out that the increase in concentration in British industry is perhaps smaller than might be imagined *prima facie*: in only twenty-seven of the trades covered was there any increase in concentration, and in fourteen trades concentration declined; there was no significant change in the remainder. The main trades with increasing concentration were: mineral oil refining, coke ovens, drugs and pharmaceutical preparations, bread and flour confectionery, watches and clocks; but since 1951 there have been important

[33] See *Company Income and Finance* (National Institute of Economic and Social Research, 1956).

[34] Listed in *A Classified List of Large Companies Engaged in British Industry* (National Institute of Economic and Social Research, 1955).

[35] Evely and Little, *Concentration in British Industry* (National Institute of Economic and Social Research and Cambridge University Press, 1960). For an alternative approach, see P. E. Hart and S. J. Prais, 'The Analysis of Business Concentration, A Statistical Approach', *Journal of the Royal Statistical Society* Series A, Vol. 119 (1956), pp. 150–91.

mergers in the motor car industry, the aircraft industry, breweries and man-made fibres, and the picture has no doubt changed in the last 10 years. In the motor car industry in 1958, for example, the employment concentration ratio was 37.3 per cent.[36] This is still rather lower than might have been expected, but part of the explanation of this lies in the fact that the industry as defined for census purposes is rather wider in its coverage than the industry as normally considered. Of the fourteen trades in which concentration declined, the most important were wallpaper, matches, boots and shoes and biscuits.

TABLE 3.4

CONCENTRATION OF EMPLOYMENT, MANUFACTURING INDUSTRY, 1951

Concentration category	*Trades*		*Employment*	
	Number	*Percentage of total*	*Thousands*	*Percentage of total*
High (67 per cent and over)	50	23	636	10
Medium (34–66 per cent)	69	31	1545	24
Low (33 per cent and under)	101	46	4188	66
TOTAL	220	100	6369	100

Source: Evely and Little, op. cit., p. 51.

The general picture of size and concentration in British industry is summed up by Evely and Little,[37] who divide trades into three main types. The first, and most important, is the group with relatively low concentration, due to the presence of a few giants surrounded by a host of 'pygmies': the iron and steel industry, the radio industry, bread and flour confectionery are good examples. The second most important type is 'the more nearly competitive type, where firms are many and there are no extreme disparities in size': clothing, building and cutlery are good examples. The third type is the least important of the three, 'where there is one or more giants controlling more than one-third of the output': motor cars, mineral oil refining, rubber tyres, aircraft and tobacco are well-known examples.

To put the question of size into perspective, there are still a lot of small firms in Britain and the concentration of employ-

[36] *Census of Production, 1958*, Part 133, Table 5.

[37] Evely and Little, op. cit., p. 14.

ment appears to be less marked than may be thought from a casual look at industry; but the biggest firms do account for most of the employment, assets and profits in the country, and their share is probably increasing. The trend is still towards an increase in the size of business units.

PRODUCTION AND COSTS IN PRACTICE

Two assumptions are implicit in theoretical discussion of costs: one is that techniques remain constant and cannot be changed without upsetting the operation of the laws; the other is that the businessman makes the best possible use of the techniques available to him,[38] and that the achievement of an optimum is due to the Law of Diminishing Returns and not to increasing business efficiency in its own right. Neither of these assumptions holds when the real world is considered. One of the most important problems which faces the businessman in real life is that of using the best available techniques and making the best possible use of them: he cannot assume that techniques remain constant, and indeed technological change is one of the driving forces of industry, the most successful businesses frequently being those who make the best use of new techniques. In addition, the assumption that the businessman always uses techniques with maximum efficiency is in itself dubious: one of the more pressing day-to-day problems of management is to achieve maximum efficiency and minimum costs with the means of production which are available. These are the practical issues with which the production departments of most firms are concerned, and they are relevant to a discussion of business economics.

The problems of production management cover a wide field, but in practice the essence of each problem is the improvement of efficiency and the reduction of unit costs. In order to achieve this aim most firms undertake some departmental specialization: under the general heading of Production Departments the firm may have departments dealing with Production Engineering, Production Planning and Control, Work Study, Materials

[38] For example, Stigler says: 'Production functions are descriptive of techniques or systems of organization of productive services, and they are therefore taken from disciplines such as engineering and industrial chemistry: to the economic theorist they are data of analysis' (Stigler, op. cit. (Macmillan, New York, 1947), p. 109).

Handling, Labour Relations, Purchasing and so on, in addition to departments based on technical requirements and usually known under the name of some process.

In general, however, these departmental specializations may be looked upon as concerned with the technical relations which underly the production function.[39] For present purposes we must accept most of the results of studies of technical relations as the data of business economics. But there are still several topics which must be considered as predominantly economic rather than technical in character (or at the very least as having a significant economic content) in that they involve a major element of choice.

Methods of Production

One of the choices which needs to be made in practice is that of a method of production. The choice of technique was discussed earlier in this chapter, but there we had to assume that we knew what were technically the best methods of production, and in real life that is not always true, and the practical problem of choice of a way of producing a product is not always purely a technical problem. The choice of a method depends partly on the techniques available and partly on the scale of production.

In practice, production may be carried on in any of three main ways (or a combination of all three), the choice depending largely on the scale of production and length of run which can be achieved. The first of these, job production, is usually small scale; the second, batch production, is usually medium scale but may also be employed in large-scale production; the third, mass, or flow production, is almost always, as its name implies, large scale. As we shall see, however, large-scale production does not necessarily entail flow methods. It is rare to find a firm which uses one method to the exclusion of the other two, but product lines or part lines are frequently specialized on this basis.

Job production is common in small businesses, but many large concerns produce some of their lines by this method, the essence of which is that the firm manufactures single products

[39] The quantitative aspects of some of these topics are discussed in Chapters VIII and X of this book.

(or at the most a few of any one product) usually to the requirements of the customer. This is sometimes referred to as a 'one-off' method of production: it suffers from the disadvantage that few economies of scale can be achieved (save for multi-purpose plant, building and staff) and unit costs are usually relatively high; but where individual requirements have to be met no other method is possible. Examples of this kind of production are to be found in the manufacture of special-purpose machinery, bespoke tailoring and similar trades.

Batch production is the typical method of manufacture in British industry. It consists as the name implies of the manufacture of a batch or 'lot' of products at one time, but is distinguished from flow production in that the process is not continuous. The manufacture of several different products for stock, as in the shoe trade and the clothing trade, or to fairly regular orders, as for components for the motor vehicle industry and the radio industry, are particularly suited to batch production. Some of the advantages of large-scale production are achieved: for example, constant use of machinery, plant, skilled staff and so on, and the consequent ironing out of indivisibilities and the spreading of fixed costs; but complete specialization of inputs is not possible. This is the type of production which is most difficult to control, and it is more difficult the larger the variety of products, and efficient production makes big demands on management. It requires good quality control and efficient programming, and the achievement of optima in the productive departments and for each product is an interesting economic problem: it is frequently solved in practice by rules-of-thumb and by trial and error, but it is capable of more systematic solution.[40]

Mass or flow production is frequently found in firms side by side with batch production, but it depends for its success on large-scale operation. In general, the word 'flow' is preferable to 'mass' in this context: mass production is often treated both by economists and in common parlance as synonymous with large-scale production, but it is not necessary for flow methods to be used to achieve large-scale production, which may well be feasible for the production of large batches. Single-purpose plant and machines of large output capacity and high cost, like

[40] See Chapters VIII and X.

the automatic and semi-automatic machinery in modern motor car factories, is usually employed, and large outputs are needed to justify their installation. Products are usually highly standardized (with minor diversifications, as in the motor industry, added at a later stage of production) and they usually go through identical sequences of operations. Industries like oil refining, cement manufacture and flour milling have to be operated on a large scale and by flow methods in order to be efficient.

The advantages of large-scale production can usually be summed up as the advantages of specialization of function, standardization of product and full-capacity use of large indivisible factors. The main danger of flow production in particular is that of over-specialization and susceptibility to economic fluctuations: a close-down of a motor car factory is clearly an expensive business and may even be disastrous, but as we have seen even a reduction of output to (say) 50 per cent of capacity may have equally serious effects. It is here that we see illustrated, *par excellence*, the need for effective co-ordination of the production, marketing and financial aspects of the business.

Two typical problems associated with both batch and mass production are those of variety and length of run.

One of the major advantages of large-scale production is the high degree of specialization which is possible; but a corresponding limitation is that specialization usually means standardization, because in order to take advantages of specialization and the division of labour small changes in routines have to be ruled out. Further, the more complex is the mass-produced article, the more components it will usually have and the more the components themselves must be standardized, with the result that even minor differences in finished products are extremely difficult and costly to introduce.

From the point of view of the market, standardization has both its good and bad sides. Standardization makes choice easier, but there is a limit to the amount of uniformity that consumers will tolerate; and in practice many large-scale producers have decided (sometimes rightly, sometimes for very dubious reasons) that the consumer will buy more of their product if some variety is introduced. Product differentiation and advertising are the consequence of this, and they can be taken to extremes, both from the point of view of the consumer who may become cynical about the whole process, but also, and more relevant to the present discussion, from the production point of view. The cost of variety in the last resort is the loss of the benefits of standardization and specialization, and the businessman has always to balance the cost of one against the benefits of the other. In modern large-scale industry the tendency is for more and more reduction of variety where it costs most, in the large-scale production lines; and its introduction where it costs least, in the least specialized and smallest-scale parts of the operation, such as the trimming processes of motor car manufacture. Usually the nearer to the finished product, the better suited is the process for the introduction of variety. Standardized products may make for duller living; they almost always make for cheaper living.

The 'length of run' problem is closely associated with the scale of production. At the extreme, the largest mass-production units require the longest feasible production runs and fullest utilization of fixed factors, maintained if possible until all of the high-cost/high-output plant can be written off. The size of the market may limit this possibility subject to the qualifications discussed earlier. But even where full-time long runs are not possible it is still desirable to use fixed factors as fully as possible and the longest possible production runs are needed. What most motor car manufacturers want and aim for is a model which will run for several years with only minor modifications from year to year: the Volkswagen, the Morris Minor and the Ford Anglia/Popular have been conspicuous successes in this sense. The problem also applies to batch production—the largest possible batches are the most efficiently produced—but this may raise problems of storage and transport whatever the form of production, and the final answer may demand a complicated operations research solution.

One way of achieving the maximum possible length of run in relation to capital is by shift-working.

The main advantage of shift-working is that it economizes on capital; its main disadvantage is that it increases the cost of labour. The saving of capital arises because buildings and machines may be used for 24 hours per day rather than for

8 or 16 and for 7 days a week rather than for 5 or 6. This reduces the cost of capital to a limited degree because less capital is required to produce a given output if it is used intensively rather than intermittently. Thus, if machinery is never idle it will be used 168 hours a week rather than the 40 that might be normal with single shift-working. Interest charges on capital and buildings will be cut by a quarter in relation to the output produced. It is only interest charges that will be cut in this striking manner; there may be small reductions in insurance costs per unit of output (although in total there is likely to be an increase); but charges for depreciation or obsolescence are likely to fall much less markedly. No hard and fast rule can be laid down on this point. Depreciation is to some extent the result of using a machine and to some extent the result of general ageing. Even without use machinery deteriorates; it may rust or perish in other ways; more likely it will become out of date or obsolescent; Stephenson's Rocket is a museum piece even though it could still haul a coach. We can assign some orders of magnitude to the typical costs of operating capital in the United Kingdom industry.

Depreciation and obsolescence	10
Interest charges or equivalent	10
Raw materials	50
Labour	30
	100

The figures given in the above table are illustrative; they are not meant to be exact and while they give an average view of industry as a whole there is no reason to suppose that they represent the situation in any specific industry or firm. Indeed, as we shall see, the significance of the figures lies in the fact that they are not typical of every industry. It is now possible to do a little arithmetic on the basis of the above figures in order to see what would be the effect of working two or three rather than one shift per day while leaving the number of days worked per week unaltered. Since interest charges do not increase when output is increased, costs per unit of output on the second shift will immediately fall by 10; there may also be some reduction in the cost per unit of output of depreciation and obsolescence; a reduction of 2 may be taken to represent this. Thus costs on the second shift fall by 12 per unit of output. There will be no further reduction in interest charges by working three shifts; these have been eliminated already. But there may be a further small saving on account of depreciation and obsolescence per unit of output. More intensive working by, say, eliminating holidays or working the machinery faster would not be likely to effect much further reduction. Once interest charges are eliminated from our calculations there is not much further scope for cost cutting by shift-working.

The savings in capital cost will almost certainly be off-set in part by the need to offer some incentive for second and third shift-working. Additional payments for shift-work vary; for an evening shift for the housewife no additional payment may be needed above ordinary rates of payment; but second and third shifts are normally likely to involve additional payments equivalent to a quarter or third of earnings on the day shift even if the times of the shifts are adjusted to minimize inconvenience. The actual increase in labour costs is often higher than this; it is not always easy to maintain standards on the night-shift or provide adequate supervision. Thus an addition of one-third to labour costs per unit of output is not an unreasonable estimate of the increase that would result. In the arithmetic example that we have chosen the savings in capital costs per unit of output would be slightly greater than the increase in labour costs that would result; but there would not be much in it. Nevertheless, if this little were not absorbed by the need to make price reductions in order to sell more output, it would make an appreciable contribution to profits.

The above example approximates the cost structure of the cotton industry fairly well and enables us to explain why the United Kingdom cotton industry has been reluctant to adopt double or treble shift-working while Japan and the United States have found it advantageous to use their equipment more intensively. It is fairly easy to account for Japanese custom on this account on the ground that it has needed to be severely competitive to win world markets; it is less easy to explain why the United States, a rich country, has adopted shift-working.

The feature distinguishing United Kingdom and United States practice is to be found in the relative modernity of their equipment. The United Kingdom industry has been declining in importance over many years; there has been little incentive to re-equip the industry with modern equipment and more than enough of older type to produce all that could be sold. The incentive to purchase new equipment was small when markets were shrinking and there was a surfeit of capacity. In the United States, on the other hand, modern automatic looms were installed; and for these to pay, shift-working was necessary. Those firms in the United Kingdom that were re-equipping in the 1950s were also keen to adopt shift-working.

From the illustration it can be seen that shift-working is favoured when:

1. Capital costs are high. This may be because a process uses a comparatively large quantity of capital in relation to output, because the cost of capital equipment is high relatively to, say, other countries, or because interest rates are high.

2. Depreciation is not closely linked to the output that is produced and is mainly the result of an ageing process. This, for example, is true of buildings but not of a high-speed cutting tool.

3. Obsolescence is a material danger and as much as possible has to be got out of the capital used before it is out of date.

4. Labour costs are low. This may be true when wages are low or because in a capital-intensive process very few men may be required.

5. Trade unions and their members do not require a substantial increase in wages for shift-working.

6. Difficulty is experienced in meeting demand because capacity is limited or because an unusually heavy flow of orders materializes.

In practice, the reasons for working shifts are often technical rather than economic. The industries in which shift-working is predominant are generally those working continuous processes such as the metal manufacturing and chemical industries or those that find it necessary to work at night, as applies in baking, newspaper printing, electricity generation and transport. But there are a number of other industries in which shift-working is important for economic reasons, for example, the jute industry, or in coal mining where large sums must be invested in opening and developing pits. Other industries, such as the motor car industry, may work shifts when demand is at a seasonal peak and occasionally a few machines or departments may work continuously because they use exceptionally expensive equipment. In a survey of shift-working, covering some $5\frac{1}{2}$ million wage earners, conducted by the Ministry of Labour in 1954 it was found that roughly 12 per cent were engaged in shiftwork.[41]

In underdeveloped countries where capital is scarce, and therefore expensive, and where some forms of labour are cheap, there are strong reasons for advocating shift-working. In the major industrial countries there is little reason to suppose that shift-working is ever likely to attain predominance. Higher real earnings make men more reluctant to work shifts and encourage them to exact a higher price for doing so. There is no reason to suppose that capital costs per unit of output will rise as time goes on and some reason for supposing that they will fall. Shift-working is thus likely to be confined to processes where it is technically unavoidable and to those exceptional industries or processes that require large amounts of capital.

Costs and Business Decisions

The economics of shift-working is one example of the ways in which a businessman must have regard to his cost structure in order to reduce costs or minimize them through the use of the best techniques and methods of production. Business decisions, since they are about the future, require the businessman to choose between alternatives, and to do this it is necessary to know the costs involved.[42]

The collection of cost and control data is useful to the firm in its aim of keeping costs down, and the development in recent years of what has come to be known as Management Accountancy is the practical approach to some of these problems. There is a growing understanding between economists and accountants about the sort of data which should be collected,

[41] *Ministry of Labour Gazette* (October 1954), p. 336.

[42] The assessment of the over-all implications of the various courses of action open to a business is a function of operations research (see Chapter X).

and about its meaning. The function of management accounting is the provision of data for business decisions, and it requires that costs be viewed as data on which to base planning and to be related to future decisions rather than simply to record what has taken place in the past. There are two main aspects of management accounting: first is prediction and planning, usually subsumed in the Budget process, discussed in the last section of this book; second is the aspect of control and keeping to plans, which is partly a question of control procedures and partly a question of costing.

The main objective of cost accounts is the analysis of records and an allocation of the main cost items to the departments and processes through which they arise. In his consideration of costs the businessman wants the answer to a whole series of questions: the effect of using new techniques, whether or not products are paying their way, how much to increase prices as a result of an increase in costs, whether to accept an order to contract, and at what price. In short he wants to be able to assess the efficiency of his firm from the records at his disposal. If his cost accounts are properly constructed they will go a long way to providing him with answers.

Cost data cannot do everything, and the businessman also needs to know something about his markets and his competitors: what his cost data will usually tell him is whether, with given production methods, or improved methods, he has a reasonable prospect of competing with others in the same field.

Several types of costing systems are used in practice, and the method employed usually depends on the nature of the productive processes of the firm; but the principle usually employed is to try to analyse expenditure in such a way that something like the correct proportion of total costs can be allocated to individual activities. For present purposes we can confine ourselves to three main types.

The first main type attempts to cost each job, or batch, or contract separately, or to allocate costs to certain departments or processes. Several names are given to these systems (e.g. Job Costing, Batch Costing, Output Costing, etc.), and although they differ in the accounting methods employed, they are all forms of 'record' or 'historical' costing. If properly constructed such records provide data for control and checks, and serve a useful but very limited purpose.

The second type, coming into increasingly common use is 'standard' costing, which has grown up because of a dissatisfaction with historical and record costing. Perhaps the most important aspect of standard costing is that it implies a point of view that what is important is not so much what a product has cost (which may relate only to a special set of circumstances in which it was produced) as what the product can reasonably be planned to cost. The three most important elements are the allocation of overheads (or fixed costs) on a reasonable basis to each product, the use of costs as controls, and the importance of the *future* element of costs. Two authoritative definitions show the thinking which underlies the process.

Standard cost may be defined as: 'an estimated cost, prepared in advance of production or supply, correlating a technical specification of materials and labour to the prices and wage rates estimated for a selected period of time, with the addition of an apportionment of the overhead expenses estimated for the same period within a prescribed set of working conditions'.[43] Standard costing, as defined by the same authority, is 'the preparation of standard costs and their use to clarify the financial results of a business, particularly by the measurement of variation of actual costs from standard costs and the analysis of the causes of the variations for the purpose of maintaining maximum efficiency by executive action'.[44] Standard costing may also be used as part of a system of budgetary control.

The third main type is what has come to be known as 'marginal' costing. The choice of title is unfortunate because it may imply that this is the process of ascertaining marginal cost as it is understood by the economist: in fact this is not the case. What the accountant means by marginal cost is in fact variable cost (cost which may be avoided by ceasing production entirely) whereas what the economist means is the increment to total cost resulting from an increase in output of one unit. Although, as was seen earlier (p. 106) in the case of firms with a flat-bottomed

[43] *An Introduction to Budgetary Control, Standard Costing, Material Control and Production Control* (The Institute of Cost and Works Accountants, April 1950).
[44] Ibid.

long-run average cost curve, marginal cost is the same as variable cost, the logic of the two definitions is different.

The philosophy underlying this principle of costing appears to be that fixed costs are unavoidable and that what matters is to cover variable cost and make some contribution to fixed costs: whether or not to accept an order or to manufacture a product depends on what 'contribution' will be made to fixed costs after variable costs have been covered; and the approach is an attempt to take account of the fact that it is difficult to allocate fixed overhead costs to production on a basis varying with the level of output. The system has the virtue that it should allow changes in costs which are the result of production to be emphasized, but in practice there is a whole class of costs, sometimes called 'semi-variable' costs which are difficult to allocate, and even the variable cost is not always easy to calculate. And the concept of fixed costs is, as we have seen, by no means unambiguous, and with firms in a state of change of techniques (as they usually are) such allocation is often arbitrary. But it is better to be arbitrary than to leave things to chance.

A useful product of the marginal costing approach is 'break-even analysis'. A business may be said to break even when over a period of time its total revenue equals its total costs: this point can be calculated *via* marginal cost analysis by working out the contribution per unit of sales made to fixed cost and from that determining how many units of output are necessary for the firm to cover its fixed costs and hence to break even; or alternatively this may be done by means of a chart.[45]

In the long run, of course, selling prices must cover fixed costs, and the success of a business which operated a marginal costing system would depend on maximizing the total 'contribution' to fixed costs over the whole range of products. In general, resources should be concentrated on those products which yield the greatest excess of selling price over variable (so-called marginal) cost; but there are so many possible exceptions to this rule that it is not necessarily so helpful as it may seem. It may be necessary to continue to supply special customers, or use certain lines as baits for other lines, and marketing policy rather than costs may dictate this approach, which may be in

[45] See Chapter VIII.

the long-run interests of the firm. Marginal costing itself does not provide information about this sort of thing, nor does it tell the businessman the effect of taking one order on other orders (there may be bottlenecks which may, for example, restrict the fulfilment of more than a limited number of orders using one group of machines). But this is the same thing as saying that a costing system does not tell a businessman everything about his firm—it is one useful tool, but that is all.

It is, however, useful to have empirical evidence about costs on which to base decisions. Accounting information and technical information are useful, but they both suffer from the limitation that they do not explain relationships: the most useful (but the most expensive both in money and time) approach is to try to find functional relationships between costs and the determinants of these costs as discussed in this chapter. Costs depend on the scale of output, fluctuations in output, the size of batch, changes in style, etc., and statistical cost analysis may be used to assess the relative importance of these and other factors.

Such analysis is not merely useful for the empirical verification of economic theories; it is also of considerable practical value. One of the pioneers of this sort of analysis was Joel Dean.[46] In a study of the costs of a furniture factory he analysed direct labour costs and its determinants: larger lot sizes and increases in production tended to result in reduced unit costs, whilst on the other hand the introduction of new styles, increased labour turnover and reductions in output all raised cost to different extents (to which it was possible to attach numerical values in place of mere statements that such might be expected to be the case).

If the components of costs and the factors influencing costs are systematically analysed in the terms of this chapter,[47] the analysis can provide a basis for both cost forecasting and cost control and for the making of business decisions.

Costs are important to business decisions inasmuch as they are relevant to plans for the future and choice between plans. These plans are concerned with the scale of production, the

[46] Joel Dean, *Managerial Economics* (Prentice Hall, 1960), Chapter 5.

[47] See also Chapter X. Both Dean (*op. cit.*) and Johnston (*Statistical Cost Analysis*) contain useful discussions of relevant statistical methods.

techniques of production and the aim of minimizing the cost of a given output.

PRODUCTIVITY

The work of cost accountants, efficiency experts and economists meet in making productivity comparisons. The interests of the first two are likely to be concerned with the efficiency of firms and what can be done to improve it, and the economist more often with the efficiency of industries and countries and the reasons for differences as much as the measures that might be taken to improve productivity.

Productivity measurements attempt to compare the output of a productive process with the inputs that are necessary for it to take place. This is not a simple operation. No productive process involves less than two forms of input; most employ at least three or four that are significant; and the total number may rise to hundreds or even thousands in some instances. The lone street trader requires both his own personal abilities and capital in some form before he can attempt to make a sale; the motor car manufacturer incorporates thousands of components into his product. Output may be as varied: the products that can be produced from crude oil are almost infinite; the retail grocer sells hundreds of lines; and the locomotive builder tailors an infinite variety of locomotives to order.

Such complexity makes it difficult to compare inputs and outputs. In principle it would be possible to calculate a rate of transformation for every product and every type of input; but in many cases this would be difficult to do and it would nearly always be very time consuming. On a modest scale such information can, however, be used to make comparisons with other firms or with other periods for which similar calculations had been made.

There are no absolute standards of efficiency in economics. Norms are constantly changing; what is good in one situation may be bad in another, standards of productivity that were revolutionary 30 years ago may be mediocre today; and as we have seen, production methods suited to one set of prices may be quite inappropriate in another. There is very little that is analogous with efficiency in the sense that this term is used by engineers in relation to heat engines.

There will be few occasions when productivity comparisons can take into account all the possible relations that can be established between input and output. Fortunately, in economic calculations quite crude comparisons can often put a new complexion on affairs. Generally it is best to confine comparisons to situations that have a good deal in common, for example, to compare the same firm at different points of time, or to compare firms with similar activities. It is often convenient to direct attention to certain principal products, particularly if these can be identified in physical terms such as tons of steel or yards of the same type of cloth. Where this is not possible useful comparisons can still be made by valuing output at the prices at which it is sold or, with more sophisticated comparisons, at constant prices, or sometimes at the prices realized in other countries or by the other firms.

The same kind of considerations apply to inputs. In the first place it may be helpful to concentrate exclusively on the number of men employed or the number of man-hours worked. Labour is not a homogeneous unit, skilled labour may be expected to contribute more to output than unskilled labour and so on; but if productivity comparisons are made between firms engaged on the same type of work the chances are that the make-up of their labour forces will not differ very radically.

One widely used method of productivity comparison is to divide the net output or added value of a firm by the number of people employed. Such a measure may be grossly misleading, the firms may not be really comparable, one may use more capital than another, one may be a specialist producer experiencing a dearth of orders and the other in the full swing of mass production. But however crude the comparison may be it will set the ball rolling and suggest further comparisons that need to be made before definite conclusions can be drawn. If the amount of capital used is thought to differ between the firms it may be possible to calculate the value of output per unit of capital employed; if the consumption of raw materials is a widely variable factor it may be possible to do the same thing for raw materials and there are many other possibilities.

Less frequently it may be possible to make an almost exhaustive comparison of the factors affecting productivity. A comparison of milling costs in four mills carried out by the

Centres D'études et de Mesures de Productivité provides a good illustration of what can be done by detailed comparisons. In this instance it was felt that as labour accounted for only a small part of production costs it was necessary to take other factors into account. Table 3.5 shows an analysis of costs per quintal produced in four mills.

TABLE 3.5

COMPARISON OF MILLING COSTS IN FOUR MILLS

	Mill A	*Mill B*	*Mill C*	*Mill D*	*Standard costs*
1. Interest on employed capital	44.10	49.50	36.90	—	44.40
2. Financial charges	33.10	33.10	30.00	33.10	33.10
3. Taxes, rates, etc.	5.30	6.80	19.30	11.40	12.90
4. Insurance	13.90	12.20	9.80	7.40	11.80
5. Depreciation	63.50	69.00	60.50	—	63.90
6. Repairs and maintenance	35.50	95.50	67.20	40.70	49.20
7. Labour (production and storage)	115.90	134.70	94.00	—	85.90
8. Power	79.40	28.70	53.20	57.20	65.00
9. Sacks	14.80	19.70	13.50	—	18.60
10. Collecting of sacks	12.00	12.00	12.00	—	12.00
11. Charges calculated on output	2.40	4.00	4.00	—	4.00
12. Office overheads	54.40	25.10	51.80	—	50.70
13. Administrative overheads	37.30	68.50	52.60	—	41.80
14. Sundry sales overheads	46.90	49.30	45.70	—	42.20
TOTAL	558.50	608.10	550.50		535.50

There are very wide differences between the costs of the various operations that indicate differences in the performance of the four mills and it is clear that there are differences in productivity. Inter-firm comparisons of this kind offer great opportunities for improvement in performance. Low productivity is often unrecognized because those responsible for running a firm do not know what is possible. Productivity comparisons bring this to light and at the same time by stimulating interest in the whole subject they indicate opportunities for further improvement in even the best practice. It is usual to find that the best practices are not confined to one or two firms and that an interchange of methods may be beneficial.

It is not always possible to make detailed comparisons of efficiencies department by department as was done in the French study. Herbert Ingham and L. Taylor Harrington advocate making inter-firm comparisons on the basis of nine operating ratios.[48] These ratios are: (1) Profit after Tax to Capital Employed, (2) Profit after Tax to Sales, (3) Sales to Capital Employed, (4) Cost of Production to Sales, (5) Cost of Marketing to Sales, (6) Cost of Administration to Sales, (7) Fixed Assets to Total Assets, (8) Sales to Average Stocks, and (9) Average of Outstanding Debts to Average Sales per Day. Such comparisons may be expected to work only if the firms being compared are of reasonably similar size and engaged in the same kind of work. It requires considerable experience to assess the significance of such calculations and they may be very misleading unless like is compared with like.

Economists have found that intercountry comparisons can be very revealing. Rostas concluded that 'A comparison of output and employment in 31 manufacturing industries shows that in the pre-war period of 1935–9, average productivity—as measured by physical output per worker—was at least twice (about 2.2 times) as high in the U.S. as in Britain'.[49] Professor Frankel writing about the period 1947–48 concluded that in general output per man-hour in American industry was a great deal more than twice as high as in British industry. Table 3.6 summarizes his comparisons.

Some part of the differences may be due to statistical incomparabilities; but the differences are too great and too pervasive for there to be any doubt that productivity in the United Kingdom lags far behind that of the United States. The differences are not universal: there are American firms and even industries that lag behind British performance; but there is sufficient uniformity in the situation for an explanation to be sought in generalizations. How far can the difference, for example, be attributed to the fact that the American market is much larger than that of the home market enjoyed by United Kingdom industrialists?—probably not very far in Rostas's view. United States' productivity was often high relative to that of the United Kingdom even when United States' plants were smaller than those in the United Kingdom, and this was true even where costs were known to fall with an increasing scale of output. There was, however, a strong presumption that far-

[48] *Interfirm Comparison for Management* (British Institute of Management, 1958).
[49] L. Rostas, *Comparative Productivity in British and American Industry*, (Cambridge University Press, 1948), p. 27.

reaching standardization in motor-cars, electric lamps, soap, etc., was to a certain extent responsible for the higher U.S. output per worker, but no exact measurements were made.

TABLE 3.6

PRODUCTIVITY IN THIRTY BRITISH AND AMERICAN MANUFACTURING INDUSTRIES

	Physical output per worker U.S./G.B. ratio	*Physical output per man-hour U.S./G.B. ratio*	*Size of market physical output U.S./G.B. ratio*	*Size of Establishment* By number employees U.S./G.B ratio	*Size of Establishment* By output U.S./G.B. ratio
Tin containers	4.96	4.97	9.49	1.04	5.43
Cardboard containers	4.20	4.24	11.75	0.94	4.59
Pig iron	4.17	4.91	5.78	0.80	3.42
Wool yarn	4.03	4.53	2.52	1.27	4.85
Radio receiving tubes	3.36	3.74	11.55	1.06	5.58
Cigarettes	3.25	3.63	3.80	2.77	16.96
Wool carpets and rugs	3.15	3.28	5.76	2.01	6.04
Glass containers	2.87	3.06	5.73	1.58	4.67
Soap	2.81	2.89	4.29	1.02	2.45
Paper sacks	2.71	2.77	10.61	1.81	5.05
Matches	2.48	2.59	5.53	2.86	7.06
Ice cream	2.11	2.14	28.24	0.73	1.43
Animal feeds	2.11	2.06	9.75	0.60	1.28
Biscuits	2.04	2.18	3.29	0.76	1.72
Malt liquors	1.98	1.98	2.13	1.53	2.40
Grain milling	1.94	1.86	2.59	0.82	1.64
Bicycles	1.80	1.88	1.37	—	—
Rubber wires	1.76	2.03	6.98	1.39	2.64
Jute yarn	1.69	1.77	—	—	—
Sugar:					
U.S., cane; G.B., beet	1.66	1.82	2.03	1.96	4.05
U.S., beet; G.B., beet	0.77	0.85	0.67	0.51	0.46
Building bricks	1.66	1.77	1.35	0.95	1.48
Paint brushes	1.63	1.74	2.65	—	—
Cotton piece goods	1.62	1.78	6.32	4.56	7.64
Boots and shoes	1.51	1.67	4.30	1.42	2.96
Rope and twine	1.51	1.61	2.28	1.48	1.94
Margarine	1.21	1.23	0.81	0.52	0.66
Cement	1.15	1.39	3.72	0.99	1.06
Razor blades	1.09	1.12	2.80	—	—
Cured fish	0.95	1.20	0.30	1.08	1.07
Manufactured ice	0.75	0.69	41.27	0.59	0.46

Source: *Productivity Measurement Review*, February 1956, p. 50: (From 'Anglo-American Productivity Differences: their magnitude and some causes by Maurice Frankel, *American Economic Review*, May 1955, pp. 94-119).

Frankel put more emphasis on this factor and concluded that standardization and specialization are the real causes of high productivity in the United States.

It may be that this is an important factor in the observed differences, for standardization and specialization permit highly mechanized manufacturing processes. These require much more capital investment per worker and it is in this respect that there are striking differences between the two countries. As an indication of availability of capital Rostas compared the amount of horse power per employed worker in a number of countries (Table 3.7).

TABLE 3.7

HORSE-POWER PER WORKER IN SELECTED COUNTRIES

	Horse-power per worker
United Kingdom, 1930	
Factory trades	2.83
All manufacturing trades	2.51
United States, 1929	
Factory trades	4.91
United States, 1939	
Factory trades	6.42
Germany, 1933	
All manufacturing trades	3.76
Switzerland, 1937	2.70
Switzerland, 1944	3.40
Holland, 1937	3.80

To conclude from these figures that it is true that more horse-power per worker invariably means more output per worker would be to over-simplify the comparisons and to misunderstand the nature of economic causation. It is noticeable, for example, that workers in Germany and Holland had more horse-power per worker than in the U.K. even though at the time the comparisons were made output per worker was in all probability less. In inter-country comparisons of this kind much depends on the industry mix; some industries require more capital than others and if they are more heavily represented in one country than in another this will disturb the comparison.

Further analysis of the figures illustrates the need to handle indicators of comparative productivity with discernment; while it is true that American output per head is shown on Rostas's figures to be at least double that in Great Britain, output per unit of horse-power would be about the same. Wages are a more important element in costs in industrialized countries than power, otherwise it would be reasonable to stress the need to economize power rather than labour. Care must be exercised in agricultural comparisons for the same reason; in arid countries output per unit of rainfall may be a much better indicator of efficiency than output per man or output per acre. This underlines the earlier point that there are many ways of developing productivity indicators, and while it is possible to combine them in various ways in order to give an overall impression of efficiency, no absolute measures can be developed. The problem is to select those indicators that are most use for the purpose in hand.

While comparative indicators of capital employed per man provide a clue to the explanation of differences in productivity, and other factors may have a bearing on the question, it is seldom possible to account fully for differences in productivity in these terms. The quality of management, attitudes to industry, systems of wage payment, the efficiency of the machine tool industry and educational opportunities are other tangible and intangible factors that have to be taken into account. Managerial skill may far transcend the importance of apparent differences in the amount of capital available per worker. High output per man, for whatever reason it is achieved, is likely to give rise to a high ratio of output to capital equipment, simply because the equipment itself is used more intensely in relation to the labour that is employed.

These general considerations may seem to be remote from the work of the production engineer trying, perhaps, to raise the output of a small section of a works by a few per cent. But they are just as germane. Much government policy has been activated by the conviction that capital investment was the obvious means to increase output per head; initial allowances are made on new investment for this very reason. But if the purchase of adequate capital equipment is all that is needed to raise productivity to acceptable standards why cannot it be carried out without the need for additional incentives? If it is more often true that the benefits of capital equipment go unperceived than that they are ruled out as being uneconomic, the remedies for low productivity may lie less in the purely economic field and more in that of education.

Government intervention in industrial affairs can be a useful adjunct in promoting productivity. The Working Parties appointed at the end of the war to report on a number of industries and the missions organized by the Anglo-American Productivity Council in the same period[50] were one device for reviewing industrial matters, sometimes with the assistance of independent outside observers. They achieved only moderate success. But their conclusions frequently pointed the way to changes in industrial practice that would stimulate output and increase productivity. The recommendations of the Working Parties were many and various; they ranged from advocating an economic intelligence service for the furniture industry and the giving of prizes for design in the glass industry, to the large-scale replacement of machinery in the cotton industry. The latter recommendation was one of the many that had been made to the industry in the inter-war years and that had still to be put into effect in 1960 when renewed efforts were made by the Government of the day to achieve the substitution of new for old machinery.

Little has been built on the reports of the working parties, but the past 10 years have seen an increasing intervention of Government in industrial affairs and a renewal of surveys of lagging industries, this time by the Department of Scientific and Industrial Research, which has considered the shipbuilding and machine tool industries. Recent proposals that some form of industrial planning should be attempted through the National Economic Development Council could also give a degree of central direction to the promotion of productivity. But too much should not be expected from any intervention in the affairs of an industry. In the last resort it is the decisions of managers and entrepreneurs that determine what is done and it is only when factors beyond their control, but within the control of outside bodies, impede their operations that outside intervention can be decisive.

[50] See Graham Hutton, *We Too Can Prosper*.

Chapter IV

PRICES

The interest of the economist in prices is mainly to discover if they are an efficient means of economic organization of society. Much of the theory of price is built up on assumptions about the behaviour of individuals and firms; but the central core of economics is concerned with the relationships of these individuals and firms through the price mechanism. Does the form of organization adopted result in the production of the right amount of commodities, an efficient combination of productive facilities and an acceptable distribution of the national income? Is the price mechanism as a means of organization the best that can be achieved? Or are other means of organization preferable?

The functions and limitations of the price system can best be understood if they are put in the general context of administration. In order to secure the economic advantages of large-scale production it is essential for the members of society to co-operate and some means of co-ordinating individual efforts has to be found. Such co-ordination lies in the answers that are given to the three key questions: What has to be produced; how is it to be produced; and how is the product to be shared?

There are those who think that problems of this nature can best be solved by a centrally directed administration. Certain aspects of them can and are. But the mass of detail which is involved in the complete resolution of all aspects of them requires devolution of decision, and it is difficult to think of sufficient devolution being achieved without the use of some system of pricing.

It might be possible, for example, to draw up production programmes in broad terms, to decide in outline how much food, how many houses, cars and refrigerators should be produced. But the programming of the components for the cars and refrigerators and the raw materials required for the production of food and houses is a task of great complexity, even if it is viewed not in terms of establishing a new programme but in terms of the modifications needed to meet changing circumstances. Such problems as those of allocating workers between farm and factory and between research and transport, while not insuperable, would be no less complicated. But without assigning some system of values to the goods and services that were produced it would be quite impossible to decide whether the programmes were optimal or whether some alternative use of resources, or a lower or higher production programme in total, would be preferable. It is not at all easy to make these decisions from a central standpoint. By using the price mechanism in a market economy it is possible to devolve most of the decisions necessary to run an economy. The price mechanism acts as a signalling device. Consumers have incomes and they signal what they want to buy by being prepared to pay for it; if the demand for a commodity rises, its price will rise; it will be more profitable to produce it; and it will be worth while to bid more for resources that are needed to produce it and if necessary to attract them from some alternative use. Thus the price mechanism enables a continuous watch to be kept on what is produced, and through the profit motive it gives a related incentive to divert resources to the places where they appear to be most needed.

There can be no doubt that the price mechanism as a means of organizing and controlling production works well, but it is not perfect. It is also clear that it does not give the same answer to all questions as would be given if decisions were taken centrally rather than by separate units combining through a market mechanism. The reason for this is fundamentally that costs and returns appear differently from different points of view. The cost to society of burning a coal fire is much greater than the cost to the individual; for the soot that goes up the chimney damages the property of neighbours as well as those who warm themselves by it. The benefits of urban development are not confined to those who initiate it but are extended to landowners who find the value of their property enhanced. Major conflicts between social and individual interests may have to be resolved by legislation designed to bring them into line. Legislation against monopoly, for example, has been introduced in several countries with the intention of ensuring that the monopolist fixes prices and output closer to levels that would appear to be desirable from the point of view of society. Revenues of a monopolist appear to be less to the monopolist himself than they appear to society and he is reluctant to produce too much for fear of spoiling his market. Thus the State is not always ready to give monopolists the right to determine the prices that they charge.

There are other occasions too when the State is not prepared to give business the unfettered right to determine prices. During the war prices were controlled by governments; this was continued in the United Kingdom and other countries during the immediate post-war years; and the Korean War prolonged price control into the 1950s. It is also common for agricultural producers to receive prices for their products that are Government determined either by the operation of support prices or by the granting of subsidies that serve to maintain the returns of agriculturists. In the United Kingdom certain other industries and forms of enterprise are subject to control and supervision that restricts their freedom to charge as they wish. This is true, for example of the iron and steel industry which is subject in this matter to the control of the Iron and Steel Board, and of the nationalized industries generally where price policy is influenced by the financial obligations imposed on them by Government. More generally industry has been exhorted on many occasions to refrain from increasing prices and adding to inflationary pressures. Although the effects of such interventions are indecisive they have some effect in modifying the prices that firms charge.

PRICE AND THE INDIVIDUAL FIRM

Even when prices are not controlled by governments it may be impossible for individual firms to fix prices. The producers of tin have no option but to accept the price that is determined by market forces or by the purchases or sales of the metal by the Tin Council with the intention of stabilizing prices. The price of wool is freely determined at the auctions; no single producer or consumer can exercise any decisive influence over it. Much the same is true of the price of jute and many other commodities that are freely traded on world commodity markets. Characteristically there are wide fluctuations in the price of primary products in contrast to the price of manufactured goods.

The bulk of manufactures, however, are sold at prices that are determined in part by individual producers. None of them can fix their prices irrespective of the policies of their competitors or of market conditions, but in each case there is some freedom of action, ranging from that enjoyed by the proprietor of a small firm with an established clientele to a monopolist who faces no direct competition in his line of business but who must nevertheless sell his product against the competing demands of other goods on consumers' purses.

It is natural to think of the bulk of sales as being made to consumers; ultimately the object of all production is to satisfy consumer wants. But goods in various forms of manufacture exchange hands many times before they reach the ultimate consumers. More prices are determined between firm and firm than are determined between producers and consumers; and firms may be expected to be knowledgable about costs, the strength of demand and the prospects of supplies. In general there will be a mutual disposition to do business over a period of years that will tend to carry with it a different attitude to the formation of prices than would emerge in a single isolated transaction. The combination of countervailing power and continuity in business relationships is likely to lead to the fixing of prices that bear some relationship to production costs and since production itself will be adjusted fairly rapidly to market conditions, prices of manufactures do not show the marked fluctuations that characterize primary production.

The typical conditions in which prices may be determined have been formalized by economists into concepts that are used in economic analysis. Primary-product markets come near to the economist's conception of *perfect competition* where in relation to the market both sellers and buyers are small, no one operator either buying or selling a significant proportion of the supplies reaching the market and being therefore, able to influence the market price. In contrast, the monopolist faces no direct competition, being the only seller in a market and consequently able to fix prices in relation to what the market will bear. If a graph were drawn relating the quantity saleable (on the horizontal axis) to the price (on the vertical axis) the curve would slope downwards from left to right, in contrast to the position as it appears to an individual firm in conditions of perfect competition in which the demand curve is pictured as a horizontal straight line, any quantity of output being saleable at the ruling market price. The opposite of a monopolist (a single seller) is a monopsonist (a single buyer); he also has a powerful influence on price and may regulate the quantity he buys in relation to the effect of his purchases on the price. In between these extremes a myriad cases are conceivable. There may be only a small number of sellers each selling a significant part of total supplies; there may be only a small number of buyers each taking a substantial part of production. And, as is not unusual, there may be situations in which oligopolists (few and powerful sellers) face oligopsonists (few and powerful buyers).[1] In the vast majority of cases, firms, whether buyers or sellers, will exercise some control or influence over prices and will have to bear in mind the fact that if they decide to increase their purchases or sales they will inevitably turn prices against themselves. It will also be impossible for them to consider their actions irrespective of consequential reactions from their competitors. A move on the part of one firm to decrease the price charged will inevitably be followed by similar moves on the part of its competitors if the initial price reduction begins to cost them part of their market. Price determination becomes a question of strategy, of assessing the reactions of competitors to some planned move and deciding in the light of this whether changes are desirable. In these circumstances firms are likely to try to move in concert with their rivals, sometimes regarding one as the price leader and by custom following his example even if there is no collusion; and they are likely to adjust prices in response to changes in conditions that can safely be seen to affect all producers, as is inclined to happen when a rise in wages is agreed with the unions or a general increase in raw material prices takes place.

What guidance can the economist give the business man on the prices he should charge? Economic analysis of this question is conducted on the assumption that the businessman is

[1] Those wishing to study these situations are referred to: J. Stigler, *The Theory of Price*, E. H. Chamberlin, *The Theory of Monopolistic Competition* and Joan Robinson, *The Economics of Imperfect Competition.*

endeavouring to maximize his profits. On this assumption it is necessary for him to equate *marginal revenue* and *marginal cost.* Marginal revenue is the shorthand of economists for the additional revenue that will result from selling one more unit of output. Marginal cost is the cost of producing and selling this additional unit at whatever level of output the business is operating. If marginal cost exceeds marginal revenue, the businessman will be adding more to his costs than to his revenue, and he will therefore not produce at that output; if marginal revenue exceeds marginal cost, he is adding more to his revenue than to his costs and it will pay him to expand. Only when the two are equal is he in equilibrium. Analytically this is unexceptionable, but it is not easy to translate into practical terms: what in effect the economist is saying is 'produce and sell up to the point at which any further increase in output will not add to profit'. At first sight such advice appears otiose. It would appear more clearly so if it were always the practice in business to fix prices in the way that would maximize profit. The value of this economic analysis lies, however, in the implications of the line of conduct advocated and in the social consequences that have to be considered.

The advice to produce and sell that output for which marginal costs and marginal revenue are equated, conceals a number of ambiguities and is not easily translated into practice. Marginal revenue is generally less than the price at which an article is sold. When conditions approximating to perfect competition prevail, the two will be the same (and average revenue per unit sold will always equal the marginal revenue from additional sales); but generally an increase in sales can be achieved only by reducing the price charged. This means that not only will less be obtained for the marginal unit that is sold but also that less will be obtained for the units that could have been sold at the existing price if no decision had been taken to increase sales. In most cases a price reduction affects all the units of output that are sold, since in organized markets it is difficult to charge different prices. If an attempt were made to do so it would often be frustrated because those who were asked to buy at higher prices would try to buy their supplies from those who could buy more cheaply. There are, of course, cases where discrimination in prices *is* possible; where, for example, transport costs make resale unprofitable, but the extent to which price discrimination can be practised must not be exaggerated. In most cases marginal revenue will be less than price.[2]

It is possible for the economist to explain his analysis by drawing a curve indicating the output that can be sold at any particular price and to derive from this the marginal revenue that will materialize from increasing sales by one unit from any given level. As we have seen it is not easy to establish precise demand curves but market research can narrow the uncertainties.

On the side of costs there are also uncertainties. Will the marginal cost curve as established from last year's production figures also apply to next year's sales? Does it take proper account of all the adjustments that are being made to productive capacity in response to changing markets and production possibilities? The marginal cost of increasing output by one unit tomorrow is very different from increasing output by one unit in 3 years' time. As time goes on it is possible increasingly to adapt a productive unit to a higher level of output. If the plant is not working to capacity the cost of increasing output by one unit will be governed mainly by the cost of the raw materials and labour incorporated in the product; there may also be some increase in the wear and tear of the machinery that is employed, but in most cases it will be very difficult to identify this as a cost item. If it continues to be necessary to increase output, there will come a time when in addition to purchasing more materials and labour it will become necessary to provide, say, more supervisory labour. At this point the production of an additional unit of output might be regarded as rising very steeply; in addition to the cost of labour and materials the cost of the wages of a supervisor would have to be added. Marginal cost would, however, drop to its previous level if it were decided to increase output further since we can assume that an additional supervisor would be all that was needed to oversee the production of a considerable number of additional units. We are faced here with a discontinuity in the cost curves due to the employment of an indivisible factor of production (the supervisor), and the significance of this for costs is discussed more

[2] Those wishing to pursue the geometry of price determination are referred to Stigler, *Theory of Price*, and Mrs Robinson, *The Theory of Imperfect Competition*.

fully in Chapter III. If output increases still further, marginal costs will once again start to rise as the plant is employed near to full capacity and it becomes necessary to work overtime at enhanced rates of pay. Finally, further increases in output may become impossible with the existing plant and the purchase of new machines may be necessary to double-up on parts of the plant; or it may become necessary to consider the construction of an extension to the plant or a new plant entirely.

Economic analysis traditionally draws a clear distinction between what is possible without new capital expenditure and what can be done if capital and equipment can be changed. The nature of the problem can be illustrated from the generation of electricity. Let us concentrate on the cost element of price determination and see what price would have to be charged if prices depended solely on marginal cost. So long as there is excess generating capacity the marginal cost of generating electricity is no more than the cost of the additional fuel that is needed to turn the generators as the load is increased. But there comes a time when existing capacity is no longer adequate to permit further increases in output and the installation of new capacity has to be considered. At this point the cost of installing new generators is relevant to marginal cost. It can be argued that if the purchase of new plant is to be justified both the costs of fuel used in generation and the cost of installing the plant would have to be met by the consumer. If the argument is followed to its logical conclusion it would appear that there would have to be a sharp rise in price in order to cover marginal costs defined in the way that we have indicated. Yet if a large modern plant were installed we might be back again in the position from which we started; excess capacity and marginal costs equal to the cost of fuel needed for generation.

We cannot escape this problem by arguing that even the largest (and perhaps most economical) generators are not so large in relation to the output of electricity that the problem of discontinuity and indivisibility does not arise. Even if this is true, the problem arises in another way through the operation of the peak load. If generating capacity is large enough to deal with the peak load, it is inevitably too large to deal with the demands that are made at other periods. Thus it might be argued that the price of electricity should be the cost of the fuel needed for the generation of electricity. If, however, the price of electricity is no more than this, the total costs of generating and distributing electricity will not be covered, for the cost of fuel used is only about one-quarter of the total costs that are involved. At this point of the argument we have reached an impasse. The temptation is to say 'make the price of electricity high enough to cover all the costs that are involved in generating electricity'. One aspect of the social cost of doing so is that at off-peak periods the consumer would be faced with a price that would be, say, twice as high as it needed to be in order to cover the (additional) cost incurred in generating the electricity required. This might be extremely wasteful because the consumer faced with a high price might not feel it worth while to buy additional electricity. On the other hand, if the consumption of electricity were not very responsive at the off-peak period to the price charged, not much harm would be done. Nevertheless, the implication of failure to charge the marginal cost of generation is that the price of electricity during peak periods may be much too low and that little incentive may be given to consume electricity at off-peak periods instead of at peak periods. In attempting to cater for a peak demand swollen in this way, generating capacity is likely to be installed on too lavish a scale.

Fortunately, more elegant solutions to the problem are possible than charging a price designed to cover full costs during both the peak and the off-peak periods. The aim of the solutions should be to make the costs of electricity generation appear the same to both producer and consumer. One way to do this would be to charge each consumer when connected to the supply a sum calculated to cover the cost of the generating equipment needed to take care of his anticipated load at the peak period. After this, all electricity supplied should be charged at the cost of the fuel needed to generate it, provided that the peak load was not exceeded at the peak period. The two-part tariff is an approximation to this solution. Alternative arrangements might be to charge electricity at different rates according to the time of the day. It is not impossible that suitable meters could be devised for it to be technically possible to charge for electricity received at prices varying from one minute to the next, depending on the load. The off-peak tariff whereby electricity is priced at a lower price when demands are light is a first approximation to this method of pricing. Whether electricity prices sufficiently reflect the various considerations outlined above is a moot point.

We have deliberately chosen the pricing of electricity as an illustration in order to be able to bring out the social implications of price fixing. The Central Electricity Authority is not expected to behave as it might be anticipated a monopolist would behave and wring out of the public the maximum amount of money that it could be compelled to pay for electricity; nor should it be expected to behave as a Santa Claus and provide electricity at less than cost. Its responsibility is to devise a system of prices that will lead to an efficient use of the country's resources in this sector. The criteria that it must bear in mind in order to achieve this can be summarized along the following lines:

1. Where possible price should not be greater than marginal cost so that those willing to pay the cost of generating electricity are not turned away. As we have seen, if this were done in a crude way it would be impossible for the industry to meet its full costs, for the marginal cost of generating electricity as measured by the fuel required is much less than the total costs that are incurred in establishing the plant as well as running it.

2. The Authority must try to avoid making a persistent loss. If it did so the consumption of electricity would have to be subsidized out of some other form of revenue. This would disturb the efficient working of the economy because it is arguable that a proper balance between the various forms of economic activity can be achieved only if they take place within the same general framework. To allow one industry to escape the competitive test of profit-making might be to encourage the activities of this industry to an undesirable extent. Moreover, the fact of having to pay a subsidy means that some other parts of the economy are penalized and charges that might properly be brought to bear on the consumers of electricity fall in some other sector of the economy. Special arguments would have to be advanced, for example, to justify putting up taxes in order to subsidize electricity consumers out of contributions made by consumers of gas. It might be possible to develop such argu-

ments, but they would be in the nature of a special case rather than a general principle to be followed in price determination. The decision to subsidize a nationalized industry must be made by Parliament and it involves the widest economic, social and political considerations.

A general argument to the effect that a particular industry or class of industries should operate at a loss can be sustained if it can be shown that sufficient social advantage will result from this policy. Thus it might be argued that in a development area cheap electricity was a powerful stimulus to the establishment of certain kinds of industry; and that the establishment of this kind of industry would help materially to revivify the area with a great saving in the cost of doing this by other means. This is a particular case of the general proposition that some kinds of economic activity generate external economies by indirectly benefiting some other kind of activity; and that even though this cannot be recouped by making an appropriate charge, it is permissible to take it into account in drawing up a 'social' balance sheet of the industry's operations and in considering claims for a subsidy to meet realized losses.

3. It may not be sufficient for a nationalized industry merely to break even. The optimum use of resources is more likely to emerge if the same profit criteria are imposed on a nationalized industry as apply to privately operated industries. Thus the object of private industry is to provide adequately for depreciation and to accumulate reserves for expansion. The need for nationalized industries in developed countries to do so may be less obvious if they have ready access to the capital market; but in underdeveloped countries the supply of capital is inadequate and every endeavour has to be made to promote capital accumulation by pursuing appropriate price policies that will enable reserves to be accumulated to finance new investment.

The social criteria involved in price policy are extremely complicated and although they have been much discussed in economic thought they have not been resolved into simple rules for action. It is not at all sure that they can be so resolved. Price determination cannot be regarded independently of social and political objectives; for apart from being a device to promote the efficient use of resources, the pricing system determines the distribution of income and the economic (and sometimes) political power of individuals or corporations. It is not surprising that when such diverse considerations are brought into contact that the economist cannot expect to have the last word and that one of the major issues of price policy—that of monopoly—should be a matter for the courts as much as for the economists.

FULL COST PRICING

One of the unresolved problems in economics is whether businessmen follow the economist's advice to determine price and output at the point where marginal cost and marginal revenue coincide. Particular doubts on this problem were raised in an article by Hall and Hitch on 'Price Theory and Business Behaviour'.[3] This article concluded, on the basis of a number of interviews, that firms made little attempt to equate marginal revenue and marginal cost; that since there was a strong element of oligopoly, prices tended to be fixed at a level which was regarded as covering full costs; that prices once fixed have a tendency to remain unchanged in relation to changes in demand, but not to changes in costs; and that some element in the prices ruling at any time can only be explained in the light of the history of the industry.

More mature consideration has thrown doubts on the universal validity of these generalizations. The truth probably lies somewhere between the extremes and it is as useful a generalization to assume that prices are determined on the basis of full costs as it is to start from the supposition that they are determined by marginal costs and revenues.

Thus it is possible to picture the businessman as fixing prices in relation to costs and modifying this somewhat according to the market situation. The procedure would consist in ascertaining prime costs, say the costs of labour and raw materials and adding to this some figure to cover overheads and profit. It is convenient to refer to this addition as the 'mark-up' applied by the firm. At first sight the mark-up may appear to be entirely arbitrary. The rules-of-thumb revealed by the Hall-Hitch survey were that it was common practice to increase prime costs first by a percentage to cover the share of overhead costs and

[3] First published in *Oxford Economic Papers*, No. 2, and subsequently reprinted in *Oxford Studies in the Price Mechanism*, ed. T. Wilson and P. W. S. Andrews.

then by a further percentage to cover profit. The share of overheads that should be covered might be decided in relation to either conventional or full loading of the plant or to actual or forecast utilization.

In practice it appears, however, that the mark-up is highly variable. A study of the movement of prices in the United Kingdom following the steep rise in import prices at the beginning of the Korean War indicated that the mark-up was not always closely related to changes in current prices of purchased raw materials and other inputs. In relation to current costs the mark-up was certainly variable.[4] There can be little doubt that this is generally the case.[5] The ratio between profits and wages shows significant variations both over short periods of time and over spans of years. Industrial commentators frequently refer to margins being squeezed and sometimes to increases in prices designed to increase realized margins. The whole feel of practical affairs is that prices are not, in fact, determined by firms solely on the basis of costs. Both supply and demand play their part.

To say that prices are determined with regard to the interactions of supply and demand is not the same thing as saying that it is marginal rather than average costs and revenues that are relevant. But the decision to cut prices in the face of competition must always be taken in the knowledge that because of the reduction in price total revenue will increase by less than the resulting increase in the quantity of goods sold. The essence of the marginal analysis is not so much that thinking should proceed in terms of the additions to revenues and costs from increasing sales and output unit by unit, as that two or more potential positions should be considered in terms of gain and loss, and a choice made between them. In other words, in practice an intention to maximize profit comes very close to the equating of marginal costs and revenues.

The price at which goods can be sold has always a crucial effect on a firm's profits. It is so much easier to make profits if a monopolistic situation gives a producer some control over the price he can charge. The more laudable activities of attaining a

[4] See J. R. Parkinson, 'The Terms of Trade and the National Income', *Oxford Economic Papers*, New Series, Vol. 7, No. 2 (June 1955).

[5] See, for example, H. F. Lydall, 'Aspects of Competition in Manufacturing Industry', *Oxford Institute of Statistics Bulletin* (November 1958).

high rate of profit by reducing costs and expanding output, which are the only ways a producer can affect his profits in conditions of perfect competition, is to some extent self-frustrating, for if carried out on a sufficient scale it is likely to be offset, at least in part, by a fall in prices as greater output is available for sale. A great deal of effort has to be extended to reduce even a small element of costs by a significant amount, and many items of cost which are essentially market determined, such as the cost of bought-in raw materials and components, offer little scope for reduction. It might seem strange that in such circumstances firms should think of themselves as fixing prices in relation to costs and that very little research is done to establish the shape of the demand curve by market research even though the price at which goods can be sold is so vital to the level of profits. Part of the reason for this may be that the concept of the just price dies hard and that there is a feeling that it is unethical to attempt to exploit the consumer. Certainly these considerations are of some importance in business. But it is possible to reconcile business practice with marginal concepts of pricing in other ways.

A good deal of business practice at the present time is in the nature of trial and error; scientific management is in its infancy and rule-of-thumb is still uppermost. To fix prices on the basis of average costs may come very near to charging the price that maximizes profit. If we exclude cases of extreme monopoly the scope for price fixing is limited. A firm cannot charge a price vastly different from that of its competitors; and the amount of profit that practice shows to be feasible is seldom very large in relation to costs. This is largely because in most industries the costs of raw materials and components often account for half the cost of production[6] and it does not require a vast amount of acumen to get on to an equal footing with rival firms. Thus price determination can be regarded as essentially consisting of a decision to add say 15 to 25 per cent to prime costs in order to meet overheads and make a reasonable profit. Few firms want to spark off 'cut-throat' competition; and most consider it reasonable to try to make some provision for covering overheads. There is also a degree of tacit understanding between firms that competition shall be conducted with due

[6] See Table 3.1.

regard to the need to refrain from spoiling the market by drastic price cuts that cover no more than prime costs.[7]

In many cases fixing prices on the basis of prime costs plus some mark-up will come near to maximizing profits. This would be true, for example, if marginal revenue was falling gently with an increase of sales and marginal costs rising gently; over a considerable range of projected output there may be very little difference between the two curves and small variations in output may be less critical than might appear at first sight. It is not at all unreasonable to think of the marginal revenue curve as being fairly flat and downward sloping; it is equally plausible to think of marginal cost curves as being fairly flat over much of their range.[8] In fact, they will be fairly flat if firms are given a reasonable period in which to adapt their production systems to greater output; frequently output can be increased with an existing unit by removing bottlenecks, increasing supervision, purchasing assemblies from other firms, working a limited amount of overtime and other comparatively minor adjustments.

The view that pricing takes place on the basis of costs as a first approximation and then proceeds by modifying the prices charged to take account of unexpected circumstances is confirmed by an investigation made by Professor Pearce.[9] In the firm he studied it appeared to be the accepted practice to base prices on the estimated full cost of production. Investigation showed that the profit margin added to costs was in fact highly variable and reflected amongst other things, considerations of good will, knowledge of competitor's prices or what the customer would pay. It was noticeable that orders for a very similar product often carried widely different margins for different customers. There was also evidence that between 1949/50 and 1953/54 there had been a deliberate application of a keener price-fixing policy designed to increase sales and so to ensure the full absorption of overhead costs. In this instance there does not seem to have been any great divergence between the views of economists and the methods used by the firm to fix its prices.

[7] This is known as maintaining an orderly market.

[8] See Chapter III.

[9] I. F. Pearce, 'A Study in Price Policy', *Economica* (May 1956), and I. F. Pearce and Lloyd R. Amey, 'Price Policy with a Branded Product', *Review of Economic Studies*, Vol. XXIV, No. 1.

PRICE AND POLICY

An economist asked to advise a firm on how to fix its prices might reply along the following lines:

(*a*) Find out what your costs are over the range of output that is relevant, distinguishing between prime costs that vary with output and overhead costs that are comparatively insensitive to changes in output.

(*b*) Take prime costs as your starting point and consider what the price would be if you added to this an allowance for overhead costs sufficient to keep you in business and the amount of profit necessary to keep your shareholders happy.

(*c*) Try to find out how your costs compare with those of your competitors. If they are much the same as yours, your competitors are likely to be thinking along the same lines; but if they are thought to be markedly higher or lower there may be reason to increase or decrease your estimated price.

(*d*) Keep a weather eye on the market; if orders are hard to get the chances are that the price will have to give a bit and competitors are likely to find themselves in much the same position. If orders come easily there is very likely to be an opportunity to raise prices a bit without running much risk of losing your share of the market.

(*e*) If the price of your raw materials and labour increase this may present you with an opportunity to raise your prices because your competitors may be expected to follow suit.

(*f*) If on the other hand costs are rising at a time when sales are hard to get you may be able to refrain from raising your prices without setting off a price war. In any case your rivals may do the same.

(*g*) Keep an eye on how you are using your factory. Production should be concentrated on the more profitable lines or the prices of the less profitable lines increased. In particular, make sure that you are not under-costing the one-off jobs.

(*h*) The good will of customers is probably better developed by an advertising campaign than by keeping prices below costs.

(*i*) If your prices seem to be higher than your competitors' although they scarcely cover costs this may indicate that your costs are too high and your production methods or factory organization defective.

(*j*) If you can sell all your output at prices that give you a substantial profit consider expansion.

(*k*) If you find that your sales vary seasonally, consider whether demand can be smoothed and profits increased by charging higher prices when demand is high and lower prices when demand is low. It is likely to be more profitable to do this the smaller are prime costs in relation to total costs.

(*l*) If your production and price problems are really complicated and you are uncertain of the rules-of-thumb that you are using to resolve them, consider whether operations research can simplify and codify the actions that are necessary.

(*m*) If you are one of a limited number of producers in an industry, what your competitors are likely to do may well be a more important consideration in fixing prices than any question of costs.

(*n*) Finally, if you are a monopolist and you pursue a price policy that is likely to be construed as against the public interest you may find yourself subject to control even though the profit made on capital employed is no more than twice as high as would satisfy you under other conditions. If your profits are unusually high beware also of new entrants to your industry or the development of unexpected substitutes.

Appendix to Chapter IV

RESTRICTIVE PRACTICES AND MONOPOLY

The interests of producers and consumers may often diverge. The consumer is interested in getting good value for money; but his choice in all these matters depends on what is offered by producers since he is seldom in a position to produce a variety of goods himself. Many producers set themselves the task of providing consumers with what they want and with good value for money; they concentrate time, attention and money on maintaining quality and improving their products. They may do this out of a sense of social duty or out of interest or because if they fail to serve the consumer they will be unable to make adequate profits or to continue in business. To many people the welfare of the consumer seems most likely to be assured if the economy is run on competitive lines. Competition invokes a mental image of a number of firms striving independently to provide the consumer with a better or cheaper product; those who succeed being able to expand their business and gain a greater share of the market, while those who fail to provide the same standard of performance are gradually driven out of production. Thus, not only does competition lead firms to strive to do better, but it automatically eliminates those who fail. There is a Darwinian process of selection with this system of the carrot and the stick.

The working of the economy does not always conform to this image. Sometimes there are a large number of firms all of which show little initiative in reducing costs, increasing sales, or introducing new products. Judging by the cotton industry competition is as likely to produce morbidity as it is to promote vigorous life. In the jute industry, on the other hand, protection from foreign competition seems to have favoured economic progress and been conducive to considerable improvements in efficiency. Even if these paradoxical results seem to be contrary to the theory of competition it may be still true that the competitive process has the effect of transferring resources between industries, to the benefit of the community. But it would probably be as wrong to assume that in practice large numbers of firms are a guarantee of improvements in efficiency as that monopolistic firms are necessarily the reverse.

In many industries small-scale production is economically impossible. The generation of electricity requires a large-scale organization to link the various stations together and spread the load. The production of chemicals is generally cheapest on a large scale; an annual production of over 500,000 is desirable for motor cars; and so on. The creation of large companies has been inseparable from raising living standards over the past two centuries.

The larger companies are assuming a dominant position in their industries; there may be a mere handful of them and they may tend to act in concert. In the absence of competitive pressure on them to be efficient there is always the danger that they will be reluctant to extend themselves for the good of the consumer. If they choose to exert their monopoly power they have every opportunity to exploit the consumer. They may sit back and fail to promote research and development; they may be slow to take up new inventions or even may deliberately suppress those that threaten their livelihood; they may be tempted to exploit labour or, more likely these days, to provide the consumer with an inferior article at a price considerably above costs. History can show plenty of instances of monopolistic exploitation, and also many instance of monopolies functioning efficiently and with the interest of the consumer at heart.

In economic literature considerable attention centres on an expected tendency for monopolists to restrict output in order to put up prices. It is not necessary to have a complete monopoly before it becomes worth while trying to keep prices on the high side. When there are a few producers of the same or closely similar products there may be another harmful effect, that of establishing production units that are below the optimum scale for the cheapest production.

Figure 4.1 illustrates these points. The marginal cost curve shows the cost of producing additional units of output in some undertaking operated on a small scale, say, a small printing establishment. It is assumed that the marginal cost of production at first falls as output increases, and then begins to rise after a period where it is fairly flat. The average cost of production is shown as being fairly high at first when the overheads of the plant have to be spread over a small number of units and then gradually falling as output expands, until a low point is reached; subsequently, rising as marginal production costs increase because, say, increasing amounts of overtime have to be worked with the given size of plant. If there were a large number of active and knowledgeable producers there would be a tendency for costs to be forced down to their lowest point. If we include in costs an allowance for profit, output would be OO_{PC} and this would be sold at a price O_{PC}.

If, however, there were only a few producers each with part of the market attached to him in some way, because, for example, some consumers imagine his product to be slightly superior to that of other firms, a different state of affairs would result. In these circumstances, each producer would find himself with a downward-sloping demand curve or average revenue curve such that if he reduced his price he would be able to sell more. We indicate such a demand curve on the diagram, and also a marginal revenue curve showing the additional revenue that a producer would get from selling an additional unit of output. Each producer following our pricing rule that marginal cost should equal marginal revenue would produce that output for which the marginal cost and marginal revenue curves intersect.

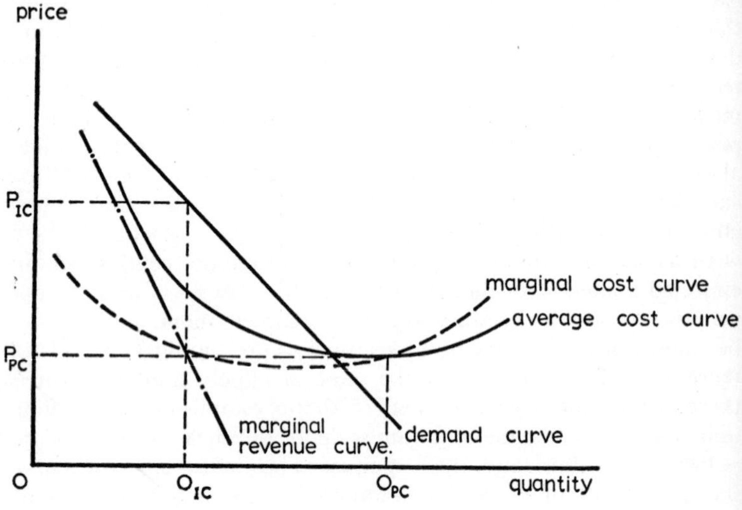

Fig. 4-1.
Price and Output under Monopolistic Conditions.

This output is OO_{IC} on the diagram and this would be sold at price OP_{IC} which, of course, is higher than the competitive price OP_{PC}. Thus, in conditions when there are only one or a handful of firms not competing vigorously, price will be higher, and output lower, than it would be under perfect competition. Since the scale of output would be lower this would mean that in industries where there is a tendency for costs to fall with an increase in the scale of operation, average cost of production would also be greater.

Many countries are strongly opposed to monopoly influences in business because they think that they result in inefficiency and exploitation. The United States has a long record of legislation against monopoly, dating from the passing of the Sherman Act in 1890. This Act forbade all activities in restraint of trade except retail price maintenance practised by an individual producer or distributor. Exclusive dealing for the purpose of lessening competition and acquiring companies for the same purpose was also forbidden. The Act and subsequent Acts has meant that companies have often been restrained from amalgamation and on occasion large companies have been broken up to promote competition and reduce their power. The threat of action under the anti-monopoly legislation has proved to be a means of curbing the power of large corporations as happened when steel producers tried to increase prices contrary to Government policy in 1962.

Other countries have not been so anxious to attempt to curb monopolies by legislation as the United States. It was not until 1957 that an Act was passed in Germany against restraints of competition, the Cartel Ordinance of 1923 being designed only to prevent abuse. Under the 1957 Act certain restraints are permitted, for example arrangements to bolster a declining industry, to rationalize production processes and in the case of agreements concerned with export markets. Anti-trust law is also of post-war origin in Sweden. A law was passed in 1946 requiring the registration of restrictive agreements and was strengthened in 1953 and supplemented in 1956. The general intention is to counteract restrictive business practices through publicity and negotiation. With the establishment of the Common Market, legislation against monopoly is being unified and in future most European countries can be expected to conform to a common code.

The United Kingdom was also late in the field of legislation against monopolies. In the inter-war years very little effort was made to control restrictive practices and in the 'thirties the climate was favourable to monopolies rather than the reverse. In 1948 the Monopolies and Restrictive Practices Act was passed. Under the Act the Monopolies and Restrictive Practices Commission was set up to investigate and report on matters referred to it by the Board of Trade. The Commission could be asked to investigate when over a third of a market was provided by one supplier or group of suppliers. By 1956, when the functions of the Commission were altered, it had prepared a score of reports on such matters as the supply of electronic valves and cathode ray tubes, standard metal windows and doors, tea, linoleum and chemical fertilizers. The reports of the Commission did not always condemn the practices that they examined. The Report on the Supply of Insulated Electric Wires and Cables concluded that price competition would tend to lower standards; and that in view of the close technical collaboration between the manufacturers it was permissible for them to inform each other before changing their prices. Other practices that could not be condoned were the subject of negotiation between the industrialists concerned and the Board of Trade. It was the responsibility of the latter to negotiate changes of practice with those concerned or to decide if new legislation was required

In practice very little impression was made on monopolistic practices by the Commission. It was left to another piece of legislation, The Restrictive Trade Practices Act, 1956, to put some teeth into the measures designed to promote competition. The Act provides for the registration of a wide number of restrictive agreements and all these agreements have to come before the Restrictive Practices Court. *Prima facie* all restrictive agreements are considered to be against the public interest, if they are found to be so they automatically become void. If a restriction is not to be regarded as contrary to the public interest it must satisfy one of a number of conditions. These include substantial benefits to purchasers, countering the restrictive measures of other bodies, being likely to give rise to serious and persistent effects on employment if abolished and leading to a restriction of export earnings.

Very few agreements have been found to be in the public interest according to these criteria. Agreements to fix the price at which bolts and nuts could be sold were found to be in the public interest because they eliminated the need for users to go shopping to make sure that they were getting the lowest price. In the cement case, the court found that the effect of the agreement was to keep prices below the levels that they would otherwise attain, because the greater certainty engendered by the agreement made it possible to attract capital on more favourable terms. In the case of the Water-tube Boilermakers Agreement it was found that an agreement which enabled a member selected to adjust the price it was proposed to quote for a contract to the lowest tender of members of the association was not contrary to the public interest: consultation in prices and market possibilities increased the chance of obtaining export orders. Too few agreements have been found to be in the public interest for useful generalizations to be made about the principles involved. The main conclusion to be reached from the operation of the court is that it is difficult to establish a case for agreements of a restrictive kind under the working of the Act.[1]

[1] For a convenient and illuminating guide to the results of the cases decided by the court consult the reports prepared at intervals by the Registrar of Restrictive Trading Agreements starting with Cmnd. 1273 and Cmnd. 1603.

The Restrictive Practices Court is concerned with the effects of agreements. Outright monopoly requires no agreement for its working, only the absence of competition; regulation of monopoly, however, is still the purview of the Monopolies Commission. It is also permissible for a manufacturer to specify the price at which his products may be sold by distributors of his goods provided that he does not do this in collusion with other manufacturers. Such resale price maintenance falls under heavy fire. Why, it is argued, should a manufacturer be allowed to insist on his goods being sold at certain minimum prices if there are retailers who are willing to sell them to the consumer on more favourable terms? The arguments against resale price maintenance are rather obvious. The arguments for it are rather more interesting and we examine them at greater length.

Andrews and Friday have been at pains to defend resale price maintenance.[2] They argue that resale price maintenance protects the consumer against deterioration in the quality of products that is to be expected with intense competition; that price cuts on some articles are generally balanced by increases on others; that it reaches the point of absurdity when two prices are printed on packets with the old price crossed out and apparently being replaced by a new and lower price; and they quote examples of price-cutting wars leaving the public distrustful of products to the point where a serious decline in sales has resulted. They show that the introduction of resale price maintenance has sometimes resulted in a fall in prices in practice, and its abolition in a rise; they also argue that the abolition of retail price maintenance would have the effect of concentrating more power into the hands of large retailers who would tend to develop their own products made to their requirements by manufacturers, and that this would have the effect of reducing competition between manufacturers. The net effect of changes in the direction of larger scale distribution systems would be to reduce consumers' choice and the service that he enjoys. Such conclusions may not be valid but they are interesting as a defence against the commonly held view that resale price maintenance is a serious drag on progress.

CONCLUSIONS

Legislation against restrictive practices in the United Kingdom have been of a somewhat experimental character. One of the weakest aspects of it has probably been the very restrained action that has been taken against monopoly itself. Some of the practices rejected by the Restrictive Practices Court might arouse no opposition if they were practised by a monopoly rather than by a collection of firms.

[2] See *Fair Trade, 1960* (Institute of Economic Affairs).

The mere abolition of an agreement does not necessarily mean that there will be a complete break with existing arrangements. Prices may no longer be maintained by agreement but price competition may be no more evident than it was before. It does not need even one firm to establish itself as a price setter for this to happen: it is only necessary that firms avoid competing on price, concentrating more perhaps on the development of new products or sales method if they are anxious to increase the size of their market. And even this may not be pressed very hard in some industries. The ultimate defence against monopoly lies in establishing a business outlook that is progressive; that is always trying to improve the quality of products and to devise new marketing arrangements and press sales because that is the only way to sell what is being produced. It may be that this kind of outlook is most effectively encouraged in competitive conditions particularly when markets are growing. But the existence of a large number of independent producers in a particular country is no guarantee that industry will be progressive. It is being realized increasingly that it is as important to stimulate competition between regions as it is within individual countries. The Common Market may have the effect of stimulating competition in European countries in this way. Unfortunately, as trading areas spread so do monopoly agreements and attitudes that wish to temper competitive forces.

Chapter V

PROFITS

Profit arises when there is a surplus of revenue over costs in a period of trading. In a sense this is a definition, but it is not much help to the economist, because it does not say anything about how profits arise, nor why they arise, nor their function, neither does it imply any relationship between profit and anything else; and it is in any case open to dispute over the meaning of the terms 'cost' and 'revenue'.

For generations theoretical economists have sought a consistent definition of profits. All other forms of income (wages, rent and interest) may be looked on as a reward to some factor of production (respectively labour, land and money [or capital]), but it has always proved difficult to isolate a specific factor of production to which profit may be said to accrue as a reward.

Several theories have been advanced. The best known of these is that profits are a reward for risk and uncertainty.[1] There is always a certain amount of risk in every aspect of human behaviour, and business activity carries at least as much risk as any other; but most such risks are calculable in terms of actuarial probability, and can frequently be insured. The risks of fire and other accidental damage to or loss of plant and stocks can usually be covered by some form of insurance. But other risks, including most of the risks of manufacture and trading are not insurable: every businessman undertakes some risk when he manufactures a product in anticipation of demand and the more specialized is a form of business activity the more risk and uncertainty there is likely to be. Anything new involves the risk that the public will not buy it, and certain trades are recognized to be more susceptible to sudden swings in demand, and therefore more risky. Fashion trades are an example, and most trades and industries which deal in goods which have relatively high price or income elasticities of demand, or for

[1] Frank H. Knight, *Risk, Uncertainty, and Profit* (London School of Economics and Political Science, Reprints of Scarce Works No. 16, 1933).

which there are several substitutes are also risky. If profit is thought of purely as a reward for risk, however, it will not coincide with what most people would think of in a general way as profit: certain wage-earning occupations (such as coal mining, jobs in the cotton industry, etc.) carry not only physical risk but also a risk of a loss of unemployment; but it is rarely suggested that an appropriate part of the wages of such employment should be thought of as profit. But even if the risk theory does not provide a complete explanation, there is little doubt that profit must provide some reward to the entrepreneur and the providers of capital for the risks which they undertake and the uncertainty which they face.

A second closely related type of theory states that 'normal' profits are a sort of managerial wage paid to a specialized form of labour, and that any surplus of revenue over costs after that is a profit due to imperfections of the market. For example, temporary abnormal profits accrued to honest traders and 'black market' operators alike during and after the Second World War, permanent profits above normal accrue to monopolies; and in general the ability to take advantage before anyone else of a shift in demand curves or cost curves yields a reward in the form of profits above the managerial wage. This type of definition is probably too wide, since it evades the problems of defining adequately the service for which the so-called normal profit is a reward and thereby fails to define the functions and aims of the normal operations of a business; but the concept of extra or abnormal profit is itself quite useful.

Another theory regards profits as a reward for innovation and enterprise, for seeing the possibilities latent in various fields of action and in new technological development. To some extent this is a variant of the risk theory, but reward for risk is not a necessary part of the profit from innovations. It may also be looked on as a variant of the 'imperfection' theory in that the innovator earns his profit from the creation of an imperfection in the market. When innovations, of technique or marketing, or indeed in any aspect of business organization, are employed, there is a short period during which the exploiters of the innovation (though not necessarily the innovators themselves, for the two are usually different people)[2] make large

[2] See Chapter VII, p. 236.

profits, which are eventually reduced and shared out by the forces of competition. Since this process goes on indefinitely profit is always earned somewhere in the economy, and profit is thus linked to change and growth. This is undoubtedly an aspect of profit, particularly important in a growing and developing economy, but although it explains why profits arise from innovations, it fails to explain the indisputable fact that, however the term is defined, profits do arise which are not a function of innovation; and at best this type of theory is only a special case of the 'imperfection' or 'friction' type of theory. But since it implies that profits are a return to a dynamism in business operations, it is a useful and acceptable partial definition.

None of the theories provides a really satisfactory explanation, but fortunately it is not strictly necessary to define a watertight category of rewards called profits. It is clear that some of what is normally called profit in everyday life is part of the reward to the various factors of production, such as rents on property owned by the business, interest paid on capital borrowed (a proportion of the dividend on ordinary share capital is probably profit). One factor of production, management, a specialized form of labour, also receives its reward partly in the form of profit. The sole owner, who manages as well as owns the business, achieves a surplus of receipts over costs, some of which is in a sense his 'managerial income' (roughly, what he would have to pay someone else to do the job), some of which is 'pure' profit, or return to enterprise. But what matters to him is that he earns something for running the firm, some possibly for enterprise, some for risk, some for innovation, and he calls this his profit.

With the increasing difficulty in modern business life of identifying the entrepreneur, particularly in large corporations,[3] it becomes increasingly hard to identify the factor of production which receives its reward in the form of profit. If, as is often the case, a business is run by professional managers on fixed salaries who use the capital of other people, the answer may well be it is not possible to ascribe anything called profit to the firm as an institution. Some of the surplus will be paid to shareholders as interest and a reward for the risks which *they*

[3] See Chapter I.

bear; some will be put by for future expansion and nothing else will be left. The most that can be said is that the successful managers receive extra high wages, or bonuses, which are partly profit, and partly a special reward to a highly skilled form of labour. Profit, in the sense of reward of some nature for some special factor of production, does not exist in the modern corporation: it all goes in payments to other factors of production or provision for the future.

But there are still senses in which profit is different from other kinds of income. It is not contractual, like wages and rent or 'fixed' interest but it is a residual item accruing as a result of producing in anticipation of demand: the businessman may be able to estimate profit fairly accurately, but he rarely receives it from anyone else as something due to him as a result of a contract: the rare cases in which he appears to do so, as in certain contracts affording him a certain level or margin of profit regardless of cost, are really to be regarded as payment for services. Since profit is residual it also runs the risk of being negative, and it is also liable to fluctuations with changes in business conditions. Thus the element of uncertainly does distinguish profit from other components of the value added by the productive process.

There is a lot to be said for the common-sense notion that profit is a reward for the successful conduct of a business. Several things go to earn this, and the several theories of profits explain what these are—it is not really necessary to go any further. And so, whilst acknowledging that they exist, we can leave aside most of the theoretical issues and for present purposes define profit as *the proceeds from and incentive to successful business activity*. This is not a watertight definition and it evades rather than solves the theoretical difficulties, but it is a convenient categorization of this complex source of income. Definition of the *functions* of profit is a separate consideration to which we return later.

THE MEASUREMENT OF PROFIT

In fact, thinking of profit as business income is much more in line with practical thinking on these matters. Businessmen, accountants and economists all tend to think of profit in real life as the surplus of the revenue from a trading operation left over after the expenses incurred in employing factors of production have been met.

TABLE 5.1

TRADING AND PROFIT AND LOSS ACCOUNT OF THE XYZ METAL MANUFACTURING COMPANY FOR THE YEAR ENDING JANUARY 12TH, 1955

			£
1.	OPENING STOCK		332
2.	PURCHASES less DISCOUNTS (Metal £2,234 Accessories £972)		3,206
3.	CLOSING STOCK		597
4.	COST OF GOODS	(1+2 less 3)	2,941
5.	WAGES		31,549
6.	SALARIES		2,040
7.	OTHER COSTS		
	Advertising		233
	Fuel and power		1,996
	Rent and rates		1,636
	Repairs		106
	Carriage		839
	Packing		81
	Insurance		219
	Stationery		271
	Travel		48
	Cleaning		157
	Telephone—Postage		212
	Legal expenses		48
	Audit fee		63
	Interest		115
	Bad debts		2,136
	Sundry (car commission, etc.)		408
		Total other costs	8,568
8.	DEPRECIATION		1,769
		TOTAL COSTS	46,867
9.	NET SALES		53,637
10.	OPERATING PROFIT	(9−8)	6,770
11.	OTHER INCOME (Rent, interest, etc.)		515
12.	TOTAL RECEIPTS	(9+11)	54,152
13.	VALUE ADDED	(9−4)	50,696
14.	TOTAL PROFIT (INCOME FOR DISPOSAL)	(10+11)	7,285
15.	DIRECTORS' REMUNERATION		4,738
16.	TAX		1,194
17.	DIVIDENDS		863
18.	RETAINED PROFIT		490

This surplus is then employed in the payments of dividends on equity capital (or risk capital), the payment of tax, and a transfer to reserves. Either in expectation or realization of high profits, 'top' management may get high salaries or bonuses in reward for its services—some of this the economist would regard as profit, the accountant would not, and most businessmen would wonder what all the fuss was about.

When it comes down to the actual measurement of profit the economist and the accountant part company. Accountants adopt conventions in order to be able to do their work, economists disagree with the conventions because, they argue, they have little economic significance. Some of the disagreements relate to terminology and are not really very important, others to valuations and the treatment of items, which are more important.

Most of these differences can be highlighted by the use of trading account and appropriation account (Table 5.1). This is an actual example, recast in such a way as to bring out the economic entities; in so doing it departs from accounting conventions.

The normal accounting definitions distinguish between gross and net profit. *Gross profit* is defined by accountants as the 'excess of sales (less returns) over the cost of goods sold directly attributable to putting the goods in a saleable condition. The cost of goods sold is the amount of the opening stock *plus* purchases (less returns) less the amount of the closing stock'.[4] *Net profit* is defined as 'the surplus remaining after charging against gross profit all the expenses, including depreciation, properly attributable to the normal activities of the particular business'.[5]

In contrast, economists usually consider gross profit to be much closer to the accountant's net profit; and net profit to be net of 'management salary', interest (both on borrowed money, and, implicitly on the company's reserves) and imputed rent on the buildings owned by the firm (if any).

Part of the difference is due to the desire of the economist to define his terms functionally in contrast with the accountant's desire to define them by enumeration. The accountant's gross profit is not profit in any sense of the term, but it comes somewhere between what the economist calls *net output* or *value added* (i.e. the value added to materials by the productive processes of the firm, which may be said to be true or net output

[4] W. Pickles and G. W. Dunkerley, *Accounting* (2nd edn.) (Pitman, 1949).
[5] Ibid.

or production of the firm) and profit: it is, in fact, simply the difference between sales and direct costs. In the example cited this is item 13 plus part of item 5. The *net profit* of the accountant is shown as item 10 (operating profit, or sales *less* costs): this is much nearer to what is generally thought of as profit.

To this is usually added the other income accruing to the firm in the form of rents, interest on securities held, etc., and the result can be called *total profit* (or income for disposal). From this sum certain allocations have to be made in the form of tax, transfers to reserves and dividends. Produced in this way the accounts tell the economist what he wants to know about the firm in a convenient and logical form: he knows the composition of costs and sales, and how the income resulting from the trading activities of the firm is distributed, and, set out thus, the pattern of the way in which costs are incurred becomes fairly clear.

But there are doubts about some of the items. This particular example was chosen because it illustrates one of the difficulties of profit measurement. The firm in question has less than 100 employees, and is controlled by three directors, one of whom is managing director. He receives one third of the *directors' remuneration* (item 7). The question is whether this directors' remuneration is profit (in the economist's sense) or whether it is all a sort of managerial wage. These three directors also own all of the shares of the company, and receive dividends of £863 (the reason why some of their reward is paid in the form of remuneration and some in the form of dividends is a function of tax law rather than logic: director's remuneration is earned income and taxed at earned income rates with appropriate allowances, a dividend is not).

Depending on how we classify these items, we get different measures of profit. If we include directors' remuneration as profit, the profit of the firm is £7385, or roughly three times what it is if the item is excluded (£2547).

In many firms the managing director receives no salary but is rewarded entirely in the form of directors' remuneration: is this profit, or managerial wage? The accountant calls it all profit and indeed the Companies Act requires him to do so, which is not logical, but at least fairly consistent. Strictly, if we wish to assess profits accurately some allowance should be made for a managerial wage in these circumstances, the remainder being called profit.

In large firms, where most of the work of the entrepreneur is carried out by salaried managers, the difference made to the final profit figure by the method of calculation is proportionately much smaller since 'top' management salaries account for a much smaller proportion of total costs.

This particular question is, however, of little direct interest to the businessman, whose main concern is with the amount which he has available for distribution and retention, or more important still, what he will get in the future and what he must do in order to get it.

There are other points at issue which are of more practical significance. Most of these stem from a difference of viewpoint: the accountant is concerned with a factual historical record, the economist with the earning power of the business. An example of the sort of problem which may arise lies in the treatment of depreciation: in formal company accounts an asset is normally valued at its historical cost (i.e. what it cost to buy it), and written off over a period of years (a variety of methods is possible but they need not concern us here); the economist argues, however, that, in order to keep the value and earning power of an asset intact, it is often necessary to make further allowances. It is interesting that many firms do find it necessary to revalue their assets in practice. An asset may depreciate in value through obsolescence, or through use, but if it is to be replaced in a time of rising prices further allowances may also be necessary to compensate for the increase in price of a replacement:[6] from all of these points of view it is more realistic to value assets at their replacement cost, and make the necessary adjustments to depreciation, than it is to use historical cost.[7] Unfortunately the Inland Revenue authorities in Britain, in allowing depreciation (or 'wear and tear') as a cost do not permit firms to make any charge for obsolescence or rising prices. The firm wishing to maintain the earning value of its assets, however, has to make some such allowance, either

[6] There is a further complication: in a time of technological advance a machine will not usually be replaced by an identical machine but by an improved model, frequently of higher price. Neither in theory nor in practice is it easy to sort out what is 'true' depreciation in a case like this.

[7] See also footnote 8, Chapter VII.

annually or in the form of extra depreciation allowances; or, when it comes to replacing the asset, in the form of an extra large payment for a new asset. This extra amount must come from profit, on which the firm will have been taxed, but this is inescapable, and it means in effect that extra allowances have to be put to reserve to take account of the extra expenditure which will be needed.

Similar problems of valuation also apply to stocks which, strictly, should always be valued at replacement cost if the cost and profit figures of the firm are to have any real meaning. In times of rising prices, valuation of stocks at historical (or original) cost will mean that cost figures are an understatement of the true position, and profits are overstated; when prices fall the opposite occurs. Again, in practice these ideals are frequently not met, and historical cost valuations are common.

Modern accountants tend to agree with economists on most of these points, but many company accounts are still made up under the old conventions, and are not therefore accurate statements of profit.

THE ALLOCATION AND FUNCTIONS OF PROFIT

After all of these adjustments have been made a surplus is available for distribution called TOTAL PROFIT, or INCOME FOR DISPOSAL in the specimen account: this is disposed of partly in the form of tax (which normally absorbs something over half the surplus), partly in the form of dividends and transfers to reserve. The two main functions of profits in the modern corporation are summed up in the last two appropriations. One function of profits is to provide a reward for the entrepreneur and the shareholder, partly in the form of dividends, partly as remunerations for directors. Dividends on ordinary shares being non-contractual and residual are more akin to profits than interest, and it is the ordinary shareholder who very largely undertakes the risk and uncertainty of business operations. Dividend on preference shares on the other hand is contractual and more akin to interest (from the point of view of the recipient) and a cost (from the point of view of the firm).[8]

[8] Fixed-interest payments on long-term debt on the other hand are usually treated as a cost (and allowed as such by the Inland Revenue authorities) and not as an allocation of profit. Dividend on preference shares, although at fixed interest is not so allowed.

In order to maintain a healthy market in the shares of a public company, very necessary if the public is to be approached for further borrowing, adequate dividends need to be paid. What is 'adequate' in this sense depends on the degree of risk

TABLE 5.2

APPROPRIATION ACCOUNT OF COMPANIES IN THE UNITED KINGDOM 1961

	£ million	*Percentage of total income*
INCOME		
Gross trading profits of companies operating in the United Kingdom (1)	3608	68.5
Income earned abroad (2)	1011	19.1
Non-trading income earned in the United Kingdom	652	12.4
TOTAL	5271	100.0
ALLOCATION OF INCOME		
Dividends and interest:		
Debenture interest	98	1.9
Dividends on preference shares	112	2.1
Dividends on ordinary shares	986	18.7
Other dividends (3)	268	5.1
Total	1464	27.8
Additions to dividend reserves	25	0.5
United Kingdom taxes on income:		
Payments	693	13.1
Additions to reserves	347	6.6
Taxes paid abroad and profits due abroad	675	12.8
Undistributed income after taxation but before providing for depreciation and stock appreciation	2067	39.2
TOTAL	5271	100.0

Source: *National Income and Expenditure, 1961* (H.M.S.O. 1961), Table 26, p. 25.
Notes: (1) Before providing for depreciation and stock appreciation.
(2) After deducting depreciation allowances but before providing for stock appreciation.
(3) Co-operative society dividends and interest, interest on building society shares and deposits, other interest paid by banks, etc.

and market pressures, and dividends usually bear some fairly close relation to those paid on shares of comparable businesses. In general, an examination of Stock Exchange prices and yields will show that the shares of the more risky enterprises have higher but variable yields, whilst those of the safer, well-established businesses usually have fairly low and stable yields.

The second main function is to provide for future expansion and in general to provide reserves for the expected and contingent future needs of the business. This is achieved by allocating the remainder of profit to reserves, either to some specially committed reserve (such as future taxation reserve) or to 'free reserves'—the actual allocation being largely a matter of book-keeping convenience. These reserves are rarely kept for long as a sum of money, but are continually used for the acquisition of assets (partly paper assets, such as securities, partly operating assets, needed for the actual running of the firm). The actual proportion of disposable income put to reserves depends on a variety of factors: it is clearly influenced by the dividend decision in the first place, but considerations of prudence play a big part. The larger and less risky the company the more it is usually able to put to reserves, and it accordingly becomes larger and less risky; but on the other hand many large and fairly speculative concerns tend to 'plough back' a high proportion of their profit in order to avoid having to go to the market for extra funds. In good years it is common to put by fairly large amounts to reserves, partly in order not to squander good fortune or the results of good management, partly in order to maintain dividend payments in times of adversity (some firms keep a 'Dividend Equalization Reserve Account' specially for the purpose) and in general to provide against possible bad times. In the years since the Second World War high company taxation (which for some time discriminated against distributed profits and in favour of retained profits) has led to a substantial fall in the proportion of profits distributed.[9] Further, whilst the quoted public company sector as a whole has retained a slightly higher proportion of its income than before the war, large industrial companies have retained less. Small firms, which have proportionately smaller profits tend to retain a larger share in the firm, partly because

[9] See S. J. Prais, 'Dividend Policy and Income Appropriation', in *Studies in Company Finance*, edited by Brian Tew and R. F. Henderson (National Institute of Economic and Social Research and C.U.P. 1959). Prais also shows (op. cit., p. 109) that in 1949 the one hundred largest companies earned over 25 per cent of total industrial profits, the remaining 2449 quoted companies earned 35 per cent, and private companies and unincorporated businesses earned 40 per cent.

they have to rely a great deal more on their own savings for any expansion which they may wish to undertake; but the very biggest public companies plough back slightly more of their profits than do other public companies.[10] As an illustration of the magnitudes and proportions involved, Table 5.2 shows, for all companies in the United Kingdom, the distribution of profits in 1960.

If any justification were needed for profits, therefore, it is simply that, in a modern business it would be impossible to continue without them. Not only are they necessary as an incentive to efficient business operations, but if such operations are to continue and growth is to take place they are necessary for the finance of such continuation. This is just as true for nationalized industries as for privately owned industries, with the exception that certain monopoly profits can possibly be eradicated in a publicly owned industry. For political reasons it may be necessary to call such profit a surplus, but it is necessary nevertheless if the industry is not to be a charge on the public purse.[11]

STANDARDS OF PROFIT

The absolute size of profit is not in itself very meaningful, and it is usual to speak of profit either in relation to capital employed or sales. Both methods have their disadvantages.

The profit on sales (or turnover) measure many be very misleading:[12] a firm with high turnover but small *value added* (for example: a firm which does little in the way of processing materials, or whose costs of processing are small in relation to material costs) may appear unprofitable if profit is measured against sales, even though its profit on assets employed may well be high, and its profit as a proportion of value added may not be far removed from average. A wholesaler may be in this position, because all he does is store, grade and resell goods, all of which are relatively cheap operations compared with the

[10] See Chapter VII.

[11] This argument, of course, does not take account of the case to be made that certain nationalized industries (of which railways are probably the best example) should be provided as social services and not made to run at a profit. There has clearly to be a substitute for a surplus in such industries, and normally it would be financed either by Government borrowing or from the proceeds of taxation.

[12] Tables 3.1 and 2.10 provide some illustrations of the way in which a ratio of profit (in this case net output) to turnover may differ for reasons which do not reflect profitability on assets employed.

costs of manufacturing. A firm with large capital and relatively small turnover on the other hand (most engineering firms would come in this category) may well appear less profitable in terms of capital employed than in terms of turnover. Profit differences between firms with similar capital structures and similar techniques may be meaningfully expressed in terms of turnover, but otherwise such measures are rather misleading.

A measure of profit on capital employed is more significant, but measurement of capital employed presents so many difficulties that here again in practice the ratio may not be particularly helpful. Practices relating to valuation of assets are so varied, and the age-structure of company assets may differ so much from firm to firm, that comparisons may be meaningless.

Profit as a proportion of value added is in many ways a more valuable measure, since this expresses profit as a function or proportion of the economic activity (production) which gave rise to it; but this is rarely employed in practice.

For the firm which merely wishes to compare its own performance now with its past performance, it does not really matter much which measure of profit is chosen, provided that definitions and valuations remain constant over time. Such a measure does not tell the firm very much about how good its profit levels are for the purposes of attracting new capital, or for providing resources for long-term growth; and perhaps most important of all, it does not give the firm much idea of its competitive efficiency. It is much more useful to compare one's own firm with others in the same industry and indeed with performance in the economy as a whole: firms do not exist in a vacuum, they have to make their living in competition with other firms, and their profitability is a reasonably good measure of their ability to do so.

In recent years more attention has been given to this problem, and the growth of inter-firm comparisons[13] illustrates this trend. Profit is only one of the measures which may be employed in such comparisons, but it is of key importance as a measure of overall success. Profit on capital and turnover are the measures usually employed.

Even within trades, however, most observers fight shy of laying down ideal standards of profitability, and differences

[13] See Chapter III.

between trades are so wide that any overall standard would be meaningless. The average ratio of total profit to net assets (i.e. the total assets of the firm less its current debt, or the 'net worth' of the firm, which may be approximately measured as the capital and reserves of the firm) in quoted public companies in Britain is about 16 per cent, for private companies it is in the range 10–19 per cent,[14] but they are very considerable differences between firms and industries. Inter-industry differences are shown in Table 5.3.

TABLE 5.3

RATIO OF NET INCOME TO NET ASSETS IN QUOTED PUBLIC COMPANIES IN THE UNITED KINGDOM, 1960

Industry	*Net income as percentage of net assets*
Food	16.9
Drink	15.9
Tobacco	15.6
Chemicals and allied industries	15.3
Metal manufactures	16.5
Non-electrical engineering and shipbuilding	15.5
Electrical engineering and electrical goods	13.2
Vehicles	18.8
Metal goods	20.1
Textiles	13.8
Clothing and footwear	19.8
Bricks, pottery, glass, cement, etc.	18.2
Printing and publishing	15.3
All manufacturing industry	15.9
Construction	15.2
Wholesale distribution	14.4
Retail distribution	19.5
All manufacturing and distribution	16.1

Source: *Statistics on Incomes, Prices, Employment and Production*, No. 1, April 1962 (H.M.S.O. 1962).

Note: Net income is gross trading income *less* depreciation.
Net assets are total capital and reserves net of depreciation.

Profits may vary both over time and between industries. Profits as a reward to innovations usually accrue in the first few years of the marketing of the new or amended product; in time these may fall, partly as a result of other firms seeing the profitable opportunities and exploiting them, thus providing

[14] Calculated from data in *Studies in Company Finance* (N.I.E.S.R. and C.U.P.) and data collected in the Small Business Survey of the Oxford University Institute of Statistics.

extra competition, partly because other innovations come along to take their place. The maximization of profits often depends on a continuous chain of innovations. Thus profits of successful firms would be expected to be high in industries where frequent innovations and changes of technique are a predominant feature; they are also likely to be high in industries where there is a long time lag between expenditure and the return in the form of profits, and the profits will be even higher, as in the case of mining and other speculative industries, when risks are greatest. In risky industries there must be a prospect of high gains in order to compensate for the possibility of loss. In new industries such as plastics and man-made fibres in the late 1940s and early 1950s, whose prospects cannot easily be assessed by reference to experience, there will also be uncertainty and similar conditions will apply. Some firms in certain industries may have well-entrenched monopoly positions and may thus be able to earn high or abnormal profits: the Monopolies Commission[15] found, for example, that the British Oxygen Corporation made exceptionally high profits on capital employed by virtue of its monopoly position.

Within industry profitability depends on efficiency and successful management; and given the basic factors, such as risk, which *may* be common to all firms in an industry, the most efficient firms will normally obtain the highest profits. For the individual firm the most important single factor likely to affect efficiency and profits is the quality of its management.

But the most important single influence on the level of profits as a whole is the level of activity: in a boom, or at any time when business conditions are good, profits are high. The reason for this is simple: when a firm can operate near to full capacity it is working at or near its optimum, at which point its average costs are at or near their minimum; sales will be booming, and revenue per unit of output will be high. The difference between

[15] See *The Supply of Certain Industrial and Medical Gases, 1957*. The Commission thought that a profit on capital of 23 to 24 per cent during the years 1952 to 1954 was 'unjustifiably high' (para. 261). In the inquiry into the supply of electrical plant (*The Supply and Exports of Electrical and Allied Machinery and Plant, 1957*) the Commission compared profits made by manufacturers in the industry with profits in seventeen other manufacturing industries and found that in 1952 '... the profit rate of 22 per cent ... was substantially higher than the average rate of 15.4 per cent for those industries' (para. 762) (it was also higher than the rate in any one of the other industries).

costs and revenue (or profits) will be highest in such conditions; if prices are also rising, profits will increase all the more. In fact, in times of rising prices, when costs tend to lag behind prices, profits tend to do exceptionally well: wage increases are usually reflected in rising prices, and businessmen, in attempting to apply a constant percentage profit margin, or mark-up,[16] try to increase profits roughly in proportion to wage increases; the consequent price increase will usually mean that in time wages will rise again, but in the meantime profits have done reasonably well. This is simply the same thing as saying that in times of rising activity most people do well, and indeed there is some evidence that at such times the share of profits in the National Income tends to increase;[17] and the expectation of higher profits is one of the reasons why rising activity tends, up to a point, to be cumulative.

It is because profits are uncertain and dependent on the right business decisions that they provide the mainspring of business activity. In the accountancy sense profits measure success, in the economic sense they are a spur to it.

[16] See Chapter IV.
[17] See E. H. Phelps-Brown and P. E. Hart, 'The Share of Wages in National Income' *Economic Journal* (June 1952).

Chapter VI

THE INVESTMENT DECISION

Consumption is the final end of economic activity. But it does not pay to concentrate all economic activities on the immediate satisfaction of consumption requirements. Roundabout processes, involving considerable preparatory activity before consumer goods are produced, are much more productive than efforts directed wholly to the immediate satisfaction of wants; indeed, most goods could not be produced at all if roundabout methods were not employed. The roots of current productive processes stretch interminably into the past. Before consumption goods could be produced a factory had to be built, and before that a blast furnace had to be constructed to smelt the ore used in the steel; and so on right down the line.

It is convenient to divide economic activities into those that are directed almost wholly to the immediate satisfaction of wants and those that are in the nature of preparatory processes. The distinction is necessarily a little arbitrary. There is generally some lapse before so-called consumer goods pass from the factory or the farm to the consumer, and the productive process can hardly be considered complete until the goods have passed through the hands of wholesalers and retailers and are ready for consumption. Even the consumer himself may not immediately consume the goods he buys but may treat them as a kind of capital on which to draw from time to time. Some goods in their nature must be consumed gradually: washing machines, cars or even bottles of whisky; and in yielding their satisfactions over a period of time they have something in common with machines which contribute to the production of consumer goods for many years. In practice it is not too difficult to classify economic activities according to whether they are to be regarded as producing consumption or capital goods. Producers of heavy generating equipment are engaged in a capital goods industry; garment manufacturers and refrigerator manufacturers for the domestic market are producing consumer goods. When there is reasonable doubt about whether a good or an activity should be classified as consumption or investment some self-imposed rule can be followed: for a long time it has been a common practice to regard the purchase of a motor car as being an investment activity if it was intended for the use of a business executive but to regard it as an act of consumption if the purchase was for private use.

The distinction between consumer and producer goods and between consumption and investment is useful because it serves to identify two types of economic activity that have different characteristics. The production of capital goods is subject to rather greater fluctuations in demand than the production of consumer goods; and is generally undertaken for other firms rather than for private persons. Firms equip themselves with capital because to do so enables them to produce more with the resources they control. But while the process of investment is going on it contributes nothing directly to the satisfaction of consumer requirements. When labour and materials are diverted to investment in conditions of full employment, fewer resources are available for the production of consumer goods. In time the production of consumer goods will be increased but until this happens consumers are worse off than they might otherwise be. Consumers and investors are different people and their actions and desires do not always synchronize or lead to the best working of the economy. It is one of the functions of economic policy to keep consumption and investment in the right balance, encouraging investment if it is thought to be too low, and reducing it if too large a growth threatens to disrupt the working of the economy. More generally investment appears to be one of the activities in an economy which needs some measure of Government oversight and in the post-war period it has been controlled or influenced by Government policy in a number of ways. We return to these aspects of investment decision below, but we start by considering the point of view of the firm. Here the basic decision is whether investment is expected to pay: whether adding to capital now will increase the profits that can be earned in the future sufficiently to justify the expense.

INVESTMENT AND THE FIRM

Investment decisions are among the most difficult in business. The value of capital employed in modern industry in 1954 may have been five times as big as annual expenditure on wages and salaries according to estimates by Professor Barna.[1] And since once money is sunk in buildings and plant there is little chance of recovering it for many years, investment decisions need to be taken with care.

Firms invest to take advantage of apparently profitable opportunities which arise in various ways. Old plant may be wearing out and must be replaced if profits are to be maintained; new markets may be opening up if new products have been developed or new production methods discovered. Investment decisions will not always present themselves in such simple terms. The need to replace old plant often gives an opportunity to change to something newer and better even if the old methods of production will still do. This is not always realized. The story is told of the efforts of one shipbuilding firm to persuade a client that a new vessel should not be an exact replica of one constructed more than 20 years before; how he nearly failed, but in the end succeeded in persuading his client to buy a new and much improved design. Change is rapid, and piecemeal attempts to keep pace with it are often unsatisfactory, while complete modernization is only profitable in certain conditions. So long as the prime (or variable) costs of operating existing plant are less than the total cost of operating new plant a change from one to the other is not worthwhile. Of course, in making this comparison full account has to be taken of improvements that may be made in the product and any other advantages that may result. But the possibilities of benefit should not be viewed too pessimistically. The older is equipment the more difficult is it to see good and secure reasons for replacing it, and it is not unknown for some equipment in the cotton industry, for example, to be proudly displayed as 'over 100 years old'! Often, however, progress depends on a willingness to do something new and perhaps to be a little over-optimistic about the outcome. There is room for both optimism and pessimism about the results of change because the outcome is seldom

[1] See the *Journal of the Royal Statistical Society*, Series A, Part I (1957), Table 5, p. 24.

certain and often depends a great deal on the efforts and energies of those responsible for it.

The more investment is undertaken with the object of doing something new and not just continuing in the old pattern the more uncertain the results of it are likely to be. Even if it is known that the demand for a product will increase there is no guarantee that it will be worthwhile increasing production facilities to meet the expanding market. It is fairly certain that the demand for cars in this country will rise as incomes rise and that the number of cars owned per head is so far below that of the United States that saturation is some time off. It is also reasonable to assume that the growth of income will be fostered by Government action as well as economic factors. It might appear safe, therefore, to plan to increase productive capacity in the motor industry. But it does not follow that it is desirable for every firm in the industry to increase its capacity, or that the individual plans of car producers will be exactly co-ordinated so as to provide for the anticipated increase in car ownership and no more. The chances are that there will be over-provision; for the cost of producing cars falls as output increases and this will encourage firms to plan for a large increase in output in the hope of being able to increase their output at the expense of their rivals and thus sell more cheaply. Excess capacity is sometimes a problem. In the 1930s it appeared to be serious because these were years of depression and there was only a slow increase in output over the whole period. The solution really lay in increasing demand but it was scarcely surprising that many industrialists here and in other countries got together to try to rationalize production facilities and eliminate some excess capacity. Today the danger of excess capacity is less because the level of demand has been high. But it is not always avoided. The reduction of Government support to the aircraft industry when a decline in the air force was planned in the late 1950s left that industry with more capacity than it could hope to employ; while refrigerator manufacturers recently overestimated the amount of capacity that would be necessary to supply the United Kingdom market for some time to come. Excess capacity can result from firms failing to take account of the actions of their competitors and overestimating the share of the market that they can hope to obtain. In some cases the amount of investment may be quite severely limited by the capacity of the market to absorb output. In the United Kingdom two Corning 'Ribbon' machines suffice for the production of all electric bulbs consumed.

The decisions to establish a plant for the production of a new product involves different considerations from a decision merely to maintain capital equipment or to increase the output of some existing product. Major uncertainties exist: about the qualities of the article that is to be produced; about the potential market for it; about the feasibility of the production processes that are proposed; and about the intentions of competitors. Since much of the new investment carried out in the United Kingdom in post-war years has been in industries where there are considerable returns to scale and where oligopolistic competition is the rule, the intentions of competitors have been major considerations in the investment decision. This applies, for example, in iron and steel, oil refining and the production of synthetic fibres. If the product is slow to catch on or is threatened by a similar article, initial investment may turn out to be too large. If, on the other hand, the product is a success and the development of rival products delayed, production facilities will be inadequate. This may still be true even when the market for the product can be viewed with confidence, as happened in the case of synthetic fibre production in I.C.I.

I.C.I. had the advantage in this field of close co-operation with du Pont which enabled them to obtain a licence for the production of nylon in 1939 and to join with Courtaulds in establishing British Nylon Spinners. On the strength of American experience the large-scale production of nylon seemed likely to be a profitable venture and it does not appear that any very close calculation of demand and cost conditions lay behind the decision to start production in this country. The potential market could clearly absorb the output contemplated and the scale of output was big enough to spread overheads. Production was first begun in a pilot plant in 1947 and the main plant started work in 1948. The original plant cost about £6 million, but it was thought that an expansion of capacity sufficient to treble output would halve the capital cost per lb of nylon. Before maximum output was attained, therefore, it was decided to carry out the investment necessary to increase output at Pontypool from 10 to 30 million lb.

Terylene was discovered by Whinfield & Dickinson and developed by I.C.I. who carried out experiments at considerable expense in time, money and ingenuity, to discover whether terylene was the most desirable fibre to produce on a commercial scale. After I.C.I. had secured a licence to produce terylene it took 3 years to get a pilot plant into production and by then a decision had been taken to set up a full-scale plant to produce 11 million lb of terylene per annum. At this stage £14 million had been committed to research and production but before the first plant was completed it was decided to set up another plant costing £18 million.[2] By 1960, however, competition in the production of synthetic fibres had greatly intensified, and with the object of rationalizing production programmes I.C.I. were bidding for control of Courtaulds who are large-scale producers of nylon and joint owners of British Nylon Spinners. Many of the advantages of synthetic fibres have been exploited and they have established themselves against natural fibres. But production capacity grew greatly in the process and it was not long before it exceeded consumption levels. Severe competition is likely even if the newer synthetics can continue to capture industrial and consumer markets.

Investment undertaken with the sole object of supplying export markets has its own problems in relation to demand. The development of countries where living standards are low is bound to disturb the structure of industry in other countries; many products currently supplied by industrial countries can be produced more cheaply where there is cheap labour; and the drive for national industrial development frequently disrupts markets for products even where cheap labour is no great advantage. In order to keep their markets many companies have found it essential to establish branch factories in developing countries. Often such investment is encouraged by special tax remissions and assurances that in the event of nationalization full compensation will be paid. But the risks remain. Much overseas investment has resulted in loss; on the other hand, if

[2] See D. C. Hague, for an account of all these developments, in the *Structure of British Industry*, ed. by Duncan Burn (Cambridge University Press).

branch factories are not established, sales are at the mercy of import duties, import restrictions and competition from both within and without the country. In chemicals, for instance, such competition may accurately be described as cut-throat and prices fixed for many products may bear little relation to long-term production costs. Overheads are high in relation to prime costs and when several products are produced jointly the distribution of overhead costs in the prices charged for products may be largely arbitrary. Thus, to invest mainly in the hope of exporting a substantial proportion of output is to run the risk that profit margins will be extinguished by some competitor disposing of chemicals which to him are something between a by-product and a waste product. In such circumstances there may be little to choose between normal exporting and the dumping of surplus products at prices bearing little relation to production costs.

It is not surprising that there must be some prospect of high yields if businessmen are to invest in overseas markets. New money for investment in underdeveloped countries, with all the uncertainties involved, may be available only if it is expected that the investment will give a return to the company of 20 per cent or more on capital and companies wishing to invest in particularly risky undertakings in this category might have to offer investors a 20 per cent return on capital before they put up the money. Many plantation shares yield investors more than 20 per cent because of the risks involved, and this is without counting money put to reserves.

From the point of view of the directors of a company investment seems worth while whenever there is a sufficient difference between the cost of raising money from investors and the return anticipated from the employment of additional amounts of capital in the business. The cost of raising money varies greatly according to the purposes for which it is needed and general economic conditions. In the post-war period it has been necessary to pay from 4 to 7 per cent for money to buy or build houses and the rate of interest that it has been necessary to offer on debenture issues has been of the same order of magnitude. The Government has been able to borrow more cheaply, but, for it too, interest rates have approached 7 per cent for short periods. The range of return anticipated on ordinary shares has been much wider. Investors have been willing to provide money for investment in some companies at a nominal yield of no more than 2 per cent. But they have done this in the hope that the profits of these companies would expand greatly and that future yields would be much higher in relation to the capital originally invested. For companies that offer no more than average growth possibilities in addition to providing a hedge against rising prices, but which are large, well known and well managed, yields have been rather higher. The yield on ordinary shares included in the *Financial Times* index has fluctuated around 5 to 6 per cent.

The yields we have been considering are, of course, dividend yields. Companies do not usually pay out the whole of their profits; and the fact that part of profits is put to reserve is an attraction to shareholders in addition to the dividends that are currently paid out to them, for they own the company and its accumulated profits. But investors set more store on the amounts that are paid out and attach rather less importance to sums put to reserve.[3] Thus it is not unrealistic to picture a large company as being able to raise new money for its operations on the strength of an intention to pay a dividend of say 6 per cent. Investors would require a somewhat larger yield from smaller companies unless they were thought to offer unusual prospects of growth.

The Economist publishes figures of profits periodically and relates them to the capital employed in various industries. One such measure takes gross profits, that is profits before tax, as a percentage of total net assets, which includes fixed assets, current assets, trade investments, and intangible assets owned by the company. The rate of return on capital, thus measured, is far from constant. In 1952 it was about 20 per cent, falling intermittently to about 15 to 16 per cent in the early 1960s. Within the total, consumer industries showed a rate of return fluctuating throughout the period from 17 to 20 per cent, the decline in profit rates taking place in capital goods industries.

Perhaps the most striking conclusion to be drawn from the figures is that there is a considerable difference between the returns that are earned on capital invested in business and the

[3] See G. R. Fisher, 'Some Factors Influencing Share Prices', *Economic Journal* (March 1961).

returns that currently accrue to shareholders. Investments yield on the average about 15 per cent on capital employed in the business, but the yield to the investor is much less, nearer 5 than 15 per cent. There might appear to be unlimited opportunities for profit in business on the basis of this comparison, and a failure of the economic system properly to confront the yields acceptable to investors with the returns obtainable in industry. It might seem worth while to invest more in industry than is currently being done. There is probably some truth in these contentions, but *The Economist's* figures show only the *average* profitability on capital employed in industry. If more were to be invested in industry the rate of profit might decline; at the margin the opportunities for profitable investment may be much less. The economist pictures the decision to invest as being a marginal one; it is the little bit more or less that really determines economic decisions. Firms are assumed to calculate the return that they anticipate will accrue from alternative investment possibilities before deciding how much capital to employ. With limited availability of capital, investment would presumably be directed to purchasing buildings, plant and machinery which offered the highest return on the capital available. With more capital, plans could be more ambitious and could include rather lower yielding investments of second priority. In practice it would be likely that additional quantities of investment would show progressively lower yields as the most profitable ways to use capital would be exploited first. The decline in yield might be slow or it might be quite sudden. If additional investment had the effect of increasing production appreciably, prices might have to be reduced in order to sell the additional output. Eventually if demand were approaching satiation there might be a sudden fall in the return expected from additional investment expenditure even though it was still possible to make a profit on the investment of smaller amounts of capital. While the yields on capital invested might be expected to fall as more ambitious investment plans were considered the cost of raising capital might be expected to rise. Investors might not want to have too much of their capital in the same business or they might consider that there was a danger of over-capacity. Thus at any given time there is a limit to the amount of investment that a firm can profitably undertake.

But even when profitable opportunities for further investment can still be seen, the rate of investment that is feasible may still be limited by the ability of the industry to absorb innovation with its existing management team. Although the opportunities for profitable investment may be limited at any one time there is likely to be a need for further investment as time goes on and rising incomes increase demand, tastes change or inventions open up new possibilities.

Opportunities for profitable investment appear to vary greatly from industry to industry. The textile industry was earning only 8 per cent on capital in 1959, when many firms must have been making losses; and although profit levels recovered subsequently the rate of return on capital remained below the average. By 1962 the shipping industry was showing a return of only 3 per cent on capital employed and was at the bottom of the scale along with the entertainment industry. At the other end of the scale companies concerned with shops and oil were getting a return of 25 and 20 per cent on capital respectively, but oil at least was not regarded as a promising industry in which to invest. A superficial reading of these figures would suggest that while investment in more shops might be profitable, great care would have to be taken in investing in new ships. Of course, the prospects would not appear the same to everybody. The prospects for the shipping industry in 1962 were far from bright; but they appeared better to some shipowners than to others. While United Kingdom shipowners were making losses, continental shipowners were seeking to add to their fleets and, presumably, saw the future in a different light. Present profitability is always an uncertain indicator of future prospects and a determined and astute businessman can make apparently unpromising ventures profitable on occasion. But in business it is generally unwise to invest unless there is a reasonable prospect of earning profits within a short period of time.

Basically, the reason for this is that it is expensive to tie up money without the prospect of immediate returns; and if initial losses or low profits are to be offset, profits have to be rather high in subsequent years. As a first step in appraising the profitability of some project, a businessman might estimate the net returns year by year that he anticipated from investing in it. He might have to choose between a number of possible projects each having its own different pattern of net returns over the years. How is he to compare the results obtainable from the various alternative uses of his talents? One way would be to try to calculate for each project the present value of anticipated future returns. Suppose that it was anticipated that the net return on one project at the end of the first year would be £100; what would be the present value of this sum? We can arrive at a value by asking what sum of money would accumulate, at interest, to £100 at the end of 1 year. And the same kind of calculation might be done for the second and all subsequent years. By adding all these results together we could arrive at a present value of all the net returns anticipated from the project; and the sum of these would give us a measure of the total benefit to be obtained from undertaking it. Similar calculations could be done for other projects under consideration and the various results compared.

The present values of the projects would depend on the rate of interest that we used for our calculations. If we used a zero rate of interest the results we would get would amount to adding up the net benefits anticipated in all future years. But if we used a very high rate of interest the net benefits to be obtained in the future would count for very little. It might be appropriate to consider a rather high rate of interest for the purpose of calculations because it appears that in some industries at least it is possible to use money very profitably. Suppose we take 10 per cent, roughly corresponding to the average rate of return on industrial investment after paying income tax. At this rate of interest £91 will accumulate to £100 in 1 year's time; thus a net return of £100 in 1 year's time corresponds to £91 now. Similarly, £100 at the end of 2 years corresponds to £83 now and so on (see Fig. 6.1). The further we look ahead the smaller the present value of future benefits becomes. Looking 10 years ahead £100 has sunk to £38 and is only some 5 per cent of the present value of successive sums of £100 discounted for 1 to 10 years. Thus, if the appropriate rate of discounting future benefits is 10 per cent, events 10 years hence are rather unimportant in most investment calculations; and, if we are considering an investment yielding £100 per year in perpetuity, two-thirds of the total benefits from the investment would accrue in the first 10 years. If the rate of interest chosen for the purpose of discounting were lower, say 5 per cent, the weight to be recorded to returns 10 years hence would be somewhat greater but the discounted value of the return anticipated in the eleventh year would be only 7 per cent of the sum of the discounted returns anticipated in the first 10 years. It might, however, be more realistic to use a higher rather than a lower rate of discount than 10 per cent and this would increase the importance of returns anticipated in the first 10 years of the life of the investment. The importance of returns in later years

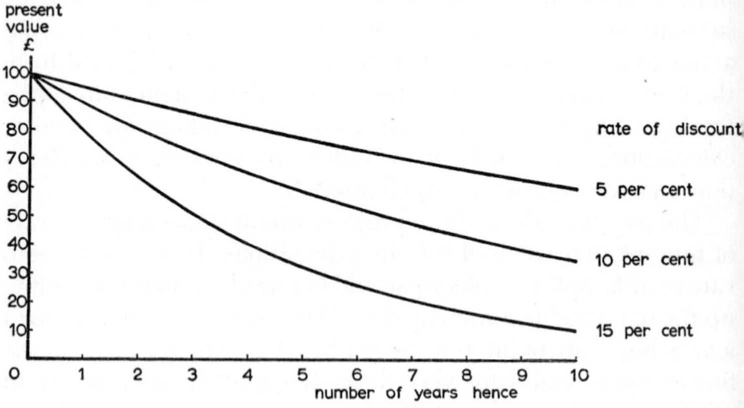

Figure 6-1. Present Value of £100 at Future Dates.

is further reduced by the uncertainty with which future events must be viewed. Not only should we discount by some factor representing the rate of return obtainable on industrial investment but we must increase this factor somewhat to allow for the fact that future returns may not materialize at all. When we are considering industrial investment it is the immediate pay-off that counts. If we considered a rate of discount of 15 per cent, 80 per cent of the investment returns would accrue in the first 10 years and with a 20 per cent rate of discount this figure would rise to 90 per cent. This explains why businessmen think mainly in terms of what is likely to happen over the next few years, seldom more than 10, and often prefer to think of investment in relation to the number of years that it will take to recover the capital sum invested out of the returns that are anticipated. To plan on the basis of an indefinite number of years of productive activity is to offer too many hostages to fortune in what is an uncertain economic world.

It is a wonder that businessmen are ever able to contemplate any but the most immediate needs. But not all business decisions are based on hard arithmetic. Imponderables figure in business calculations as in others. Carter and Williams, in *Investment in Innovation*,[4] have cautioned against assuming that businessmen are calculating machines. They demonstrate that investment is frequently undertaken irrespective of yield considerations in order to keep ahead of competitors, to expand, to introduce new products and to give effect to invention and innovation. They also stress that even when yields are calculated there are frequently wide divergencies between what is anticipated and what eventually transpires.

Investment in research might be difficult to explain in terms of the investment calculations that we have been discussing. The results of research are always uncertain and the benefits often delayed and because of this there is a strong temptation for firms to neglect research, or if they do attach importance to it, to concentrate on immediate applications rather than fundamental research. It is often appropriate to leave the latter to other institutions established for the purpose. For the larger firms, however, which can afford substantial research programmes, research is less chancy because failure in some line of research may be compensated by success in another, and some fundamental research can be carried, and sometimes profitably carried, in and amongst research intended to be directed to the immediate need of the firm. The justification for industry investing in research, apart from the better managerial attitudes that it engenders, is that the benefits from research, even though delayed and uncertain, can be very large and more than adequate to ensure a satisfactory return on research activities. The more these results can be disseminated beyond the firm that discovered them, the greater can they be made to be. But apart from the social aspects of research a firm is always at the mercy of its competitors if they succeed in discovering some new product or process to which there is no effective answer. If the whole of the profitable activities of a firm are at stake,

[4] Oxford University Press, 1958.

research may be the most rewarding form of investment that a firm can undertake.

INVESTMENT AND THE COMMUNITY

One of the economic responsibilities of the State is to ensure that there is the right amount of investment and that it goes into the right things. It is not easy to decide how much investment should be carried out. Sometimes the major consideration is whether investment will be large enough to prevent unemployment, given some anticipated level of other types of expenditure. Sometimes it is a question of balancing future benefits against present sacrifices, in conditions of full employment, and there may be differences of opinion about the proper balance between the two. Still another approach to the question starts from the assumption that investment is the best means of ensuring growth in national income. Past experience has been that the ratio between capital employed and the income of the community has been of the order of 3:1. It is only a step from this, but often a rash one, to assuming that an increase in capital formation will automatically give rise to an increase in the national income in the same proportion. If, for example, it is thought that an increase in the national income of 5 per cent is desirable it might be concluded that investment ought to be three times as much, say 15 per cent of national income (quite apart from the need to make good depreciation).

Other comparisons are also made in an effort to judge what level of investment is desirable. It has been fashionable to compare the United Kingdom effort with that of other European countries by calculating investment as a percentage of each country's gross national product. Comparisons of this kind have almost invariably shown the United Kingdom to be near the bottom of the list. The statistical comparison of the percentage of the gross national product invested by various countries is a little uncertain in spite of efforts by international organization to compile figures on the same basis. Countries differ somewhat in the type of activities that they are prepared to consider as investment; the extent to which repairs are regarded as investment or treated as current expenditure on maintenance is one issue. But the difference between the percentages of the national income invested by the United Kingdom and other countries has been so large in many years as to leave little doubt that there was a real underlying difference. More recently the United Kingdom investment effort has compared favourably with that of the leading industrial continental countries. In 1961 the United Kingdom invested 21 per cent of the gross national product and this is as much as most other countries have been able to sustain for any length of time.

Throughout the post-war period the level (and direction) of investment has been the subject of Government policy. Until 1955 investment was controlled by licensing. Demands on the economy repeatedly exceeded the resources that were available and the weight of Government intervention was directed to keeping investment in bounds. The intention was to ensure that sufficient resources would be available for producing exports and that the standard of living would not be too depressed by a higher investment effort or the working of the economy swamped by inflationary price increases that might be generated if consumption were brought under pressure. But because investment was restricted, industrial capacity was developed more slowly than businessmen would have liked had they been free of control. There is also evidence that investment licensing affected entrepreneurial initiative. It took entrepreneurs some time to react to the abolition of investment licensing in 1955 and it seemed that they had lost the habit of making investment plans because they felt that there was little chance of seeing them implemented in the face of Government restrictions. After some delay, industrial investment increased when investment control was jettisoned and in so doing strained the country's resources and contributed to an exchange crisis both by increasing imports and by limiting exports with the diversion of a greater proportion of the output of industries producing investment goods to the home market.

It is impossible to decide if investment would have been higher if the resources invested had been decided by market forces rather than by Government intervention in the immediate post-war period. Forces making for increased investment might well have been nullified by pressures for higher wages or greater distribution of profits. Nor can it be concluded that Government intervention is not needed to increase investment levels in other circumstances. Countries in Europe that planned their investment programmes succeeded in achieving a higher rate of investment than the United Kingdom. Indeed, much of the success of French industrial efforts in the post-war period had been attributed to planning. In the United Kingdom, also, restraint in investment imposed by controls has given

TABLE 6.1

GROSS FIXED CAPITAL FORMATION BY INDUSTRY GROUP AT CURRENT PRICES

	£ million										
	1950	*1951*	*1952*	*1953*	*1954*	*1955*	*1956*	*1957*	*1958*	*1959*	*1960*
Housing	331	376	494	630	645	619	633	617	591	658	753
Social services	80	93	102	105	109	119	144	172	179	189	198
Other public services	54	70	72	80	82	88	107	111	135	168	190
Total	465	539	668	815	836	826	884	900	905	1015	1141
Mining and quarrying	33	34	46	62	79	86	91	103	105	117	91
Gas, electricity and water	195	217	239	265	304	343	340	360	389	421	429
Transport and communications (2)	215	199	205	264	275	288	363	460	467	500	535
Total	443	450	490	591	658	717	594	923	961	1038	1055
Distribution and other services (1) (3)	179	200	217	233	280	369	382	412	468	540	615
Manufacturing (1)	444	514	549	547	581	678	845	931	921	874	1034
Agriculture, forestry and fishing	93	94	97	94	100	110	102	114	134	147	140
Building and contracting (1) (construction)	25	33	36	35	44	50	53	57	62	61	63
Legal fees, etc.	51	54	45	40	43	47	44	42	44	50	55
GRAND TOTAL	1700	1884	2102	2355	2542	2797	3104	3379	3495	3725	4103

Notes: (1) The figures for 1956 onwards are on a business unit basis, those for earlier years on an establishment basis.
(2) Excludes load haulage, taxis and private-hire cars.
(3) Includes load haulage, taxis and private-hire cars.

place to fiscal encouragements to invest, in the form of accelerated depreciation allowances which postpone taxation payments and the introduction of initial allowances which have had the effect of subsidizing investment activity. The operation of the National Economic Development Council is also seen in some quarters as an attempt to adapt the French system of planning to this country.

Increasing investment in the so-called industrial sector of the economy at the expense of other forms of investment has been suggested as one means of accelerating industrial development. It is surprising at first sight how small a proportion of investment takes place in industry. In recent years it has been about one-quarter of the total.

But the fact of the matter is that industrial investment can be increased at the expense of other forms of investment only for a short period. The provision of capital for other purposes is as essential in the long run as investment in the industrial sector. Industry cannot function without the provision of power, transport and shops; and houses and education are just as indispensable. The United Kingdom is not peculiar in being able to invest only a limited proportion of its resources in industry. It is a characteristic of investment in all countries and over nearly all periods that the infrastructure of the economy (roads, schools, houses and requirements of Government) makes the heaviest demand on investment.

There is also a danger of exaggerating the effect of investment in industry on production. Even without any increase in the quantity of capital available some increases in production would result from technical progress. Reddaway and Smith have suggested that in the period 1948–54 'progress' was sufficient to increase the output of manufacturing industry by some 2 per cent per annum.[5] Manufacturing provides about 35–40 per cent of the gross domestic product so that an increase of 2 per cent per annum in this sector would have the effect of increasing the national income by about ¾ per cent per annum. Progress is not confined to the manufacturing sector although it may have more marked effects in this sector than elsewhere, and a somewhat higher rate of increase in income might be anticipated in total than ¾ per cent. Doubts arise, however, because the rate of 'progress' in the period 1948–54 may have been unusually high, it was certainly higher in the period 1948–54 than from 1951–54.

The benefits of progress can be more easily spread if a large investment programme can be sustained. The renewal of capital equipment will help, but substantial net investment will

[5] 'Progress in Manufacturing Industries in the period 1948–1954', *Economic Journal* (March 1960), p. 17.

accelerate the process. In countries where population is increasing this will still apply even if the investment is no more than is necessary to keep pace with the increase in population. In underdeveloped countries it is not uncommon to find that population is increasing at the rate of 2 or more per cent per annum. To keep pace with this increase an investment programme of 5 or 6 per cent of the gross national product may be necessary. Existing capital must also be maintained and it is not unusual to find that 10 per cent of the national income must be invested in order to keep the economy standing still.

Investment probably responds more readily to the need to broaden the capital structure in response to an increase in population or an increase in demand than to other factors that might be expected to influence it. Much investment can be seen as a response to increasing demand. Demand increases and industrialists seek to expand the capital they have available in order to keep it in some accustomed relation to output. There may be some economies of scale in the use of capital as output increases and this will enable capital to be economized; but there will seldom be a tendency to retrogress to some method of production requiring less capital in relation to output because capital equipment cannot increase in line with rising demand. Industry is, above all, a capital-forming sector of the economy which depends only in part on the savings of persons and institutions outside industry for the finance needed for capital equipment and it is likely to react with vigour against financial difficulties that deprive it of capital it thinks it needs. In recent years industry in this country has provided between 50 and 60 per cent of the finance needed for its investment programmes out of retained profits. Thus it is useful to regard capital as being expanded roughly in proportion to output. The relation is not, of course, fixed for all time. In recessions output is reduced without capital being reduced to begin with, though its accumulation may be slowed down; at times, also, it may be possible to increase output by working existing plant more intensively; while, in the long run, there is no reason why the accumulation of capital should not proceed more slowly than the increase of output if it happens that technical progress makes possible economy in the use of capital; or why it should not increase more rapidly, if the greater wealth or developed saving habits of the community increase the rate at which capital can be accumulated. If this occurred it would be open to industry to adopt production methods requiring more capital and less labour or other factors of production per unit of output, unless much of the additional capital flowed to other sectors of the economy.

It appears doubtful whether the amount of capital used in industry would be greatly increased if interest rates were to fall by some small amount. We have already pointed out that a large gap exists between the rate of return that is available to investors in companies and the rate of return that companies earn on the average or their capital. Much economic theory has been written on the supposition that investment in industry is sensitive to interest rates with the implication that lower interest rates would lead to a substitution of capital for other factors of production. But, in fact, the scope for substitution of capital seems to be rather limited at present interest rates. It might be thought that with low interest rates there would be scope to increase the use of capital until interest became a more significant item in costs. The fact that this is not done may seem to imply that the scope for substitution of capital for other factors of production is determined by technological factors in a rather rigid way. In underdeveloped countries, for example, it is usual for industry to use the same kind of production methods as are in use in advanced industrial countries; even though labour is much cheaper in relation to capital. Another important factor making the use of capital in industry rather insensitive to interest rates lies in the risks and uncertainties that are inseparable from industrial operations, and this reduces the importance of interest rates as factors affecting business decisions.

This suggests that changes in interest rates about their present level are not likely to have very significant effects on the amount of capital used in industry in relation to output. In other words, somewhat lower interest rates would not lead to a 'deepening' of the capital structure, that is the use of more capital per unit of output.

Econometric studies on the whole confirm the conclusion that the use of fixed capital in industry is relatively insensitive to small changes in interest rates. There may be some reason for believing that investment in railroads and the electricity industry in the United States have been affected by interest rates but for the most part there is little evidence of close association.[6] If rates of interest had been higher during the period for which studies have been made the results might have been different, for there is little doubt that if interest rates were high they would exert more influence over business decisions.

The amount of capital required by industry depends greatly on the type of industries that are being developed. In 1954 the amount of capital invested in china and earthenware, shipbuilding, leather, biscuits and the manufacture of wood and cork was less than £1000 per head. The capital required for general chemicals was £5000 per head and oil refining nearly £13,000. By comparison the industries pictured as fully automated were only moderate capital users. Fixed assets in the motor car and aircraft industries and in engineering amounted to less than £2000 per person.[7]

Taking a long view the most powerful stimulus to the use of capital is undoubtedly innovation. The whole process of accumulating capital in this country can be seen as the reaction to a succession of discoveries starting from the development of the steam engine and mechanization of the textile industries and leading to automated flow processes of the type used for the production of chemicals today. Thus the investment decision might be said, as a half-truth, to be influenced primarily by technical progress, the discovery of new processes and new products, rather than by economic considerations. But the practicability of producing new products depends on being able to produce them at a price at which they can be sold, and on the existence of a rising level of demand; while the ability to produce goods requiring large amounts of capital depends on the community's willingness to provide the capital needed out of its current income. But as we have seen, the provision of capital for industry is only part of the total capital needed for industrial and other purposes, and shortage of capital or the cost of obtaining it is not likely to be a very serious obstacle to a well-established company in a developed economy if the market

[6] See *The Investment Decision*, Meyer and Kuh (Harvard University Press), p. 8.

[7] See T. Barna, 'The Replacement Cost of Fixed Assets in British Manufacturing Industry in 1955', *Journal of the Royal Statistical Society*, Series A, (1957), p. 25.

prospects for a new product have been proved. If large numbers of industrialists see profitable opportunities for investment simultaneously, it may be extremely difficult for the Government to keep the level of industrial investment in bounds and we have the phenomenon of an investment boom. Often it will be self-liquidating, but in the short run the effects on the economy may be harmful if investment activity exceeds the capacity of the economy to supply it either in total or at a number of key points. The investment boom in 1955 led as we have seen to a foreign exchange crisis and this in turn led to the level of demand being reduced throughout the economy until there was substantial unused productive capacity.

It is not only investment in private industry that is inflexible. Investment by nationalized industries, too, is only partially responsive to Government policy. The Government has found it necessary to supervise the total investment programmes of these industries in order to tailor them to the economic situation. Investment in other public sectors of the economy has also been subject to Government influence largely because the finance for investment purposes has been provided from Government sources.

The Government is also concerned with the geographical distribution of investment. This has been mainly in the interests of developing various areas of the country where unemployment is high and communities are likely to disintegrate without active Government intervention. The areas most affected have been South Wales, north-east England, Scotland and Northern Ireland, parts of Lancashire and west Cumberland. The decline of economic activity was marked in these areas during the depressed years of the 1930s and they have not shown the same rate of growth since as the rest of the country. For 30 years successive governments have sought to channel investment into these areas, with some success though not on a sufficient scale to eliminate undesirable unemployment, particularly in Northern Ireland. The availability of labour has probably been an attraction to firms when labour has been scarce elsewhere; and refusal to grant licences for development elsewhere in the early post-war years was a means of enforcing a prescribed distribution of industry on expanding firms. Specific encouragements to investment have also played their part. The provision of industrial estates for easy development, the construction of special factories and the lease of factory space at nominal rentals have been encouragements to incoming and expanding firms. They may have been important to firms that otherwise could not have found the money to carry out the investment that they needed if they had been forced to buy their factory as well as to provide the capital equipment to go with it. But the provision of factory space at subsidized rentals can have only a moderate effect on costs, particularly if the firms that occupy the factories are handicapped in other ways, and would not have considered establishing themselves in a development area without some form of Government assistance. The purpose of providing special facilities in a development area is largely to tip the scale when a firm is not opposed to moving to it; and in this respect they seem to have succeeded. But the measures so far taken have done little to alter the attractions of various areas for industrialists in any more fundamental manner and the pull of the south-east of England remains strong.

There are, however, dangers as well as advantages in attempting to promote growth in areas where it would not otherwise take place. In underdeveloped countries it is frequently desired to provide centres of growth throughout a country so that all may share in development even to the point of restricting development in areas where it is going ahead of its own volition. The net effect of a policy of this kind, however, may be to retard the rate of growth if businessmen are not allowed to place their industries in places where conditions are most conducive to growth and where the interactions between growing sectors of the economy act as a further stimulus to expansion.

When both the interests of firms and the interests of the State have to be reconciled the investment decision becomes extremely complex, as may be seen in the discussion in the Appendix of the decision to build a strip mill to be operated by Colvilles in Scotland.

SUMMARY

The main points made in this chapter may be summed up briefly:

1. Investment enables more roundabout processes of production to be used which are more productive than attempting

to concentrate all economic activity on the production of consumer goods.

2. The level of investment is as much a concern of the State as it is of the private sector of the economy

3. Investment may be undertaken to replace existing plant, increase output or improve production methods, for example by reducing costs. In practice it may do all these things simultaneously.

4. In general, plant should not be replaced if the prime cost of operating it is less than the total cost of operating new plant of greater efficiency.

5. It is desirable not to be pessimistic about the benefits to be anticipated from investment even though 'excess capacity' is a danger in some circumstances.

6. It is difficult to decide how much to invest in the production of a new product because of the uncertainties involved. But all investment involves uncertainty and particularly investment in overseas countries.

7. The relative profitability of different investment projects can be compared by discounting estimated future returns. The higher are interest rates, the more does the profitability of investment depend on the results anticipated in the first few years. Uncertainty about the future has the same effect.

8. The State considers investment in relation to unemployment and the growth of the gross national product. Recently over 20 per cent of the gross national product has been invested and about one-quarter of this in industry.

9. Capital accumulation may respond to the need to increase output, to changes in the industrial structure and to invention, but it does not appear to be greatly affected by small changes in interest rates. This is one reason why it has proved necessary to exercise some direct control over investment in the post-war period.

Appendix to Chapter VI

LOCATION OF A STRIP MILL[1]

The decision to establish a strip mill in Scotland concerned not only Colville's and their shareholders, but the various pressure groups campaigning for new industry in Scotland, the Government and the Iron and Steel Board. Investment in steel-making capacity is planned to some extent. The Iron and Steel Board, which was set up in its present form in 1953, has the responsibility of reviewing the investment plans and requirements of the steel industry periodically. Such reviews inevitably take the form of attempting to assess the movement of demand for steel products over a period of years along the lines discussed in Chapter IX. As a result of this assessment views are formed of the increase in capacity that is likely to be needed, and attempts are made to co-ordinate the plans of the independent steel companies. The production of cars and domestic appliances has increased the demand for strip steel considerably. In 1955–56, when the Board carried out one of its periodic reviews, it was anticipated that the demand for sheet steel would continue to expand rapidly and the expected increase between 1956 and 1962 was of the order of 50 per cent. Even with the retention of some 300,000 tons of output from obsolete, mostly hand, mills it was anticipated that home production would be deficient by almost half a million tons in 1962.

The Board had been saying as early as 1955 that additional strip-mill capacity would be necessary. The choice of site for expansion was the issue. In Wales neither the Ebbw Vale nor Port Talbot sites appeared to be as suitable as Newport, which was being considered by Richard Thomas & Baldwin's. Pressure groups outside the industry favoured Kidwelly and Swansea in Wales, and Grangemouth in Scotland. Another proposition not sponsored by any firm was to build a strip mill at Immingham. On mainly economic considerations the choice appeared to lie mainly between Immingham and Newport. In choosing between them the Board came down in favour of Newport. But the matter was not allowed to rest. There was great pressure from Scotland for the establishment of light industry and it was thought that the provision of a strip mill might be the first step to the reintroduction of the motor car

[1] The following discussion draws heavily on: Duncan Burn, *The Steel Industry, 1939–59* (Cambridge 1961), Chapter X.

industry to Scotland since its eclipse in the 1920s. It was decided that there should not be one but two strip mills, one in Wales at Newport and the other in Scotland, an extension of Colville's at Ravenscraig. In order that finance should be no obstacle the Government arranged to provide capital for both companies to the extent that they were unable to provide it.

This particular investment decision gives us an opportunity to study some of the issues that underlay the decision to have a new strip mill and its proposed location and to recognize that the decision to have two strip mills, one in Wales and one in Scotland, while mainly a political one, had a measure of economic justification.

1. The first issue is the basis for believing that a new strip mill was required. The calculations of requirements rested essentially on the projection of certain past trends into the future. It was reasonable to suppose that technical change and the growth of incomes would continue to increase the demand for sheet steel over a period of years. But the rate of growth was more difficult to determine. At what rate was it reasonable to assume that the consumption of sheet steel would increase in relation to the growth of industrial production; and how fast could industrial production itself be assumed to increase? In the post-war period the rate of expansion of steel consumption had generally been underestimated. Was the judgment about the future expansion of steel requirements over-correcting for previous errors?

2. The second issue hinged on the decision to base the production of strip on imported ores, which was unavoidable if production was to be localized at Ravenscraig. The industry seemed increasingly to have lost sight of economic factors in its pricing policy as determined by the Iron and Steel Federation. In the post-war years prices were fixed too low and insufficient allowance was made for depreciation and re-equipment; imported iron ore had been subsidized to users through the operation of the Industry Fund which exacted a levy on scrap and ingots in order to reduce the costs of imports of iron ore, scrap, pig-iron and semi-finished steel; and there was a long-established custom of charging all steel users the same price irrespective of their nearness to sources of supply. Had a comparative disregard of price economics made the industry insensitive to the comparative economies of using home and foreign ore? The indications were that home ore was cheaper where it was mined than foreign ore at other places. Certainly there might have been an opening for the production of wide strip steel on a site in the East Midlands or on the East Coast.

3. Another major issue involved in the decision to build two strip mills instead of one, or to attempt to increase the output of existing capacity, was that of productivity. In most steel operations productivity in the United Kingdom was far below that of the United States. Scale of operation was certainly a major factor in this. By 1959 the minimum economic capacity for a wide semi-continuous mill was said to be 2 million tons per year. Against this could be set the decision that Colville's should aim at an ultimate capacity of 1 million tons in sheets and light plate while Richard Thomas & Baldwin's were scheduled to make not much more than half a million tons. The implications of these decisions have been said to be that Colville's would run at about half their sheet-steel capacity and the Newport mill at much the same loading.

4. For Colville's the production of sheet steel was something of an act of faith. It would be difficult to think of any steel maker in Scotland embarking on the production of sheet on the scale envisaged without Government prompting and support. At the time the decision was taken to build the strip mill there was very little demand for sheet steel in Scotland, and the argument that since continental producers had found it profitable to sell sheet steel in this country, it would prove possible for Colville's to find export markets to load the mill fully, was scarcely convincing. By 1962, however, the hoped for expansion of the motor industry in Scotland was under way, offering at least some measure of domestic demand.

5. The decision to construct two mills rather than a single one originally meant that neither were to be fully continuous, although this decision was later reversed for the Newport mill. Continuous strip mills gave lower costs and better quality at the expense of some flexibility. For Colville's a fully continuous mill was not thought to be justified though if demand increased sufficiently the mill might be modified for continuous working at rather greater expense.

6. The issues of location were both economic and political. The availability of steel-making materials was drying up in Scotland. The Ravenscraig site is removed from a deep-water anchorage and imported ore has first to be unloaded in Glasgow and then transported by rail to be smelted. The supply of good coking coal was becoming exhausted and the cost of mining it was greater than in Wales or Yorkshire. If it had been charged to Colville's at the cost of mining it, it would have cost at least 14s. more per ton, the difference between mining costs and sales price being made up by the National Coal Board's policy of subsidizing the operation of inefficient pits. Newport was better placed in respect of access to raw materials and, at the time the decisions were made, to markets. But the most

advantageous location appears to have been Immingham. It would have been comparatively better for supplies of home ore had these been used and at least as well placed for imported ore as Newport. It would have had access to markets in the north-east and would have been able to serve London, Luton and Coventry almost as well as Newport, though not the West Midlands where Newport was at an advantage. The main advantage of Immingham lay in the cheaper cost of coal from the Yorkshire coalfields.

7. The final decision on location, and the construction of two mills rather than one, comes under the heading of socio-political considerations. The development of both Wales and Scotland has been a major consideration since the years of heavy unemployment in the 'thirties. Scotland has found it difficult to attain a balance of industry that could reduce its dependence on heavy industry sufficiently and give impetus to growth by the introduction of new and expanding industries. The traditional output of Colville's was heavy plates used by shipbuilders and, as the 'fifties wound up, the prospects of selling steel for ships on the same scale as previously seemed to be receding. Colville's needed new outlets and Scotland new industries. The decision to instal a strip mill was rapidly followed by news that the motor-car industry was moving part of its activities to the North. It is extremely unlikely that this would have materialized if local supplies of sheet steel had not been available. If the establishment of a strip mill is the means of getting more light industry it may prove to have been justified even if the location appears wrong on narrowly economic grounds. The effect of slightly more expensive sheet steel (say, as had been suggested, 5–10 per cent more expensive) than would have been produced elsewhere on the costs of vehicle production may be more than offset by advantages to be found in Scotland. But decisions taken on social and political grounds are possible only if the economy is wealthy enough to underwrite them.

8. Nowhere is there available an account of the discussion that must have taken place on estimates of costs and returns anticipated from the construction of the two strip mills. They must have been made; for it is doubtful if Colville's would have embarked on the construction of a strip mill in an unfavourable location without first verifying that the provision of Government loans at a reasonable rate of interest would be sufficient to assure the venture of profitability. But much of the decision to invest and the decision to locate the mills in Wales and Scotland was carried out without close reference to profitability. The need for the mills in the first place rested much more on assumptions about the movement of quantities

likely to be used than in terms of demand curves or cost functions. It might not have done so if the United Kingdom had been a member of the European Coal and Steel Community at the time, closely weighing the dangers of foreign competition, and thinking less exclusively in terms of producing for national requirements and using international trade only as a means to balance out supply and demand. Attitudes might also have been different if investment were carried out in a less ordered fashion in the steel industry and threats of nationalization had less bedevilled the industry and made it both easier and essential to raise money for the ventures from the market. But then there might have been no new steel mills or so much excess capacity that profits disappeared.

CHAPTER VII

FINANCE

FINANCE is not, as is often imagined, entirely the province of the accountant. The decisions which the firm has to make about forms of finance are influenced largely by economic considerations, and this chapter is devoted to an examination of these.

Broadly, the firm has three main[1] sources of finance: *internal funds*, or *self financing*, derived mainly from the retention of past income in reserves, or through the sale of assets which the firm has acquired in the past; *long-term external funds*, in the form of loan and share capital; and *short- or medium-term external funds*, mainly in the form of bank credit, trade credit, hire purchase and similar shorter-term obligations. We shall consider each of these in more detail in this chapter. The extent to which the main sources of finance are used in Britain is shown in Tables 7·2, 7·3 and 7·4 at the end of this chapter (pages 237–9).

There is no such thing as an ideal way of financing a firm—the individual circumstances of each firm differ so much that each one has different requirements—but certain principles do underly any financing decision and, from the purely practical point of view, it is desirable to examine the possibilities in the field and the advantages and snags attached to them.

There are four main considerations to be borne in mind:

1. The amount of money needed.
2. The time when it is needed.
3. The purposes for which the money is needed.
4. The form of finance to be used.

There is a further consideration—whether it is profitable and worth while to undertake the expansion (or to start production

[1] There is a fourth aspect of finance, frequently neglected, which is not a form of finance in the same way as the others, but is more strictly an allocation of available funds, or the improvement in the utilization and movement of funds within the firm. This, which may be called *internal financial control or management*, is dealt with separately in Chapter VIII since, although it has the same aims as other financial decisions, the factors affecting it are rather different.

at all). This question was considered in the discussion of the investment decision in the preceding chapter, and for the purposes of the present chapter is assumed to have been answered; but clearly the one consideration will always depend to some extent on the other. Related to this, however, is yet another consideration: whether the proposed capital expenditure is to be used for the expansion of the business or in the maintenance of existing business (under which heading it is frequently convenient to consider not only replacement of assets but also such special requirements as safety and welfare). The distinction between expansion and maintenance of business underlies the whole financing decision.

Determination of the amount of money required is largely a matter of budgeting and forward planning. Overestimation of requirements is wasteful, since it involves the firm in payment of interest on funds which are not being put to any useful, profit-earning purpose; but it is on the whole less serious than underestimation, which leads to the firm running short of funds before the project reaches a stage where it begins to pay its way (not only does this lead to financial embarrassment *per se*, but it may also lead to greater difficulty in getting the extra funds which become necessary).

Timing is also largely a matter of budgeting: much capital equipment not only takes a long time to instal and reach the stage of profitable operation, it may also have a delivery date a long time ahead: at the extremes it takes several years to sink a coal mine, build a steelworks or a ship, or construct a power station or dam and even in less extreme cases the installation of much plant and equipment and the building of new workshops may take several months. Increases in working capital also need to be budgeted and provision made in good time, and possible seasonal variations in supplies and markets have to be taken into account.

The purpose for which the money is needed largely determines the form of finance which will be used. Long-term capital (internal or external) is almost always needed for the large-scale extension of productive capacity in the form of heavy plant, equipment and buildings. It is preferable, though not essential, that the capital for such purposes should be permanent, or, at the very least, not subject to withdrawal before the plant has started to pay for itself. The long-term criterion of such finance is that the capital expenditure should pay for itself (or amortise itself) out of the profits earned from the plant.

Plant of a less durable nature—such as vehicles, contractors' plant, machine tools, etc., which can be written off over a period of 3 to 5 years—can be financed by medium-term funds; though it is possible and sometimes desirable to finance such equipment, along with durable plant, from long-term sources, and, in the case of a major investment decision, to bring all equipment into one long-term capital budget. Similarly, the financing of a very long contract—road building, factory building and so on—is often a good candidate for medium-term funds; and the financing of the sale of capital goods (particularly in the export market) is also frequently undertaken from such funds.

Short-term funds are usually restricted to debt which is self-liquidating. Examples of this are the monthly payment of creditors, the financing of short-term contracts (up to 6 months), the financing of seasonal stock peaks, and the financing of production lags (of the seeds-to-harvest variety).

To some extent the form of finance used depends on the legal form of the firm. The unincorporated business initially has to rely for long-term capital on the contribution of the partners or the sole owner plus what they can borrow privately; later it may borrow from the bank, or it may acquire new capital *via* retained income, by bringing in new partners, or by a change to company status and the issue of shares; or it may at any time (it if can find lenders) raise funds by long-term borrowing on mortgage or by the issue of debentures. The private company can issue shares, but generally, as will be seen, is restricted in the amount of capital it can raise in this way. The quoted public company can use the resources and contacts of the New Issue Market and can, in general, command access to much larger resources, both in total and proportionally, than its smaller brethren. Change from one legal form to another (e.g. from private to public company) may well be a way of raising funds by tapping new sources of finance, but before this is possible certain economic and legal conditions have to be fulfilled, and there are other implications, to which we return later.

Two further considerations have to be borne in mind: ownership and liquidity. Some forms of finance, of which ordinary share capital is the prime example, constitute a form of ownership, and raising funds in this way means that some ownership of the firm, and some degree of control, *via* voting rights, passes out of the hands of the existing owners of the equity[2] of the firm. The degree to which this is acceptable to the firm depends on the existing structure of ownership and the attitude of the existing owners to any potential diminution of their power and control over the firm: one reason why many small firms are unable to expand is that their owners are loath to part with any share of the ownership—or, as they usually call it, their independence—and many of their potential lenders will not consider putting any money into the firm without receiving in return some degree of control. Other forms of finance, such as renting, hire purchase or any other form of finance which requires payments at regular and specified intervals, whilst they do not raise the ownership problem, do represent obligations of the firm which may from time to time impair its liquidity, or its ability to settle its debts in cash or other acceptable forms of money at short notice: sensible budgeting can avoid most of these problems.

INTERNAL FUNDS

Internal funds consist of amounts retained from income in the past. The precise way in which profits are transferred to reserves is largely a matter of accounting convenience and convention,[3] but there is a reasonably clear theoretical economic criterion of what is retained profit. Any amount of income transferred to reserves over and above what is required for the maintenance intact of the net worth of the firm (the assets of the firm, less the current liabilities; or, alternatively, the equity or share in the firm of the shareholders or owners of the firm[4]) is retained profit. In practice, however, it is often difficult to

[2] Equity in this context means ownership and a right to a share in the earnings of the firm.

[3] See Chapter V.

[4] This is analogous to personal net worth (see Table 2.4), and it can be represented in balance sheet terms as the Total Issued Capital and Reserves of the Company (although in practice these only represent historical cost valuations plus any revaluations which may have been undertaken, and rarely represent real net worth).

determine this amount with any precision, and the determination of real net worth at any one time is frequently impossible. The answer may be in terms of earning capacity, or profitability of the assets of the firm, or of the replacement cost of the assets, but all of these are difficult to assess in practice (for example, the resale value of assets and earning power of assets both depend on the fact that the firm is a going concern,[5] and are rarely related to the historical cost of the assets); but in practice the valuation of assets is usually on a historical cost basis, which is of little value in the formulation of economic judgments.

Part of the answer to these problems lies in the firm having a sensible attitude to and policy towards the valuation of assets, based probably on replacement prices, and making its accounting provisions for depreciation and replacement in accordance with such policy; though the policy of the Inland Revenue authorities of allowing such provisions on a basis of historical cost alone as a tax-free expense, taxing all other provisions as profits, is not very helpful to such policies; and accountants have an aversion from valuing assets at any other than historical cost.

Strictly, therefore, depreciation provisions are not a source of funds, since they do not add to the net worth of the company; but in a purely practical sense many firms treat such provisions as amounts of cash or resources becoming available in a certain period, and use them (in the short run, since in the long run this is clearly not possible if assets are to be maintained intact) as a source of funds.

The availability of internal funds depends on two things: the

[5] Contrary to what many accountants claim, this is a meaningful term. The valuation of a firm as a going concern is a measure of what the assets of the firm may be expected to earn in their present occupation; a historical cost valuation merely represents what the firm paid for the assets at the time of purchase. Historical cost valuations are economically meaningless: a firm's assets are either worth what they can earn or what they would fetch if sold. If the firm is sold as a going concern or if the assets are sold as working assets, they will fetch a sum calculated on a basis of what they could earn; if sold as scrap they would fetch another (much lower) sum. What the assets cost is irrelevant to either of these calculations. An experienced valuer should be able to put a 'going concern' value on the assets of a firm in the same way as he can assess the market value of a house or a motor car. From the book-keeping and auditing point of view historical cost valuations are perhaps reasonable, from the business point of view they are not. In any case, a reasonable compromise is a replacement cost valuation, which is not open to the objection that it is based on subjective elements.

past profits of the firm and its past policy with regard to the retention and distribution of profits. Policy in this respect may be complex: the firm cannot distribute all of its profits, even to keep shareholders happy with dividends, and indeed shareholders would themselves be unhappy to see nothing being put to reserve; but equally some dividend payments must be made and public companies in particular have to keep a healthy market in their shares if they are to use the capital market for raising new capital in the future. If too much is retained and used for the accumulation of liquid assets (mainly cash or marketable securities), the firm may lay itself open to the danger of take-over bids. The ability of small firms, whose directors own a majority of the shares, to pay out profits (up to a point) as directors' remuneration alters the form, but not the nature of dividend policy. Taxation also plays a part, largely determining how much is left out of earnings for distribution: in the years following the Second World War, for example, high taxation led to a fall in the proportion of profits distributed as compared with the position before the war; but on the other hand, with the exception of the giant companies (who both distributed and saved less) public companies retained a higher proportion of their earnings than before the war.[6]

Internal funds are frequently the most important (sometimes indeed the only) source of long-term funds for small firms; and many of the industrial giants which we know today financed the early stages of their growth by this means, many of their owners going to what would nowadays seem extreme lengths in thrift and self denial in order to plough back profits for growth.[7]

[6] S. J. Prais, 'Dividend Policy and Income Appropriation', in *Studies in Company Finance*, edited by Brian Tew and R. F. Henderson (National Institute of Social and Economic Research and Cambridge University Press, 1959).

[7] The case of the Walker Brothers of Rotherham, ironfounders, illustrates the importance of savings as a source of finance in the Industrial Revolution. They started business in 1741, both of the brothers working part time (Samuel teaching in a local school); in 1743 Aaron was employed full time, in 1745 Samuel gave up his school (the value of the concern was put at this time at £400); and from this time they allowed themselves 10s. per week each. Not until 1757, when the stock had reached £7,500 did they allow themselves a dividend—of £140, and throughout their lives dividends remained small. By 1774 their capital had reached £62,500; in 1812 the assets of Samuel Walker & Co. were estimated at nearly £300,000 (Samuel Walker had died in 1782, but his financial policies were continued by his heirs). See T. S. Ashton, *The Industrial Revolution, 1760–1830* (Oxford University Press, Home University Library, 1948), pp. 95–7. Ashton quotes many others who built up their firms in a similar way, including Wedgwood, Newton

Recent surveys[8] show that small firms tend to save more out of their profits than do large firms. They pay smaller dividends, less tax, and save more: private companies in 1954–56 saved 31.7 per cent of their trading profits, public companies saved 27.3 per cent; private companies saved 3.5 per cent of their net assets, but public companies saved 4.1 per cent. But more important, private companies relied on retained profits to the extent of 44.7 per cent of total funds, public companies to the extent of 32.4 per cent; and within the private company group there was a tendency for small private companies to rely more on savings than their slightly bigger brothers.

This tendency for small firms to save more than big ones is partly due to the fact that they have to do so in order to grow at all (as will be seen later, they have particular difficulties in raising long-term capital). It is also partly due to the fact that they are less profitable than large firms, and simply in order to keep on relatively even terms they have to plough back a larger part of a relatively smaller sum. Even industrial giants, however, cannot rely entirely on external finance, even if they want to, and do finance a large part of their expenditure internally. The large British oil companies for many years after the Second World War never went to the capital market for funds, but financed all of their growth from retained profits: this may have been partly due, as has been claimed, to the fact that their enterprises are rather speculative, and borrowing may have been expensive and difficult, but it also reflects the high profitability of such companies: the claim which is sometimes made, that the sums required were too large for the resources of the capital market, is not substantiated.

LONG-TERM EXTERNAL CAPITAL

In this field the first distinction to be made is between Share and Loan Capital. Both involve the sale of some sort of security

[8] Tew and Henderson, op. cit.; James Bates, 'The Finance of Small Business,' *Bulletin of the Oxford University Institute of Statistics* (May 1958); James Bates, 'The Finance of Small and Big Business', *Bankers' Magazine* (April 1961); and James Bates, *The Financing of Small Business* (to be published by Sweet and Maxwell in 1964). These will be referred to in the remainder of this chapter as the 'National Institute Study' (Tew and Henderson) and the 'Oxford Survey' (Bates). See also the tables in the Appendix to this chapter.

Chambers and several more. He concludes: 'Industrial capital has been its own progenitor': to a lesser extent this is still true today.

by the firm: share capital, as the name implies, is in the form of a share in the ownership or a prior right to a share of the profits of the firm; loan capital in the form of a prior right, both to interest and usually also over the assets of the firm, in the form of a mortgage or debenture. Share capital is never repayable save by permission of the High Court, though in quoted public companies it is marketable and is bought and sold on the Stock Exchange; long-term loan capital is repayable, the period varying from 10 to 50 years, and occasionally even longer; lenders cannot demand repayment before the 'term' of the loan, but are entitled to a fixed rate of interest, whether the firm is profitable or not; and the security is usually marketable. If the firm defaults, loan creditors have the right to put it into liquidation in order to recover their principal and interest from the proceeds of the sale of its assets.

Share capital carries with it some share in the equity of the firm, and may be of two kinds. Ordinary share capital carries with it a vote proportionate to the number of shares held and receives a dividend in the form of part of the residual income of the firm after prior charges have been met. Preference shares rarely carry a vote, but have as compensation a prior right to dividend over the ordinary shares. There are several varieties of each of these types of share, but they need not concern us here; neither need the Stock Exchange implications of shareholding, but there are important policy considerations which affect the firm's attitude to, and distribution of, share capital.

First is the question of *gearing*. The gearing ratio (or leverage as it is known in the U.S.A.) of a firm may be defined as the ratio of the annual amount payable on prior charges, or fixed interest (on preference shares and long-term liabilities) to the annual income available for disposal; this clearly acts as a limitation to the firm's freedom of choice in the raising of finance. The following calculation illustrates the point:

	1950	*1960*
A. Fixed interest dividend payable	£25,000	£25,000
B. Disposable Income	£50,000	£500,000
Gearing (A/B × 100)	50 %	5 %

Clearly gearing matters less in good times (when a firm is

making high profits, as in 1960 in the illustration) than in bad times (as in 1950 in the illustration), because fixed interest then represents a smaller burden on the firm. Since it is not always possible to predict profitability in advance, however, a reasonable guide to gearing may be obtained from the ratio of Preference Capital plus Long Term Liabilities to Ordinary Share Capital—where this is high, gearing is *potentially* high, and the owners and ordinary shareholders may be unhappy about the position—but in the last analysis it is the ratio of fixed interest to profit that matters. The gearing ratio in the National Institute study of quoted public companies in the years 1949–53 was 8.5 per cent; 60 per cent of companies had gearing ratios in the range 0 to 10 per cent; 18 per cent were in the range 11–20 per cent, 12 per cent were in the range 21–40 per cent; 6 per cent were over 40 per cent (and 4 per cent had negative income). Gearing was particularly high in the brewing industry. In the Oxford Survey half of the firms did not have any fixed interest commitments; 27.5 per cent had gearing ratios in the range 0.1–9.9 per cent, 7 per cent in the range 10–19.9 per cent, 4 per cent in the range 20–39 per cent, and 30 per cent were over 40 per cent.

From the ownership point of view most firms would prefer to issue preference shares, but they have to bear in mind that this would give them a high gearing ratio, which would commit an excessive proportion of their income each year, and would deter potential shareholders.

The possibility of obtaining fixed interest finance is also limited by the existing equity of the firm. Few outside investors would be willing to contemplate lending to a firm whose owners had what was thought to be an inadequate stake in the firm: this is particularly true in small firms with no long record of profitability, and, since many such firms are in particular need of funds and unable to contribute much in the way of self-financing, this is yet another factor which may retard their expansion.

Ruling market conditions and the existing structure of interest rates in the country would influence the rate of preference interest which the potential preference share investor would want, and a time of high interest rates is rarely the best time from the point of view of the firm since, once committed to a rate of interest, this has to be paid regardless of the profitability of the firm or the economic climate and the later structure of interest rates. In fact, the timing of any sort of issue is important and, since the raising of long-term external funds is in any case a fairly long drawn out procedure planned well in advance, the firm usually has a fair degree of latitude and, within limits, can choose its time to suit market conditions. The raising of ordinary share capital is usually easier at times of good trade and high Stock Exchange share values, and it is at times like this that the issue of shares tends to be over-subscribed (which simply means that there is a bigger demand for the shares than the supply of them).

The New Issue Market in Britain is a fairly complex organization, consisting of a small group of issuing houses and merchant banks specializing in the issue of new share capital, and whose prime function is to act as an intermediary between those who wish to issue share capital and those who are willing to invest in share capital. They will usually advise on the best form of capital, work out a financial plan, make sure that the complex Stock Exchange regulations are complied with, arrange any underwriting which may be necessary (underwriting is simply a guarantee by a financial institution to take up any part of an issue which is not bought), and—perhaps as important a function as any—lend the weight of the house's name and reputation to an issue.

There are five main possibilities for the firm wishing to make a new issue of shares:[9] the offer for sale; the issue by prospectus; the placing; the Stock Exchange introduction; and the issue to shareholders. With an offer for sale, an issuing house buys the shares from the company and offers them to the public; with an issue by prospectus the issuing house undertakes to find subscriptions for the new issue of shares: both of these methods are expensive, and involve the issue of advertisements, and are rarely worth while for issues of less than £200,000 (the percentage of costs tends to be rather too high for smaller issues, since there is a fairly high fixed-cost element). The private placing is a method by which an issuing house will sell shares

[9] The reader interested in a fuller discussion of these topics is recommended to read F. W. Paish, *Business Finance* (Pitman, 2nd edn., 1961), R. F. Henderson, *The New Issue Market* (Bowes & Bowes, 1951).

through brokers or jobbers on the Stock Exchange, and thence to private investors (it is possible to do this without reference to an issuing house): this method is relatively cheap, and can be effected without a Stock Exchange quotation (although, since the shares of unquoted companies are not marketable, buyers are cautious of their issues, and the method is only likely to succeed if a firm's record and prospects are thought to be good). The Stock Exchange introduction is a method by which the issuing house makes application—on behalf of the shareholders—for the shares of the firm to be quoted on the Stock Exchange. The issue to shareholders (sometimes called a 'rights issue' if the company is public, since the existing shareholders have preferential treatment) is a relatively cheap method, since it does not involve a prospectus or advertisement; it is usually made in proportion to the existing holdings of shareholders. Whether or not this method is used depends partly on the size of the new issue and its relation to the size of the existing equity of the firm—if this is too large such an issue would be unlikely to succeed—and partly on the past record and prospects of the company. In general the main disadvantage of the issue to shareholders is that it only taps existing sources of funds, and is therefore only worth while for relatively small issues, but for the small company it is frequently the only possibility in the field of long-term capital.

The small firm has particular difficulties in the field of long-term finance. Most small firms only require relatively small sums for expansion, and raising these may be too expensive for the normal processes: R. F. Henderson[10] estimated that the average cost of new issues in 1926, 1937 and 1945–47 ranging from £160,000 to £270,000 was between 7½ and 15½ per cent of the sums raised. Small firms are also handicapped by the increasing dependence of the capital markets on institutional investors (such as insurance companies) who prefer quoted and marketable securities, only want a limited number of equity shares, and do not in any case like small holdings of less than £10,000. The private company is further handicapped (as is the unincorporated business) by the fact that it cannot use the resources of the New Issue Market (unless it becomes a public company); and, since its number of shareholders is legally

[10] Op. cit., p. 141.

limited to fifty, its field of influence is very restricted and depends on the prosperity of shareholders (which to some extent depends on the prosperity of the firm).

In fact, small firms rarely use the capital market at all for their finance—this is part of the explanation of their reliance on self-financing—but quoted public companies make much more use of this facility. In the Oxford Survey few private companies made any share issues at all, and these were usually small issues to shareholders; in public companies in the National Institute study, on the other hand, 32 per cent of firms made new issues between 1949 and 1953. Loan capital is subject to much the same considerations as share capital in this respect, and less than 1 per cent of private companies in the Oxford Survey made issues of long-term liabilities, compared with 10 per cent of public companies.

The problems of the small firm have been recognized for several years,[11] and the Macmillan Committee commented on them in 1931: 'It has been represented to us that great difficulty is experienced by the smaller and medium-sized businesses in raising the capital which they may from time to time require even when the security is perfectly sound.'[12] Since then several institutions, of which the Industrial and Commercial Finance Corporation is the best known, have been established in an attempt to overcome the difficulties; but, although they do valuable work, they operate on too small a scale and too selectively to do more than solve a part of the problem, and the Radcliffe Report still found it necessary to comment on the problem in 1959.[13]

SHORT- AND MEDIUM-TERM CREDIT

There are two main sources of short- and medium-term finance for the firm: bank credit and trade credit.

British bankers have traditionally maintained that it is no part of their function to provide long-term funds for industry, and have concentrated in the past on the finance of relatively

[11] For a fuller discussion of these issues see James Bates, 'The Macmillan Gap—Thirty Years After', *The Banker* (July 1961); James Bates, 'The Macmillan Gap in Britain and Canada', *The Bankers' Magazine* (March 1962).

[12] *Report of the Committee on Finance and Industry* (June 1931) Cmd. 3897, para. 404.

[13] *Report of the Committee on the Working of the Monetary System* (August 1959), Cmnd. 827.

short-term needs of the seeds-to-harvest variety. In this they are sharply contrasted in particular with German banks, which do have a large stake in German industry. Occasionally, however, within cautious limits, British banks are prepared to offer longer-term finance.

The main disadvantage of the traditional bank overdraft is its relatively short duration—in practice banks usually review their overdrafts half-yearly, and once an overdraft has been granted it is not very common for it to be withdrawn, so that it is in fact possible to use this form of finance for a longish period. But not for typical long-term borrowing: the bank usually wants to know what the money is wanted for, and bankers are not happy about lending for long-term projects. The fear of withdrawal of an overdraft, and its short-term nature in general make it a bad form of finance for anything requiring finance for longer than a year. Following a recommendation of the Radcliffe Committee the Midland Bank and its Scottish associate the Clydesdale and North of Scotland Bank introduced a scheme of term loans (loans of up to 7 years' duration, repayable in instalments); and any spread of this type of finance is likely to be of help to the smaller firm, which often finds it difficult to raise finance for that sort of period. Unfortunately this particular facility was withdrawn at a time of credit restraint in 1961, and other banks have not yet introduced such measures.

In private companies in the Oxford Survey bank loans accounted for 6.5 per cent of total assets, compared with 2.8 per cent in public companies in the National Institute study.

Bank borrowing provides a convenient illustration of the need for realistic planning and control within the firm. It is always easier to borrow from banks if it is possible to indicate to the bank manager in advance that borrowing will be necessary. Good budgeting facilitates this, and shows the bank manager that the firm is not merely trying to borrow because it is in difficulties, but because of a planned and conscious intention to grow with adequate financial backing. The same is true of all good financial control; it not only helps the firm to keep a check on money flows and to economize in the use of cash, it also helps in raising money outside.

Table 7.1 shows the magnitude and direction of bank

advances in Britain in August 1962. The biggest advances in total are to personal and professional borrowers (about 15 per cent of the total); followed by the engineering industries (about 12 per cent), agriculture and the retail trade.

TABLE 7.1

ANALYSIS OF BANK ADVANCES IN UNITED KINGDOM, AUGUST 1962

Industry	*Advances (£ million)*
Coal mining	0.5
Quarrying, etc.	12.4
Iron and steel and allied trades	112.2
Non-ferrous metals	17.5
Engineering, etc.	534.1
Shipping and shipbuilding	111.9
Transport and communications	34.3
Cotton	23.8
Wool	60.1
Other textiles	93.3
Leather and rubber	38.6
Chemicals	70.9
Agriculture	397.8
Fishing	13.6
Food, drink and tobacco	216.5
Retail trade	388.0
Entertainment	26.5
Builders and contractors	174.6
Building materials	37.4
Unclassified	273.2
Local government authorities	75.6
Public utilities (excluding transport)	77.8
Churches, charities, hospitals, etc.	21.8
Stockbrokers	8.1
Hire purchase finance companies	107.3
Other financial	355.7
Personal and professional	722.0
TOTAL	4005.3
Of which:	
To nationalized industries	70.8
To other borrowers:	
By London clearing banks	3934.5
By other banks	574.9

Source: *Bank of England Quarterly Bulletin* (December 1962), Table 10, p. 285.

Trade credit is a form of finance which tends to have been neglected by economists in the past. It works in two directions: the firm gives credit to its customers, and this credit tends to vary directly with variations in turnover; it receives credit from suppliers, and this tends to vary, as would be expected, with variations in stocks. In most firms debtors (accounts receivable) exceed creditors (accounts payable), partly because of the time lag between receipt of accounts and the payment of them, and partly because of the value added in production, which makes the price of finished goods higher than the stocks which go to their manufacture or processing. Both accounts receivable and payable tend to be higher in small firms than large: trade creditors form the major part of outside debt of firms in the Oxford Survey, accounting for 19 per cent of total assets, compared with 14 per cent in companies in the National Institute study, and 30 per cent in unincorporated businesses; debtors account for 26 per cent of total assets in private companies and 19 per cent in public companies (and 30 per cent in unincorporated businesses).

To the extent that these two items balance each other, there is no net flow of funds within the firm, but one way of raising funds, in the short period at least (and it is a method that has dangers), is to take more money from creditors on loan than is lent back to debtors. Rapidly growing small firms tend to do this, pointing again to their special difficulties in raising funds. The biggest danger in this form of finance is that of overtrading, or expansion to the point that short-term commitments (notably in the form of wages and raw material accounts) exceed the liquid assets (or the ability to meet these payments) of the firm. Again intelligent budgeting can avoid these dangers.

Trade credit is a convenient and easy form of finance for stocks, and it has the additional virtue (from the point of view of the entrepreneur) that it is one of the less easily influenced forms of finance in times of credit restraint: one way in which some firms in the past have avoided the effects of a credit squeeze has been by taking extra credit from suppliers, who, if the firm is doing well, are reluctant to apply any excessive pressure. But since most trade credit is subject to a fairly substantial discount for prompt payment, this can be an expensive form of finance. And also it is dangerous since it is always liable to dry up. The bankruptcy courts are full of firms which have expanded, have increased their turnover, but have not been paid for the goods and who at the same time have been pressed by their suppliers, or, in the most extreme cases, have been told by their suppliers that they cannot have any more materials until past accounts are paid. The use of trade credit as a source of funds demands sound financial control and a knowledge of the structure of the trade in which the firm is operating.

In the United States the importance of trade credit is much more widely recognized than it is in Britain, and it is appreciated that the typical firm may well have large sums of money tied up in the form of accounts receivable (debtors). Accordingly the practice of 'factoring receivables' has developed, by which the firm sells its debts at a discount to a factor, who collects them when due. This liberates the cash for the firm and does away with part of the need to raise extra funds outside the firm. In Britain this practice is hardly developed as yet, but there have been developments in recent years in the factoring of export credits (which are frequently long term and unreliable): an interesting development is the Amstel Club, which is a series of reciprocal agreements between financial houses in Europe and the U.S.A. for the finance of exports and imports.

A new method of financing the sale of manufactured goods has also been developed in Britain: by this method, the manufacturer would sell his goods for cash to a specialized finance company (not directly to the customer on credit terms); the finance company would then appoint the manufacturer as agent to sell the goods. This development, which is still in its infancy, overcomes the disadvantage of ordinary factoring that the selling of debts in the ordinary way might suggest instability.

The Bill of Exchange is another way of financing trade credit: it is in essence a post-dated bill drawn by one trader on another. Although fairly common in the export trade and in some domestic trades where stock purchases are an important part of total costs, bills of exchange are rarely used by manufacturing firms.

It is possible to make other arrangements with creditors (who are usually the firm's suppliers) and debtors (who are its customers). Long-term credit can sometimes be arranged with the supplier, particularly if the production cycle is fairly long. There is also a system in some industries, particularly engineering, where the customer, with whom a contract is arranged, provides the materials for fabrication without charge to the manufacturer, making provision for excess scrappage penalties. This system, known as the use of Free Issue Materials, is however, restricted in its application. Similarly, large organizations sometimes finance their sub-contractors by making loans for the purchase of materials. Small contracting engineering firms can also come to arrangements for the finance of machine tools: sometimes the customer buys them and loans them, or charges the contractor at the completion of the contract; and there is a variety of possibilities.

Any of these formal arrangements is preferable to letting the bills run up in one direction or another; and any arrangement which liberates cash tied up in trade credit is worth considering.

Hire purchase is another form of medium-term credit which may be used. Big companies rarely buy in this way, but hire purchase is frequently used by small firms[14] for relatively small purchases of machinery and motor vehicles. A quarter of the firms in the Oxford Survey used this method of finance: they were mainly small, rapidly growing concerns hungry for funds for their rapid development. It is an expensive source of funds, costing from 10 to 20 per cent per annum, but it is convenient and frequently easier to arrange than a bank loan, and many businessmen feel that the expense is amply compensated by the convenience and the fact that the earning capacity of the machinery is usually sufficient to meet the burden of repayment. Since the banks developed close links with hire purchase finance companies, bank managers are recommending their clients to finance part of their requirements by overdrafts and part by hire purchase.

Another possibility which may be considered at the same time is that of leasing plant and equipment. For some years now a few large British firms have leased their cars, but it is only relatively recently that the idea has spread to equipment (the boot and shoe industry has long been accustomed to machinery leasing, complex office machinery has also often been leased, and bowling alley equipment is usually leased from the manufacturers, but there have been special reasons in all of these cases). Renting is similar to leasing save for the

[14] See James Bates, 'Hire Purchase in Small Manufacturing Business', *The Bankers' Magazine* (September and October 1957).

fact that leasing is usually for a specified period, whereas a rental agreement may be for any period which need not be specified in advance. The decision to lease, which commits the firm to regular payments for a defined period, obviously depends on an assessment of the advantages of capital economy weighed against the disadvantage of not owning the machinery (not very serious) and the possibilities of earning profit from the equipment. The total cost of rentals can be charged against tax, but naturally, since the leasing company owns the equipment, the lessee cannot charge wear-and-tear allowances. Leasing has other advantages: it avoids the problems of obsolescence of machinery to some degree, it requires no balance sheet entry (this is not important but it may well satisfy those who are more attached to the form of things than to their reality); it frees not only working capital, but also the bank overdraft for normal operating needs, and it makes budgeting easier.

Borrowing from individuals, such as directors or members of the family is not very common in large firms, but it is fairly frequent in smaller concerns and particularly in unincorporated businesses. About a quarter of firms in the Oxford Survey used directors' loans, but they accounted on average for only 1.3 per cent of total assets. Such borrowing may well help the firm out of a temporary difficult position, and it is a convenient way of borrowing from a fellow director without giving him extra control in the company via the ownership of ordinary shares. But this last fact points to one of the difficulties: many directors will not do this sort of thing unless they get some such advantage, and it is not unknown for a lender to use his loan as a lever to get more equity, by threatening to withdraw the loan (or to enforce liquidation) unless some such offer is made. Bank managers, too, are rather suspicious of directors' loans on a balance sheet since they may well give a false impression of the liquidity of the firm, and managers are alive to the ruse of temporary borrowing of this sort in order to give a favourable impression.

FURTHER CONSIDERATIONS

A special form of finance, which does not fit readily into a classification by term or period of borrowing, is the sale of assets. There are two main possibilities: the straight sale of an asset and the sale and leasing back of the asset. One form of sale of assets has already been considered (the factoring of debts), but it is also possible to sell either real, operating assets (plant, equipment, land, buildings, etc.) or paper assets in the form of marketable securities. The general principle underlying such a straight sale is quite clear: the asset will be sold either if it is no longer needed (as in the case of a piece of equipment bought for a special purpose which the firm is not fulfilling any longer) or if it is not needed so urgently as the money. Sale of a security involves sacrifice of liquidity and of the interest receivable from the security, sale of an operating asset involves the loss of its earning capacity, and both of these have to be weighed against the desirability of the finance and the prospective returns from the use of the money. As an alternative to borrowing, this method clearly has its advantages but the scope is limited by the availability and value of such assets in the firm. Sale and leasing back is a form of external finance which has become popular in recent years, particularly in connection with take-over bids, the seller disposing of one asset in order to liberate the funds for the purchase of other assets. The method is largely restricted to buildings, and is particularly useful for firms whose buildings represent a substantial part of their assets, and hence of their illiquid capital. Since mortgages on industrial property are not common such arrangements as this are frequently much more practical than attempting to finance the continued ownership of the property.

Special problems are associated with the finance of innovations.[15] The Radcliffe Committee examined this problem and commented:

'There are certain special problems about the provision of finance for the commercial development by small businesses and private companies of new inventions and innovations of technique. One problem is that the amount of capital required to finance a development may be larger in relation to a small company's capital structure and apparent earnings prospects

[15] See James Bates, 'The Finance of Innovations', *The Bankers' Magazine* (July 1962).

than the financial institutions would ordinarily feel justified in putting up.'[16]

The problem of financing innovations is essentially one of reconciling the risks with the long period of development and the attendant wait for rewards (which may never accrue, or, when they do, may not accrue to the person responsible for the innovation). The risks are in development, the rewards are in marketing; and the major risk is that the innovation may not be a commercial proposition.[17] The larger firms can usually take care of the risks of innovation: they have specialized research facilities, the cost of which is justified by the scale of operation, and the finance of innovations is part of the process of growth of larger firms. Small firms can rarely do any of these things. A survey in the U.S.A.[18] showed the advantages of larger firms: only 8 per cent of manufacturing companies with less than 100 employees had research programmes, compared with 94 per cent of companies with over 5000 employees.

A new firm, Technical Development Capital Ltd, was formed in London in 1962 to cater for some of these problems; but it is still doubtful whether what has come to be known as the 'Radcliffe Gap' has ceased to exist.

There are still other financial possibilities which need not be considered in detail here. The Exports Credit Guarantees Department, a British Government institution, helps the exporter by insuring his export credits—an extremely valuable function in some of the more unreliable export markets; there are some special factoring concerns specially concerned with exports; and in general the finance of exports has attracted a great deal of sympathetic attention in recent years.

The Government is also prepared to offer help to firms in development districts (areas suffering from or threatened with large-scale unemployment) by means of grants, loans, provision of premises at low rents, provision of houses and grants for key workers, preferences in the award of contracts put up for tender and, in Northern Ireland in particular, capital grants.

[16] Cmnd. 827, para. 948.

[17] The experience of the National Research Development Corporation in Britain and similar organizations overseas suggests that 5 to 10 per cent of suggestions put to them succeed in this sense.

[18] National Science Foundation *Science and Engineering in American Industry* (U.S. Government Printing Office, 1956).

But these schemes in the development areas and the field of exports, are for particular problems: where they are applicable they are useful, but it must be remembered that such schemes

TABLE 7.2

SOURCES OF FUNDS OF SMALL FIRMS, 1950–56

Source	*Number of firms using source*
A. *Retained profits*	
No retained profits	29
Profits ploughed back in:	
1–3 years	39
4–6 years	253
Not ascertained	14
TOTAL	335
B. *Overdraft*	
No overdraft	162
Overdraft in:	
1–3 years	49
4–6 years	121
Not ascertained	3
TOTAL	335
Average duration of overdraft:	
Up to 6 months	143
6 to 12 months	27
C. *Other sources of funds*	
New shares issued to shareholders	35
New shares issued outside firm	16
Debentures, etc., issued	10
Loan from parent company	15
Directors' loans	76
Other sources:	
Institutions	37
Other	9
Hire purchases of plant and equipment	108
Total other sources	306
No other sources used in period	193
TOTAL*	499

Source: James Bates, 'The Finance of Small Business' *Bulletin of the Oxford University Institute of Statistics* (May 1958).

Notes: This table includes unincorporated businesses.

* Since more than one source may be used at once (i.e. sources in group C are not mutually exclusive) total sources exceed total firms.

only exist because of the particular problems involved, and these problems in themselves may constitute sufficient disadvantages for the firm not to consider operating under conditions where they might be eligible for such assistance.

TABLE 7.3

BALANCE SHEET AND SOURCES AND USES OF FUNDS OF PUBLIC AND PRIVATE COMPANIES, MARCH 31ST, 1956

	Percentage of total assets	
	Public	*Private*
Capital and liabilities		
Issued capital	28.9	26.4
Reserves	37.0	38.8
Long-term debt	10.0	2.2
Bank loans	2.8	6.5
Directors' loans	Nil	1.3
Trade creditors	14.4	18.9
Other	7.0	5.9
TOTAL	100.0	100.0
Assets		
Fixed assets	39.3	32.2
Stocks	30.2	32.1
Trade debtors	19.0	25.8
Liquid assets	11.5	9.9
TOTAL	100.0	100.0
Average amount	£4,855,000	£97,546

	Percentage of total sources/uses	
	Public	*Private*
Sources of funds		
Issued capital	16.9	33.4*
Bank loans	0.4	−3.9
Directors' loans	Nil	1.6
Creditors	12.0	−16.6
Other accruals	3.0	1.0
Retained profit	32.4	44.7
Depreciation	24.8	34.3
Future tax reserves	3.2	−9.5
Other	7.3	15.0
TOTAL	100.0	100.0
Uses of funds		
Fixed assets	54.5	71.8
Stocks	16.3	−25.6
Trade debtors	16.2	37.0
Other capital payments	6.1	0.2
Liquid assets	6.9	16.6
TOTAL	100.0	100.0
Average amount	£466,300	£5,546

Source: Data from Small Business Survey of Oxford University Institute of Statistics, Tew and Henderson, op. cit., and *Economic Trends* (February 1957).

* This total is inflated by large issues by three companies.

Many firms dislike the use of additional external finance, whether long term or short term, and some even go to the point of restricting expansion to the availability of cash from retained earnings, even though this may mean ignoring profitable earnings. This reflects a desire for independence, not only of outside ownership, but of any form of control: even bank loans sometimes carry restrictions on the use of funds, and many other lenders insist on 'a seat on the board'. It is also sometimes argued that there is another factor which owes its

TABLE 7.4

THE SAVINGS OF PUBLIC AND PRIVATE COMPANIES, 1954–56

Profit and Loss Account (annual average)

	Percentage of total profit	
	Public	*Private*
Trading profit	117.9	110.1
less Depreciation	21.4	24.5
plus Other income	3.5	14.4
TOTAL PROFIT	100.0	100.0
Tax on current income	53.8	49.8
Dividends (net)	18.9	18.5
RETAINED PROFIT	27.3	31.7
(N.B. Director's remuneration	2.0	40.0)
Annual total profit	£536,800	£7,823
	Average annual profit as percentage of net assets	
Trading profit	17.2	13.1
Total profit	14.5	11.9

Source: As Table 7.3.

existence to the Managerial Revolution and the consequent divorce of ownership and control. The rewards of professional management—usually a salary plus some share of profits (which may be small in relation to the salary) and promotion—are not usually closely geared to the profits of the firm; and since managers frequently regard their security both from dismissal and from the bankruptcy of the firm as fundamental, they are disinclined to take extra risks (such as change of ownership) involving the use of external finance. The importance of this motive is questionable.

The decision about the finance of the firm depends first on the expected profits or gains from the expenditure balanced against what may be termed loosely the costs of borrowing (in terms of theoretical economics, the entrepreneur balances the marginal efficiency of capital against the costs of borrowing). These costs include not only interest and repayment obligations (which may indeed be relatively unimportant), but also considerations of the use to which the money is to be put, the actual amount required, the timing, and the form of finance to be raised; which in turn raise questions of ownership, control, convenience, liquidity, capital structure, field of influence and, to some extent, personality.

Chapter VIII

CONTROL AND PLANNING

THE NATURE OF CONTROL

By control of an enterprise we mean the ability to shape it in some desired way. We can think of this ability as depending on certain individuals having the power, or right, to control and on their being able to devise methods of control that will enable them to achieve their objectives. In most of this chapter we examine methods of control that are directly linked to economic planning and the attainment of economic objectives by the enterprise. There are many other aspects with which we are not concerned. The exercise of authority, the interrelations of those engaged in the enterprise and the organizational structure adopted lie largely outside our approach with its roots in economics. Nor are we concerned with legal aspects of control, with the rights of shareholders or the powers of directors. Nevertheless, we must recognize that the power to control is legally circumscribed, and that the fortunes of the enterprise depend on the actions of those seeking to control events from outside it as well as on the ability of those within it to use their powers effectively. The Chancellor of the Exchequer, financiers and shareholders exercise some control over the enterprise as well as the managers most closely concerned with it. It is useful briefly to examine the nature of this divided and overlapping control before we turn to considering the enterprise in isolation.

CONTROL BY THE CHANCELLOR OF THE EXCHEQUER

The Chancellor of the Exchequer seldom intervenes in the affairs of individual firms. There are too many to consider individually and the Chancellor has not got, and could not possibly get, the information that would be necessary to do so. In general, the higher the level of control the less detailed can it be and control must be exercised by indirect means. The Chancellor makes regulations that apply to all firms, or to certain sections of them, and which have the effect of altering the economic framework in which they work. Thus from time to time he alters the regulations that apply to hire purchase; or he may alter the system of taxation, instituting or changing certain taxes in a way that he expects will make industry and the economy move towards the objectives he has set. The Chancellor cannot be sure that the measures that he takes will produce the effects that he desires. Our understanding of the working of the economy is imperfect; altering the conditions in which business works sometimes produces unexpected results, and the broad administrative methods of control that the Chancellor is forced to use cannot always be sufficiently refined to produce more than a close approximation to what is intended.

These limitations apply, to a greater or lesser degree, to control at all levels. Control is often more a power to influence the actions of others than a means to prescribe them. Indeed, the first requirement of a successful controller is the realization that his powers are limited, for he must work by combining the activities of individuals or bodies in a constructive way. Often this can best be done by setting broad objectives, and prescribing certain limits of action, leaving others to change, initiate and shape on their own responsibility within their own spheres of control. Many people find this more difficult to accomplish, with its attendant devolution of control, than to attempt to attend to all the details personally. One of the tests of the good manager is his ability to devolve his responsibilities on to others while still maintaining broad control and, perhaps even more important, his ability to devise the framework of control or methods or systems by which he operates to bring about the desired results.

CONTROL BY SHAREHOLDERS AND OTHER BODIES

Control by shareholders, like that by the Chancellor of the Exchequer, is also highly indirect. For the most part shareholders cannot interfere in the day-to-day management of the concerns in which they hold shares. Only rarely are shareholdings sufficiently concentrated for shareholders to be able to establish their power to influence the affairs of the companies they own. Even when they are, shareholders often do not wish to do so, holding, perhaps, as do some insurance companies with large shareholdings, that the conduct of a business should be left exclusively to those engaged in it. Control in this case is seldom more than that conferred by the power to change the personnel who are concerned with day-to-day direction of the company. When shareholdings are widely spread, it is unusual for even this form of control to be exercised; if it is, the reasons are generally that the company is making losses and that some shareholder is sufficiently involved to be prepared to organize a body of opposition to the existing board of directors or sees a way to forward his personal ambition by doing so. In continental countries there is greater opportunity for intervention on the part of shareholders for it is more usual to appoint banks as proxies to vote at meetings than to appoint nominees within the company, and a more unified view of shareholders, in relation to the company which they own, may emerge in consequence.

The type of control exercised by holding companies over their subsidiaries has resemblances both to that employed by the Chancellor of the Exchequer and that exercised by shareholders. It may consist of no more than setting objectives and in laying down certain broad policies to be followed; or it may reside largely in the appointments that are made to subsidiaries. In some circumstances even this power may be lightly exercised and the subsidiaries may be free of most control so long as they continue to function successfully according to some criterion: Mr Roy Thomson gives the impression of controlling his newspapers mainly in this way. More detailed control may be needed, however, if the activities of subsidiary companies are to be closely integrated.

Control by the 'City' follows much the same pattern. General impressions about the economic scene and more detailed views about the prospects for particular products, industries and firms are the starting point. Control consists of fashioning the flow of finance in line with these views so that money is available for promising ventures and not for those that offer little prospect of success. Often a major control at this level lies in making suitable appointments to the boards of companies. Once this is done, the future of the enterprise may be left to its directors, further intervention being necessary only if the members of the board do not fulfil their promise.

Only as we come down the scale of control should the

amount of detailed policy specification increase. But it should not increase too quickly. It would be a mistake, for instance, for the board of a large company to attempt to control all the details of the company's operations. Sometimes it may be remote from the actual operations of the company, and this may render attempts at detailed control abortive; but it is not a matter of geographical nearness that is at issue in matters of control so much as the general principle of good administration—that it is the function of the board to determine broad matters of policy and its responsibility to see that others more closely in touch with day-to-day events and detailed matters carry out its general instructions. The board should determine apparently detailed matters of administration only if they are really vital to the success of its operations and if, in consequence, only the board can be asked to take the final responsibility for them; otherwise the detailed implication of the board's policies should be left to others, or to a limited number of its own ranks if they are full-time employees of the company and responsible, as individuals, for certain aspects of its operation. One test of the effectiveness of such a board is whether it can develop a system that will enable it to prescribe and supervise the work of others. It may do this by setting objectives and verifying from time to time that they have been achieved. But if it does no more than this, it is in danger of playing only a passive role. A good board of directors should not only receive reports but should also initiate them; it should not only accept the policies and objectives that are suggested for it by the policy makers that it appoints for the purpose, but should also be ready with suggestions of its own. But in all its deliberations it must recognize that its function is to lay down the broad lines of policy and to create the kind of institution that can carry them out. It should never attempt to take decisions that can be taken better by its subordinates.

KNOWLEDGE, THE FIRST REQUIREMENT FOR EFFECTIVE CONTROL

The first requirement for effective control is knowledge; the second is the means to use this knowledge for the formulation of policy; the third is the means to ensure that what is intended materializes.

Shareholders are often said to have lost effective control of their companies because, individually, they own too small a proportion of the shares to have a decisive voice. But even if this were not so, it would be extremely difficult for shareholders to formulate policy on the basis of the limited information that they normally possess. Each year (and sometimes at more frequent intervals) they receive an account of their company's operations. The amount of information given varies, but it may be no more than the minimum laid down by statute and often the

TABLE 8.1

CONSOLIDATED BALANCE SHEET

Wilson Bros Ltd and a Subsidiary Company

Liabilities	£000 1960	£000 1961	Assets	£000 1960	£000 1961
Share capital	210	210	Fixed assets	416	655
Revenue reserves	392	431	Current assets:		
Future taxation	92	83	Stock on hand	152	175
Current liabilities	148	257	Debtors and payments in advance	122	149
			Deposit on leasehold property	23	—
			Government securities	29	—
			Cash	100	2
	842	981		842	981

accounts are presented to shareholders only some months after the end of the year for which they were prepared. The amount of information given is very limited and it would generally be considered to be totally inadequate for the purpose of deciding policy by those responsible for the company's operations. Such accounts are not instruments of control so much as formal accounts of stewardship. It may be useful to look at them from this point of view before going on to consider what information is necessary in order to be able to exercise more than formal control over a company.

One conventional way of accounting for stewardship is to draw up a balance sheet which sets out the assets and liabilities of the company and shows, when compared with similar statements prepared for earlier dates, how the company's position has been changing.

Table 8.1 shows a condensed balance sheet relating to Wilson Bros Ltd.

Liabilities of the company are shown on the left-hand side of the statement and assets on the right-hand side. The liabilities of the company are shown under four main heads: liability for the share capital of the owners of the business; liability for the reserves that have been accumulated over the life of the company (for on dissolution these belong to shareholders); provision for future taxation (a liability to the Board of Inland Revenue); and current liabilities, to creditors, bankers, shareholders and for taxation payments. On the credit side are placed first property and plant, after allowing for depreciation; and second current assets consisting mainly of the stock of raw materials, semi-processed and finished goods owned by the company; cash (largely in the form of bank balances); and the debts owed to the company by its debtors which are claims to the receipt of cash in the future.

For the sake of comparison, figures are shown for both the company's financial years 1960 and 1961. Some substantial changes are noticeable between the two dates. On the side of liabilities there has been an increase in revenue reserves (which have to be accounted for to shareholders) and to this extent the shareholders' stake in the company has been increased; it will also be seen that there is a considerable increase in the amounts owing to creditors. The increase of liabilities has been matched by an increase in property owned by the company, partly offset by a fall in holdings of Government securities and a marked reduction in the amount of cash available. The picture given is one of expansion of the firm's activities, imposing some strain on liquid resources and tying up shareholders' reserves in the business. In fact, at the end of 1961 the company was holding no reserves of cash and would have been dependent on bank finance to maintain its liquid position. On the average, companies appear to keep about 5 per cent of their net assets in liquid form (mainly cash less borrowing from banks plus marketable securities).[1]

The change in the balance sheet reflects the results of the previous year's working as well as changes resulting from

[1] See *Studies in Company Finance*, (Cambridge University Press) edited by Brian Tew and R. F. Henderson, Chapter I by Brian Tew, p. 20.

expenditure on capital account. The consolidated profit and loss account is shown in Table 8.2. Profits have fallen from the previous year, and there was some fall in taxation. After paying dividends, a substantial sum remained for transfer to reserve and this helped to finance the investment that was made.

TABLE 8.2

CONSOLIDATED PROFIT AND LOSS ACCOUNT

Wilson Bros Ltd and a Subsidiary Company

	£000	
	1960	*1961*
Trading profit	294	279
Deductions for directors' fees, depreciation and bank interest	41	57
Profit before taxation	253	222
Deduction for taxation	119	113
Deduction for dividends	70	70
Transferred to reserve	64	39

The shareholders would be greatly handicapped even in determining whether companies were profitable if it were not for the fact that the preparation of financial accounts is closely supervised by professional accountants and auditors according to certain accepted conventions. But the shareholder would do well to note that balance sheets are not the final word and that the valuation of assets involves some element of judgment. What value should be ascribed to fixed assets which often have value only because the company that owns them has prospects of using them profitably in the future? How much allowance should be made for possible bad debts in calculating profits on hire purchase transactions? What values should be assigned to stocks, and is a fall in profits due to a fall in the price of stocks really an indication of reduced potentialities for profit in the future?[2]

The shareholder might examine the accounts of a company in order to see it it was profitable, if it appeared to be adding to its assets in a desired way and if it were in a position to continue to do so in the future. He might well feel satisfied with the progress that his company was making; without more information

[2] See Chapters III and VII.

he would only rarely be in any position to suggest changes in policy, much less to put them into effect. It does sometimes happen, however, that balance sheets and profit and loss accounts throw up facts that are apparent to shareholders and apparently ignored by company boards. Shareholders in Courtaulds might well have inquired from their board why at the end of March 1962 net current assets had reached some £44½ million and whether it would not have been wiser to have used some of these resources in the extension of their manufacturing activities in earlier years. In a wider setting, information along the lines given in company reports and covering a number of years might enable shareholders to review their company's operations to greater purpose; economists are used to drawing conclusions and suggesting policies from historical series of figures, and investment analysts sometimes use the same techniques. But very little can be said about the operations of a company on the basis of the limited information contained in a single set of accounts, and for the most part, shareholders and would-be shareholders should be chary of drawing conclusions from them. The following comment by the *Daily Telegraph* (August 18th, 1961) on the report of a Select Committee on the gas industry illustrates the point. Consider how much additional information would be needed before the conclusions could be accepted without question. 'In particular the report convicts it of the besetting sin of all nationalized industries—that of failing to return enough profits to maintain and develop its capital equipment. Nationalized gas started with a capital of £187 million, and has raised £424 million from outside sources. It has increased its borrowed capital by over 120 per cent but the amount of gas sold has increased by only 6 per cent.' Such a sweeping conclusion cannot be reached on the basis of the four figures adduced in its support. What happened to profits? Was it possible to justify the expenditure on the grounds that costs were reduced? What was the state of the gas industry before nationalization? Presumably this comment rested on wider appreciation of the operation of the gas industry than was possible in a brief leader. Shareholders would often be misled if they attempted to control their companies on the basis of such limited information and more complete and illuminating company reports are often needed to keep shareholders informed about their company's position. But it is also true that many of them would pay little attention to more informative reports; the bulk of private shareholders are more likely to guide their appreciation of a company's progress and potentialities by reading the chairman's speech or digesting financial commentaries than by detailed statistical studies. The latter they may well leave to those who operate the companies they own.

THE FLOW OF INFORMATION IN A FIRM

The directors of companies are in a vastly different position from that of shareholders. They are able to devote themselves much more exclusively to the affairs of their company and they command the means to secure the knowledge, both internal and external, which is necessary for company control. Information about matters external to the company is required for setting the wider objectives of the firm; to help in suggesting profitable lines of production; to enable an appreciation to be made of the prospects of getting labour; to allow the firm to anticipate changes in the Government's economic policy; and so on. We leave the discussion of this and a brief description of appropriate sources of information to later chapters, concentrating in this chapter on information relating to the firm itself.

Information about the internal working of the firm must be sufficient for:

1. Objectives to be set for the firm, bearing in mind, of course, that external factors must also be considered.
2. A plan to be prepared for attaining the objectives.
3. Management to be able to verify whether objectives are being attained and to see what deviations have occurred from the plan.
4. Management to be able to establish the causes for deviations and either remedy them or adjust the plan to changing circumstances.

Much of the information needed for these purposes is financial. The performance of a firm is measured in terms of profits or, if expansion is the main aim of the firm, in terms of additions to the value of assets. By the criterion we are using, firms are successful if they earn profits and increase the value of their assets; they are not successful merely because they have increased production or added to their capital equipment in physical terms. But financial data is not enough by itself; physical quantities are also needed for the purposes of control as we shall see.

It is common experience that great flexibility is needed in the preparation of statistical data. An analysis of data that is adequate for one purpose is not suited to another; figures that have proved to be perfectly adequate in customary circumstances need to be developed and analysed in greater detail as events change or the emphasis of the company alters. This suggests that the aim should be to collect data in a form that permits of variety in analysis if this can be done with economy. Consider sales: the company may want to know the value of everything it has sold in a given period, or in divisions of that period; it may want to know how the total of sales was distributed between products, salesmen or districts; it may require totals grouping products according to certain main characteristics, say, according to whether they were affected by a change in hire purchase regulations or by the weather. It is a great advantage if a variety of analyses can be made available with a minimum of effort even if many of them are required only occasionally. There is a need, however, to strike a balance between extreme flexibility and keeping statistical operations within bounds. Some managers prefer to collect the minimum of routine information and rely on *ad hoc* compilation of data for specific purposes. Fortunately the mechanization of statistical work and the use of electronic computers is tipping the balance in the direction of being able to provide copious statistical information in useable form with the minimum of delay. But although it is desirable to make provision for a variety of statistical analyses, particularly in order to have sufficient information for the formulation of policy, the actual amount of detailed information considered by individuals will depend on their functions. A foreman will need detailed information about the operations for which he is responsible, but the production manager will be most concerned with the totals relating to his department. Attention to ten or a score series of key aggregative figures is likely to be all that is needed to keep the managing director in touch with what is happening in the business and will give him warning of points that require attention and suggest additional information that is needed to follow up indications of deviations from anticipations. If the statements he receives are well chosen and prepared, he will often be able to assimilate the figures they contain while removing his coat in the morning.

It is not possible to prescribe in detail the figures that are necessary to run individual businesses. Information on sales and orders, on purchases, production, man-power, costs, stocks, credit and capital expenditure will be required in concerns of any size. Much more information may also be needed since requirements differ very greatly in detail. As we have seen, the guiding consideration is that the data must be as adequate as is economical for the determination of policy, for the preparation of a plan of operations, and for the supervision of the execution of the plan once it has been prepared. The latter requirement means both that the data provided and the plan itself must be related to the administrative divisions of the company; otherwise it will be difficult to integrate the company's operations with the plan of operation prepared for it.

Finally the more speedily data can be compiled the more use it is likely to be. Data relating to periods long since past serves neither as a warning, a means to put things right nor as a starting point for future planning. Information needs to be presented at sufficiently frequent intervals for changes in the circumstances affecting the company to be discernible with little delay. It also follows that information that gives a more up-to-date view of a company's operations is to be preferred to a series that is up-to-date and speedily available but refers to events taking place some time ago; thus figures of sales are generally of more value in controlling a business than receipts, which reflect sales in some previous period.

PLANNING

In a small company planning can be carried on without any great apparatus. In the one-man business there is no great need to commit much information to paper and, perhaps, not even much need to decide clearly what is intended for the future. But for the larger business it is different and a plan is indispensable. A. K. Cairncross has described how programmes (or plans) serve several distinct functions: how they register and communicate decisions and allow decisions to be delegated; how they serve the purpose of clarifying and forcing decisions and provide a measure of success in what is attempted.[3]

A fully developed plan of business operations has thus considerable administrative advantages. The various departments can regard the budgetary plans as forming a basis for their operations; the rate and amount of purchases is written into the plan; the production scheduled gives a close indication of the number of men that will be required during the period for which the plan has been drawn up; and financial requirements can be mapped out. This will not eliminate the need to co-ordinate activities, but it will facilitate it by ensuring that conflicting requirements are reconciled within the context of the plan. The plan is also an important means of administration since it sets limits to the expenditure of departments or individuals. An increase in expenditure over the levels laid down in the plan requires authorization and in consequence is brought to notice earlier than would otherwise occur.

The administrative uses of plans must not be allowed to obscure the importance of a plan as a formulation of policy. A good plan is an essay in imagination as well as an administrative instrument, for it concerns itself with what the business can become as well as with what it is, and it incorporates arrangements for development as well as for continuation. Those who belittle planning often do so because they think too much in terms of continuation of the present and too little in terms of the need to shape events as well as to accept them.

There is generally some starting point to the formulation of a plan. It may be no more than a consideration of what modifications need to be made to some previous plan to bring it up-to-date; or it may be an intention to improve on some previous performance. Sometimes the starting point will represent a radical departure from what has gone before: the desire to expand on a grand scale, or an opportunity to move into some new branch of industry. In many cases, but not in all, one aspect of the operation of a business will appear to be dominant; for example, the need to expand sales or make the

[3] *Scottish Journal of Political Economy* (June 1961), p. 88.

best use of productive equipment. But whatever the starting point may be, all the aspects of a business's operations must be integrated and seen as a whole; production, sales and stocks must be consistent with each other and likewise costs, returns and profits must be related.

Integration can best take the form of a series of interlocking budgetary accounts. These provide both a means of formulating a plan and serve as instruments of execution and verification. The future operations of the business will be portrayed in a series of financial accounts for the next operating period or periods.[4] For the whole of the company's operations these will show the total expenditure anticipated, forecasts of the value of sales and the profit that is expected to materialize from the company's operations. In a large company the budget will have to be spelt out in considerable detail. Each major department will have its own budget, which will lay down in effect what is expected from it in operating results during the budgetary period. The budget for the sales department will specify the value of sales that it is hoped will be made and underlying this figure will be estimates of the quantities of various products that can be sold and the prices that will be realized. Expenditure by the sales department will also be budgeted, the figure allowed depending on the number of salesmen to be employed, the average salary and commission earned and selling expenses likely to be incurred. The authorized expenditure will be judged adequate for the task in hand and the sales department will be expected to adhere to its budget. For the production department output will take the place of sales, and expenditure will be based on the supposition that production programmes are adhered to. Table 8.3 shows the expenditure budgeted for a production department during the current year and shows how expenditure and the budget compared after 9 months of the year had been completed.

This is a relatively simple control statement. Departmental budgets are often prepared in considerable detail and rest on a number of assumptions about the distribution of work, wage rates, scrap percentages and so on. The departmental budget itself may be broken down further into sub-departments and foremen may also be required to work within a budget. In a

[4] See, for example, Harold C. Edey, *Business Budgets and Accounts* (Hutchinson).

large company there may be a large number of such budgets covering every aspect of the company's operations.[5]

They should also cover such matters as the investment programme for the company. Investment cannot be planned on a hand-to-mouth basis and it is necessary to estimate what finance can reasonably be expected to be available for this purpose for a number of years ahead and to specify the sources of the funds that are likely to be available.[6] A cash budget is no less essential to make sure that the company will not be impeded in its operations by an avoidable shortage of cash, and that it makes proper provision for overdraft facilities as a precaution against financial stringency; indeed, the fact that budgets have been prepared to cover all the operations of the company, and particularly its financial requirements, may be of considerable help when seeking an overdraft from a bank because it is possible to show that the company's requirements have been carefully worked out.

Budgetary planning is less formidable than might appear; plans seldom grow out of nothing and must generally bear some relation to what has gone before, and as a properly conducted planning exercise will incorporate the view of those who are expected to carry out the plan as well as those who have responsibility for the formulation of policy and perhaps little close connection with the shop floor; there is no reason to expect a divorce between theory and practice. Departments will be asked for estimates of their anticipated future expenditure in relation to certain broadly determined objectives and after verification and sifting these will be incorporated in the draft budget. If these methods are followed, it is possible for the plan to be fully accepted by those who have to carry it out and lack of co-operation which could completely nullify budgetary planning can be avoided.

[5] Those interested in the details of budgets are referred to *An Introduction to Budgetary Control, Standard Costing, Material Control and Production Control* (The Institute of Cost and Works Accountants).

[6] The significance of this in practice can be gauged from the action taken by United Steel to deal with an expected increase in capital expenditure in 1948. A special return forecast expenditure for the following 5 years, distinguishing expenditure already sanctioned from that likely to be required over the next three financial years. The total expenditure forecast was £27½ million, and substantially greater than the resources that were likely to be available. New projects were therefore reduced, and after consultation with branches some £5.6 million of expenditure was postponed (P. W. S. Andrews and E. Brunner, *Capital Development in Steel* (Blackwell, 1951), pp. 313–14).

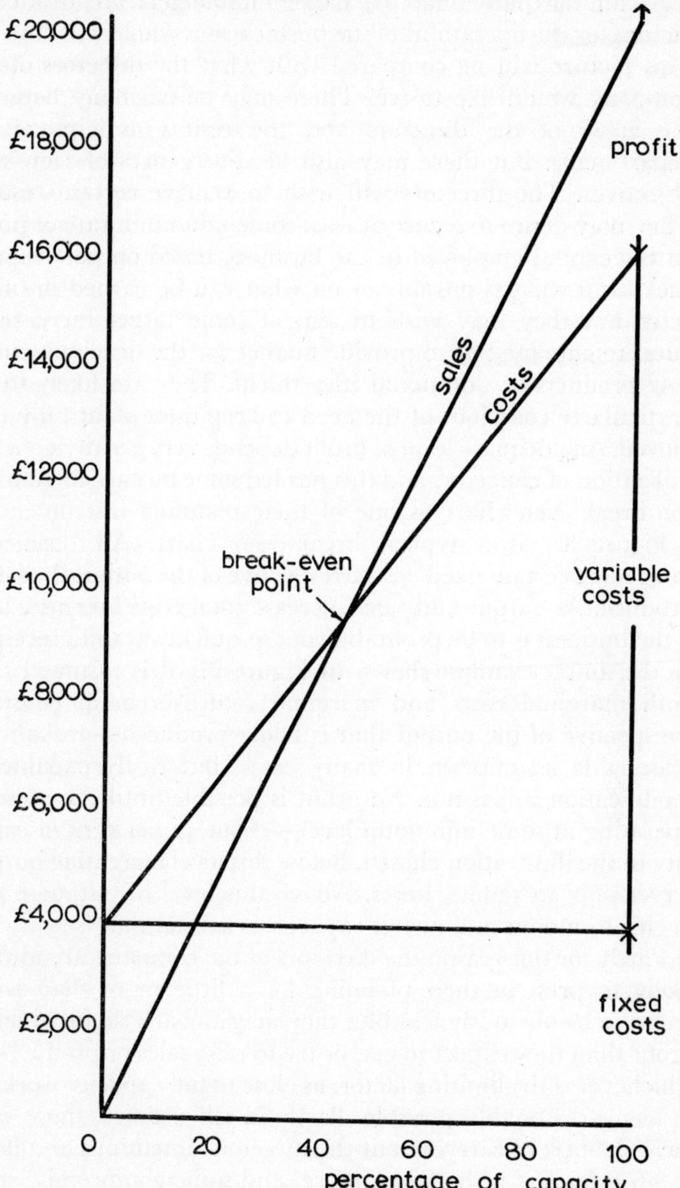

Figure 8·1. The Break-Even Chart.

As all the individual departmental budgets are drafted a picture for the operations of the business as a whole will emerge. This picture will be compared with what the directors of the company would like to see. There may be harmony between the views of the directors and the results anticipated by departments. But there may also be divergences of view and objectives. The directors will wish to achieve certain results. They may desire to secure at least some minimum rate of profit on the capital employed in the business, based on past experience as to what is possible or on what can be earned in other activities; they may wish to aim at some target increase in sales; to cut costs; or to provide finance for the development of new products or additional investment. They are likely to be particularly conscious of the need to keep their plant fully employed. An adequate level of profit depends very greatly on a full utilization of capacity, and this has led some businessmen to use the break-even chart as one of their planning instruments.

Figure 8.1 is a typical break-even chart. All businesses must meet certain fixed costs irrespective of the output that they produce. As output and sales increase total costs increase, but, if the business is to be profitable, not so quickly as total receipts. In the simple example shown in Figure 8.1 it is assumed that both marginal costs and marginal returns remain constant irrespective of the output that is being produced—probably a reasonable assumption in many cases, but easily capable of modification if it is not. No profit is possible until the plant is operating at some minimum level—about 40 per cent of capacity in the illustration chosen. Below this level increasing output serves only to reduce losses. Above this level of output profit begins to mount and at full capacity is substantial.

Partly for this reason the directors of the company are always likely to press in their planning for a little more than what seems to be obviously feasible; they may aim at a slightly higher profit than they expect to get, or try to raise sales or production, whichever is the limiting factor, as close to full capacity working as seems reasonably possible. Partly in self defence, those who have the task of carrying out the directors' intentions are likely to press for less rather than more, and some compromise may have to be reached. In the event the directors may be pleasantly surprised or disappointed; the future seldom turns out completely as anticipated but a good plan will be sufficiently flexible to take account of most eventualities and may provide for a variety of outcomes.

Flexible budgeting is designed to be responsive to changes in activity that are due to outside and uncontrollable influences. Obviously it would be absurd for a production manager to refuse to produce more than was provided for in his budget if capacity and markets were available for additional production and enhanced profit. Such an eventuality can be covered in budgetary planning either by developing a number of plans for different levels of output or by making it explicit in the first place that departures from the budgets laid down are permissible within certain limits. In the latter case fulfilment of the budgetary requirements will depend on adhering to recognized standards of productivity, and on costs varying with fluctuations of output in a reasonable way. Thus, adherence to a budget becomes more a matter of comforming to certain norms than of achieving certain expenditure figures and particular totals. The use of standard costs in budgetary control is one aspect of the establishment of recognized but not unchanging norms. It is obvious that if major departures from plan are made the whole of the company's operations will need reconsideration if they are not to become unco-ordinated.

DEVIATIONS FROM PLAN

The essence of budgetary control as a check on operations is to compare what has been achieved with what was intended. Routine checks are needed to verify whether the company's operations are going according to plan or whether there have been significant deviations. Some deviations are to be anticipated; sales may not materialize as expected; new capacity may be late in coming into operation; raw material costs may rise or fall. If deviations from plan are due to factors outside the control of the company there is nothing for it but to accept the fact that the plan is unlikely to be fulfilled and to modify it accordingly; but if the deviations are due to factors within the control of the company, remedial action is possible and, if the plan was well conceived in the first place, desirable.

When deviations are noted the first step is to establish their cause. Table 8.3 suggests some simple procedures that are

TABLE 8.3

MANAGEMENT ACCOUNTING STATEMENT

Production Department costs for 9 months to August 31st

	Year to date				*Total budget*				*Per cent of total budget used*(1)			
	Basic labour cost	*Overtime cost*	*Expense cost*	*Total*	*Basic labour cost*	*Overtime cost*	*Expense cost*	*Total*	*Basic labour cost*	*Overtime cost*	*Expense cost*	*Total*
	£	£	£	£	£	£	£	£				
Production administration	8,325	225	296	8,846	12,444	400	400	13,244	66.9	56.3	74.0	66.8
Manufacturing departments	144,313	45,303	17,254	206,870	203,853	42,500	29,000	275,353	70.8	106.6	59.5	75.1
Assembly departments	50,359	13,284	2,605	66,248	67,395	13,100	10,000	90,495	74.7	101.4	26.1	73.2
Plant engineering	26,058	9,140	30,496	65,694	36,185	9,300	31,000	76,485	72.0	98.3	96.4	85.9
Production control	79,183	18,808	2,882	100,873	112,721	18,800	5,000	136,521	70.2	180.0	57.6	73.9
TOTAL PRODUCTION COST	308,238	86,760	53,533	448,531	432,598	84,100	75,400	592,098	71.3	103.2	71.0	74.9

(1) To be compared with the completion of 75 per cent of the budget year.

necessary for this. It will be seen that the costs of the Production Department were roughly in line with the budget after the elapse of three-quarters of the budgetary year; but while this was so in total, overtime costs were somewhat in excess of what had been planned. This deviation would certainly call for explanation. Was it due to difficulties in recruiting, excess rates of overtime pay, failure to keep production on target without excessive overtime, or slowness in installing new machinery? What effect on ultimate costs and profits might the deviation be expected to have? And what remedial measures, if any, should be proposed? Management by exception, as it is known, consists of finding out the reasons for deviations from intention and taking action on them. Not every departure from plan is necessarily bad. In the illustration, more intensive working of existing machinery through working additional overtime might have had the effect of reducing costs rather than increasing them as might be assumed at first sight.

It is obvious that in order to establish the causes of the deviations additional information would have to be sought. Some of this might be contained in supplementary budgets on which the accounting statement was based. The rate of pay for overtime working, for example, would almost certainly have had to be specified in preparing the budget as would the number of operatives it was intended to employ. Very likely the causes of the deviations may be known to those responsible for operations without the need for detailed scrutiny of budgetary figures. There might have been a problem of recruitment throughout the year that made overtime working unavoidable and efforts to remedy this might have had little success. But whatever the cause, the departure from the accepted norm calls for inquiry and reconsideration of accepted views.

By no means all control is exercised through budgetary statements and in some senses the budget is the end-product of control. Many critical operations will almost certainly be controlled without immediate reference to the budget. It is often simpler to control output in terms of the number of units produced than in terms of the financial contribution that is being made to the affairs of the company, and comparison of the output produced with the target rate of production laid down may be all that is needed to keep operations according to plan. If a high rate of operation is the key to success, which is likely to be true if there is a rapidly expanding market for some product, control may centre on output statistics. Sometimes performance may be so critical that hourly reports of the number of units produced may be required; it is not that the loss of an hour's production would be irreparable so much as that even momentary relaxation of efforts to increase output can destroy the accelerating tempo of working up to a high target.

Detailed stock control is also likely to be carried out without regular reference to budgetary requirements. The budget will certainly provide for carrying certain levels of stock, but it may not specify how these levels are arrived at or the procedures to be gone through to ensure that stocks are maintained at desired levels. The special problems of stock control are discussed in the next section.

STOCK CONTROL

The control of stocks requires special techniques and may be extremely complex if thousands of items are involved as sometimes happens. The purpose of holding stocks is to bridge the interval between the availability of a new supply of an article and an immediate requirement for it. But the average level of stocks held must be related to a number of economic factors and the benefits to be derived from holding stocks must be balanced against the costs of holding them.

The cost of holding stocks is often higher than is realized. It is not unusual for one-third or even one-half of the assets of a manufacturing business to be in the form of stocks or work in progress and exceptionally the proportion may be much higher, the tobacco industry being a case in point. The cost of holding stocks includes the interest charged on money borrowed for the purpose (or the loss of profit involved in tying up the company's capital in financing them), warehouse and insurance charges, the cost of supervision and the risks that stocks will become obsolete or prove to be unsaleable. In some types of production the costs of holding stocks and the risks associated are so great that production is only undertaken to order. This is always the case when a product has to be tailored to the needs of specific customers, as happens with many capital goods.

Stock control in industry is not confined to control of stocks of finished goods. It includes the control of stocks of material and the issue of these materials for production; the amount of work in progress that is permitted, or unavoidable; as well as control of stocks of finished goods or spare parts awaiting delivery or customers' orders. It is thus an integral part of the whole production process and of production control. The effect of running out of raw materials and components used in production is almost always to cause a very costly hold up in production. But this does not mean that excessive stocks should be held and it is necessary to establish some systematic way of verifying when stock levels are adequate but not excessive. A number of considerations have to be borne in mind when determining stock levels, and the methods that are adopted to control them. Some compromise has to be effected between the size of orders which are placed, and costs of holding stocks. Generally speaking, large quantities of goods can be purchased more cheaply than small quantities, and this points in the dircction of ordering in large amounts; on the other hand, at any given rate of consumption the larger the orders placed the larger will be the average level of stock held. On certain assumptions it is possible to determine the optimum size of an order having regard to these conflicting considerations.[7]

[7] Let the cost of placing an order be C, irrespective of size of order; let N orders be placed each year; let the value of the material purchased and used each year be U; and the cost of holding stocks to be a fraction R of their average value per year. Assume that consumption takes place perfectly evenly throughout the year and that deliveries are made just as stocks become exhausted. The average value of the inventory held will be $\frac{U}{2N}$ since the quantity ordered will be $\frac{U}{N}$ and stock levels will vary between this and zero just before a new delivery is made.

The cost of holding this inventory will be $\frac{UR}{2N}$ per year.

The cost of ordering will be NC per year.

The quantity ordered will be $\frac{U}{N} = Q$.

Total costs per year (K) of holding inventory and ordering

$$K = \frac{UR}{2N} + NC = \frac{QR}{2} + \frac{CU}{Q} \text{ (substituting for } N\text{).}$$

Differentiating with respect to Q and minimizing we have

$$\frac{dK}{dQ} = \frac{R}{2} - \frac{CU}{Q^2} \text{ and for } \frac{dK}{dQ} = 0$$

$$\frac{R}{2} = \frac{CU}{Q^2}$$

$$\text{or } Q = \sqrt{\frac{2CU}{R}}.$$

Another consideration in determining stock levels and methods of control is uncertainty about consumption rates and delivery times. Suppose that the system of stock control used is to order a fresh supply of some component whenever stocks fall below some level. How should this level be fixed? In most cases, some time will elapse before the order can be delivered, and it will be necessary to have sufficient stock on hand to ensure that supplies of the component can be maintained until the new supplies arrive. Thus the level to which stocks can fall before a new order is placed must be related to the level of consumption that is anticipated, and the time to make delivery (the lead time). Both of these are subject to some uncertainty: the time of delivery may vary and the rate of consumption fluctuate. It is often possible to appraise the extent of such variations from past experience, modified if necessary to allow for alterations in future conditions, and various statistical techniques are available to assist in this.

It would be possible to devise detailed methods of controlling the stock of every component and raw material used in manufacture. But in practice it is wiser to reflect on the degree and method of control that appears to be worth while for different components and raw materials. Study of the composition of inventories has shown that it is usual to find that about 15 per cent of the items held in stock account for about 85 per cent of the value of the raw materials and components consumed. This suggests that inventory control should pay most attention to the relatively few items that account for a large percentage of value and give much less attention to items that bulk insignificantly in this respect.

In one manufacturing concern it was found useful to group components and raw materials according to certain characteristics. The first group was composed of items that represented an appreciable proportion of the value of components used and which were required in very varying quantities. It was decided that the stock and future delivery position of these items would be kept up-to-date at all times and in advance of assembly, so that supplies could be made available to meet requirements. A second group included parts which represented a medium to high proportion of the value of components utilized but were consumed in reasonably constant quantities. It was decided in this case that the components should be manufactured, assembled, or purchased by schedule and that stock holdings should be no more than what was necessary to smooth out small irregularities in supply. No stock records would be kept but a strict watch would be kept on the floor stock at frequent intervals. Such a procedure is not without its dangers when it relates to goods that are purchased from outside for it means that continuity in production hinges on the ability of suppliers to maintain deliveries. A strike at S. Smith & Sons, producers of motor accessories, in 1961 made it impossible for car producers to finish the cars they were in the course of constructing, for the stock of components gave out after a few days. It is also obvious that there must be very close co-ordination between the production plans of producers and their suppliers. A third group of components consisted of items representing a medium to high proportion of the value of components used, and which were subject to some fluctuation in use. The appropriate method of stock control for these items appeared to be that they should be ordered in 'economic order batches' along the lines of the formula shown in footnote 7, page 261. Finally, another major classification included parts that were much in demand but of small value. In this case the 'two-bin method of control' was used whereby immediately one of two bins or store locations was empty, a replacement order was put in hand. The effect of this decision was that supplies of these parts were assured at all times without it being necessary to pay particular attention to the stock position. Moreover, little supervision was exercised over the issue of these components.

One of the effects of the introduction of the method of stock control outlined above was that there was an appreciable reduction in stock levels, a considerable reduction in the chance of running out of stock of the various items in use and a saving in setting time needed for internally produced parts. The latter saving arose because it was not necessary to break production runs and reset machines to produce parts that had been used up unexpectedly.

The system of stock control just described is geared to production requirements. In some industries it is necessary to pay particular attention to the effects of price fluctuations on the business. It used to be said that the wool textile industry made most of its profits out of successful speculation on the course of wool prices rather than out of processing the raw material. It may be expedient in some cases to build up stocks when it is thought that prices will rise and to live from hand to mouth when it is thought that a fall in prices is imminent. But not all producers take this view; many hold that the risk of running short of supplies or of misreading the market outweighs the chance of speculative gain.

It is clear that the volume of work in progress depends largely on the effective planning of production. Minimum levels of work in progress in particular operations are determined by the technical requirements of the process, by the speed of a conveyor belt or by the time needed for paint to dry, and so on. The total inventory can be controlled by regulating the production of partially finished products so that there is a smooth flow of production and relating the production programme closely to the delivery pattern or the orders that are being received. Thus, the control of work in progress is much more likely to be a by-product of production control than something in its own right.[8]

The considerations that affect stock control of finished goods ready for delivery are fairly similar to those of raw materials and components. If the product is always built to the order of customers the question of having a stock of finished products does not arise. It may be, however, that to some extent the finished product is a particular arrangement of components that are themselves standard, and in this case the problem of stock control appears at one remove. Where the firm is functioning as a supplier of components to another industry, the penalty of running out of stock is likely to be high. It may involve the loss of future custom or taking emergency and costly measures to expedite production which interrupt the production flow, dislocate other programmes and result in excessive amounts of overtime. The cost of such happenings must be weighed against the cost of holding inventories at a level designed to meet orders with little or no delay. There is also a dilemma in reconciling optimum rates of production (particularly where batch production is involved) with minimum stock levels and

[8] For an extreme example of this readers may care to consult Mark Spade, *How to Run a Bassoon Factory*, Chapter V.

service to the customer. The simplest administrative solution to this kind of situation is to keep inventories on the high side, but this is unnecessarily expensive and may not be a solution at all if capacity is limited and the required inventory cannot be accumulated. In practice the problem may be resolved by laying down certain rules about the replenishment of stocks when they fall below certain levels and control may be reduced to the automatic verification of stock levels. If this is done at regular intervals it may be adequate and an improvement on an unsystematic approach to the problem. But a more complete solution lies in a thorough investigation of the various cost functions that are involved; the costs of failing to make delivery to the customer on time or of being out of stock when he wishes to make an immediate purchase; the cost of stockholding; and the costs of operating alternative production programmes. It is possible to carry out such calculations and there are many instances where with the recent progress that has been made in this kind of work and with the use of electronic computers the benefits to be derived far exceed the costs that are involved. Once the problem has been analysed for a particular undertaking the necessary decisions can be taken comparatively easily and considerable flexibility can be introduced into the production programme.[9]

For most firms refined methods of programming production and relating the control of stock levels to the programme will not be possible. The main form of control in such cases is making sure that the problem of stock control is not ignored. Automatic rules for the replenishment of stocks aid considerably in this and the indirect methods of budgetary control that we discussed earlier also come into their own. Deviations from expected or habitual stock levels may call for explanation, and such verification may be an effective check on stock levels if it is combined with periodic reviews of stock levels to assess whether circumstances have altered or new methods of production or changes in market conditions require alterations in accepted practice.

Control of stocks is an essential function of day-to-day

[9] For a full discussion of these matters see Charles C. Holt, Franco Modigliani, John F. Muth and Herbert A. Simon, *Planning Production, Inventories and Work Force* (Prentice-Hall International, Inc.).

management. Higher up the management tree, stock levels are likely to fall under broader scrutiny, such as the comparison of variations in figures of stocks with changes in production levels and comparisons with other firms. It might appear that when attention is paid to the regulation of stock along the lines we have been discussing that nothing would remain to be done, and that little could be discerned from general considerations. It is surprising that this is not true. But things do not always work as intended, and problems viewed from different points of view and with different considerations in mind often result in different solutions. There is still room for the chairman of a large company to urge economy in stock accumulation on his various departments when credit is tight or money has to be husbanded for other purposes.

QUALITY CONTROL

Quality is said to sell goods as often as price. We are concerned with only one aspect of the control of quality, that of making sure that finished goods or components do not fall below certain measurable specifications. In a production run there are always some variations in the measurable characteristics of the articles that are being produced. The length of nails varies from one to the next, the strength of wire is not the same throughout its length, and the value of resistors is seldom that indicated by the nominal values shown on them. It is common in engineering to think of dimensions as being subject to tolerances. If the value assigned to some article falls within a certain range it will do for the job; if the value lies outside this range difficulty will be experienced and the article will have to be rejected. The function of quality control is to ensure that the production process is controlled in such a way as to minimize the number of articles that fall outside the tolerances that are prescribed. The advantages of quality control are that it reduces rejects, provides the customer with a more uniform and reliable product and avoids the waste of time, materials and effort that results from the incorporation of a faulty part in subsequent processes.

Statistical methods are used to control quality. The dimensions (whether length, strength, resistance or some other measure) of a series of similar articles can be regarded as varying about some central value. This is evident in Fig. 8.2 which shows the number of matches found in successive counts of samples of four boxes. It will be seen that the contents of the box vary from 33 to 40. Quality control operates by ensuring that the central value about which variations take place is that specified for the dimensions of the article and that the variations are kept within the prescribed tolerances either completely, or so far as the process permits. In order to do this it is necessary to be able to decide when the production process is really off-beam. Some deviations from the prescribed values are to be

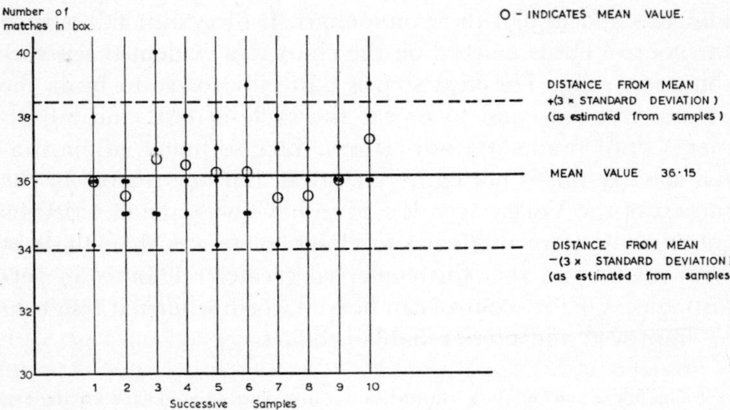

Figure 8·2. Numbers of Matches in a Box. (Samples of four).

expected. When are they so great that they indicate that something is not as it should be? And how many measurements have to be made in order to detect this? In many cases it is too costly to test all the components coming off the production line because the tests require a long time to perform. In other cases universal testing may be impracticable; if, for example, the longevity of a component is in question and this can be established only by using it until breakdown or disintegration occurs, universal testing would leave no components for subsequent use.

It is possible to provide statistical answers to all these questions. It is known, for example, that it is uncommon for the mean value of a small sample taken from the production line to differ from the mean of all the articles that are being produced by more than a certain amount. On the chart these limits are shown by the two dotted lines.[10] If the average number of matches in the samples exceed these limits, it is fairly certain that control is not being maintained. Similar rules can be used to judge whether samples indicate greater variability in the value of the articles than is specified, even though their average is about right.

Although setting up these tests calls for some specialized knowledge, their operation can be reduced to routine. All that is needed is to take sample measurements at appropriate intervals and to plot these on a chart. If the values fall outside the control limits marked on the chart it is evident that something is wrong. The next step is naturally to try to bring the process into line and to repeat the cycle of tests and adjustments until results are satisfactory. Like so many administrative devices this is not entirely costless. But one reason for the success of the Volkswagen is said to have been the fact that its components were produced to closer tolerances than those of rival makes and that this conferred greater reliability in performance. Quality control can be well worth while if it results in an improved and more reliable product.

[10] The filling machinery is adjusted in the first place to attain the standard of performance desired and to give no more than an acceptable number of rejects. The process of control is to ensure that these results are maintained subsequently. Statistically this is a question of making sure that the numbers contained in the sample could have been drawn by chance from a population of the characteristics originally laid down. One test of this is whether the means of the samples differ from the mean of the population by more than three times the standard deviation of the means of repeated samples drawn from the population (or three times the standard deviation of the population divided by the square root of the numbers included in the sample). This is, of course, a rather wide range and the percentage of cases falling outside it by chance is very small.

Chapter IX

FORECASTING

In Chapter VIII we discussed planning as one of the instruments of control. We assumed that the directors of the company would set certain objectives and that from this would emerge a plan of action set out in the form of budgets. We touched briefly on the divergences from the plan that might arise because the future had been imperfectly foreseen and suggested that flexible budgeting might be one way of maintaining control in the face of unexpected events. In this chapter we are concerned with forecasting, that is, with trying to foresee what is likely to happen in the future. In the next chapter we complete the planning picture by touching on some quantitative methods that are available to assist in the planning process.

WHY FORECAST?

Any form of planning involves some view of the future. It may be an optimistic view, a pessimistic view, one based on hunch, or a simple assumption that the future will be rather like the past. Sometimes the precise view that is taken is not critical; if it proves to be wrong plans can be easily and speedily adjusted. But on other occasions, when resources have to be irrevocably committed to some purpose, accurate forecasting may make a great deal of difference to the fortunes of a company or the economy of a country. The price of natural fibres can vary by 10, 20 or even 50 per cent in the space of a year; the same is true of certain other materials, such as tin, lead and rubber; and of foodstuffs such as butter and tea. It is not surprising that textile manufacturers find that their profits are affected very substantially by fluctuations in prices and there is no doubt that some have the reputation of being shrewder buyers than others. The latter buy when they think the market will rise, and sell, or keep themselves short of stock, when they think prices will fall. A view that the market will rise or fall is in effect a forecast even though the extent of the rise or fall anticipated may never be precisely formulated.

Some of the most important forecasts in business are connected with sales. Most production is carried out in advance of sale; to produce too much is expensive, to have too little on hand may be to miss substantial profits if demand proves to be unexpectedly high. The demand for some products varies markedly; economic crises cause the Government to cut back on demand and this falls heavily on certain types of goods; hire purchase sales fluctuate with some regularity; the demand for oil increases from year to year but by varying amounts. Forecasting may enable such changes to be anticipated. When it comes to investment plans, forecasts of demand are often even more important. The ships that were laid up in 1959 as soon as they were completed would not have been built by their owners at the time if they had realized that too many ships would be seeking cargoes in 1959.

By no means all types of outcomes can be forecast. Low freight rates in 1959 might well have been forecast; the effect of the weather on the yields of jute grown in Pakistan in 1960 could not have been forecast with the techniques then available. Forecasting is concerned with the future, but we have information only about the past and present. The future is uncertain; how far it is capable of prediction depends on the extent to which it is related to the past and whether the relationships between past and future events can be discovered. In the natural sciences the future does appear to be deducible from the past for many relationships that we have so far been able to observe. We may feel confident that the sun will rise tomorrow and that the proportions of oxygen and hydrogen contained in water will remain the same. So far we have not been disappointed in these beliefs. But many of the relationships established for the natural sciences are approximate: they are useful generalizations that may have to be modified quite considerably as time goes on and our understanding of the true relationship grows. Economic relationships are always of this nature and a useful relationship established at one time and having all the appearance of an acceptable approximation may cease to be so as the nature of the economy alters or as knowledge about it becomes more complete.

The view that economic events can be forecast depends as we have seen on the assumption that they reflect past events in some degree. This is a reasonable assumption: economic events do appear to have continuity and there is, therefore, a presumption that the past can tell us something, but not everything, of what is to come. If there were no relation between the past and the future there would be no basis for forecasts and we could only guess at what would happen. This is thought by some observers to be true of stock exchange forecasts, for example.

The purpose of developing forecasting techniques is to try to exploit the relationships that are thought to exist between past and future to greater purpose. Although forecasts are sometimes made as though the value of the variable to be forecast will, or will not, attain a particular value, complete accuracy is not to be expected. A point forecast should be taken to convey the notion that the future value of the variable is uncertain but that of all the different values that could have been chosen one appears to be more likely than the rest. A forecaster might be rather surprised if, in the event, his point forecast proved to be dead on. But equally he would be surprised, or at least disappointed, if the value materializing proved to be remote from the forecast figure. Ideally a forecast would take the form of giving a picture of all the values that might be assumed by the variable to be forecast with an estimate of the likelihood that they would be attained. This type of information might be summarized by saying that the most likely value for the variable would be v and that it would be unlikely to deviate from this value by more than a certain amount. The accuracy of forecasts could be improved in this sense if an alternative value of the variable could be shown to be more likely; if it could be shown that the possible range of values was smaller than supposed; or if it could be said that the variable would lie within given limits with a greater degree of certainty.

It is sometimes said in business that it is no good trying to forecast because forecasts are almost always bound to be wrong. There may be some truth in this observation if the accuracy of a forecast is thought to depend on its coinciding exactly with what transpires. But, as we have seen, this is not what a forecast is intended to do. One forecast is to be regarded as more accurate than another if it reduces the margin of uncertainty about future events. And the test of whether forecasts are to be preferred to guesses is whether on the average they lie nearer the truth. In business the criterion to be used in judging a forecast is whether it enables better decisions to be taken: whether, in short, forecasting techniques result on the average in more profit being made than using methods based on hunch or guess-work. In the evaluation of the usefulness of forecasts account must be taken both of the consequences of the forecast being successful, that is of the forecast event falling within some critical range, and of the possibility that the forecast will fall outside with dire consequences. Thus, a number of good forecasts may not be enough to compensate for some disastrous deviation from the value anticipated. But a consideration of this possibility and its implications would carry us too far afield.

Following out this general line of reasoning it appears sensible to suggest that the decision of a business to spend money on forecasting should be based on the following considerations. If the use of forecasting techniques increases the accuracy of assumptions made about the future for planning purposes, and improves the quality of managerial decisions in consequence, forecasting may be worth while. But it will be so only if the increase in profits that results from improved foresight exceeds the cost of making the forecasts. If the forecasts result in no better profits than would have been realized without them there is no point in forecasting, just as there may be no point in planning if policy changes are costless. If profits can be increased by greater accuracy in forecasting, it will be worth while increasing expenditure on the preparation of forecasts up to the point that the additional cost just offsets the increase in returns that results. Some forecasting techniques are relatively costless but, if accuracy involves nation-wide surveys, costs can mount rapidly.

METHODS OF FORECASTING

The methods of forecasting used will depend very much on what it is hoped to attain. There are some things that it is appropriate for a business to forecast and others that it is not. It is obvious that all businesses will be affected by the rate of growth of the economy; but few businesses in this country have the resources to devote to estimations of this kind. In most cases it may be best to rely on forecasts made by bodies specializing in this field, such as the National Institute of Economic and Social Research, or to take guidance from forecasts done by other research teams with the specialist knowledge required. It is possible that target figures published by the National Economic Development Council will be useful in indicating to business what scope there is for expansion.

The first step in attempting to forecast the growth of output in the economy is to attempt to understand the various interrelations between major sectors of the economy. What, for example, determines the level of consumption? In the model used for forecasting in the Dutch economy consumption is decided according to the amounts spent by wage-earning and entrepreneurial families and it is assumed that each of them spends different proportions of their incomes remaining after taxation. The proportions spent broadly reflect past experience. Similarly prices are supposed to depend on wage rates, the price of imported goods and tax rates. The relationship between the various types of price index and the variables explaining them are again constructed from past experience, modified if necessary to take acccount of any changes that can be anticipated in these variables in the period for which the forecasts are made. In all, the 1955 system for the Dutch economy consisted of twenty-seven equations, twelve of which were definitions and these equations acted like a working model of the economy.[1] It was possible to tell from them what might happen if, for example, wage rates rose, production increased, or a number of changes took place simultaneously. Prediction proceeds by feeding into this system a number of plausible guesses or assumptions, about certain variables, for example, wage rates, stock changes, and import prices and the consequences of these changes for the development of the economy can then be estimated in detail.

There is a decided advantage in using a system of equations in such estimates but the same types of exercise can be carried through solely in terms of arithmetic. Some increase in pro-

[1] See H. Thiel, *Economic Forecasts and Policy*, (North Holland Publishing Company). p. 52.

duction can be assumed, for example, and the consequences of this for wage incomes and profits deduced by assuming certain relationships between production and wages and profits. These in turn may be held to determine consumption and investment which together may be regarded as governing production and must, therefore, be consistent with the increase in income postulated. This is, of course, a very simple example, but the principles remain the same when much more complicated systems are considered.

The assumption made about an increase in production in the previous example might itself rest on conclusions drawn from observations of the past working of the economy. It might have been noted that increase in production had averaged 3 per cent in the past 10 years, or it might have been assumed that the increase would be the same as in the previous year. To some extent the rise in production may be determinable, from, say unfilled orders or entrepreneurs' expectations at the beginning of the year. In any case, the forecast will rest on past experience in some form or another and the test of the reasonableness of the assumption may be whether it fits into the observed pattern of previous years.

If forecasts of the general state of the economy are required for business purposes, when no official forecasts are available, it may be easier to attempt to pick one or more 'leading' series than to attempt to make a full national income forecast. Stock exchange price indicators have been used for this purpose and some success was claimed for them before the war when it appeared that their movements anticipated changes in business conditions. The reason that they did so may have been that they reflected movements in new orders known to stock exchange operators from business contacts. Post-war stock exchange indices appear to have been a less reliable guide and other indicators have had to be developed for forecasting purposes. Direct inquiry from a representative sample of businessmen is now carried out in a number of countries. In this country the Federation of British Industries has been asking businessmen what changes they anticipate in business conditions and whether, for example, they anticipate increasing the level of their investment in some future period or whether it will fall or remain unchanged.

The search for leading series is of general application. A rise in import prices in the United Kingdom does not affect retail prices immediately but will do so after a lapse of perhaps 3 months. A decision to construct a new dam will give rise to orders for new generating equipment at some later date; a fall in new orders for ships will affect steelmakers only when existing orders have been completed. An increase in the rate of utilization of plant and capacity is likely to give rise to orders for new plant; and a fall in retailers' stocks to new orders for wholesalers and manufacturers. A rise in the population will affect the demand for houses, and so on. Relationships of this kind, though they may be obvious, are valuable. They are likely to play an important role in business forecasting.

A more interesting relationship is that between the price of jute and rice in the area of land planted for jute in some year and the relative prices of jute and rice in the previous year. Research carried out by the Food and Agriculture Organization of the United Nations shows that there is a discernible relationship between the two, such that an increase in rice prices or a fall in jute prices will tend to reduce the acreage put down to jute in the following year. The mechanism behind this relationship is understandable. A high rice price will tend to make farmers increase the output of it either on the supposition that high prices will continue to rule in the following year or, because the high price is a sign of hunger and it is not intended to run the risk of starvation the following year in the hope of maintaining previous proceeds from the cash crop. A relatively low jute price will reduce the value of the cash crop and suggest a change to the production of apparently more worthwhile crops. It appeared that from 1910 to 1940 a 1 per cent increase in the price of jute relative to that of rice increased the acreage put down to jute by about half per cent. Thus the supply of jute was in some measure determined a year ahead of its harvesting.

The relationship for jute did not hold exactly from year to year. For a more complete explanation additional variables would have had to be introduced. Perhaps some measure of the opportunity to prepare land for sowing, having regard to the incidence of floods and rainfall, or the addition of other price series to that for jute might have improved the 'explanation'.

Generally greater confidence is felt in a forecast that depends on some understandable relationship. It is reasonable to proceed on the assumption that the jute acreage is related to prices in the way that has been indicated. Forecasting the jute acreage by the above method would not, however, necessarily be ruled out even if no easily understandable explanation of the relationship could be advanced. If observation suggests that two series are related in some way it is perfectly possible to use the one as an explanation of the other. But considerable doubts might well be felt about the reliability of such forecasts if the variables involved could not be connected with any kind of economic model. The relationship might be a chance one holding over a limited period of time but without real underlying validity.

There may be more justification for other comparatively simple forecasting procedures. The demand for some article may be forecast on the assumption that it will increase in the future at much the same rate as it has done in the past, and a more complicated forecast may be built up out of a number of such simple assumptions relating to separate items in a composite whole. Such relationships sometimes seem to rest on insufficient foundations but they may be more reliable than alternatives that would otherwise be used. One company found, for example, that they were more reliable indicators of sales than the anticipations of their salesmen.

Another example of the future course of a series of figures being related to values assumed at some earlier date arises in the case of the replacement demand for certain types of capital goods. Thus, if machines have a life of x years and n of them were installed x years ago, n will now be due for replacement. Relationships of this form are certainly evident but they are generally of a much more variable form than that postulated above. The life of capital equipment is not predetermined; the decision to replace some existing machines depends on a number of uncertain events such as the cost of repairs as the equipment becomes older, the extent to which replacement may be advanced or retarded, obsolescence and the state of the market for the products being made by the machines.

Similar types of relationships may exist for hire purchase expenditure. Mr J. R. Cuthbertson has suggested that individuals tend to sustain a certain level of hire purchase payments so that the completion of a series of payments on one article tends to be followed by the conclusion of another hire-purchase agreement.[2] If such a relationship held it might be possible to anticipate a resurgence of demand for durable consumption goods in the future from looking at the anticipated maturities of existing contracts.

Observed relationships are not always so simple as this. For many years economic forecasts of saturation of the demand for durable consumer goods have proved to be wrong because young consumers in the middle and upper income brackets were willing to enlarge their instalment debt for the sake of upgrading their possessions.[3]

This means that it is useful to know something about consumers' buying intentions as well as other factors in predicting the demand for durable consumer goods. The demand for motor cars was dependent in the early days of production on potential consumers realizing the value of motor cars to them. At the present day the demand for motor cars depends on second-hand prices realized for the sale of used vehicles, the level of incomes, and the price of cars in relation to other consumer goods. In the United States it appeared that a 1 per cent increase in the level of disposable income increased expenditure on new cars by 2.5 per cent; and a 1 per cent increase in the ratio of the prices of new cars to the index of consumer prices was associated with an average decrease of 1½ per cent in new car sales.[4]

The National Institute of Economic and Social Research prepared a long-term forecast in 1961 of the demand for cars in 1965 and 1970. The method adopted was to see what factors appeared to have influenced the stock of cars in Britain from 1948 to 1960 and to use the relationship established for the purpose of prediction. The stock of cars was compiled by depreciating the value of older cars in line with second-hand prices, thus giving what might be described as an index of the

[2] 'Hire Purchase Controls and Fluctuations in the Car Market', *Economica* (May 1961), p. 125. See also: A. Silbertston, 'Hire Purchase Controls and the Demand for Cars', *Economic Journal*, (March 1963.)

[3] See George Katona, 'Changes in Consumer Expectations and Their Origin', *The Quality and Economic Significance of Anticipations Data*, (National Bureau of Economic Research), p. 81.

[4] See G. Maxcy and Aubrey Silberston, *The Motor Industry* (George Allen & Unwin, 1959).

value of all the cars owned in the country. This stock value was then related, with a time lag, to income levels, the price level of cars in terms of other goods, changes in hire purchase regulations and a time trend. The predominant influence was found to be disposable income though an upward time trend was of importance. They found that an increase in income of 1 per cent might be expected to increase the car stock required by 2½ per cent, a somewhat similar relationship to that found for the United States. On the basis of various assumptions about the continuation of observed relationships and the rise of national incomes, forecasts were prepared for future years.[5]

A motor car agent might do well to consider how the main factors affecting the demand for cars would be likely to move before ordering cars for a new season and in planning expansions to capacity of sales premises or repair shops.

In *Planning Production, Inventories and Work Force*, Holt, Modigliani, Muth and Simon describe how they set about forecasting sales of paint 1 month ahead. They found that sales in the first half of a calendar year could be accurately forecast from sales for the second half of the preceding year. Sales for the entire year could be forecast from the real gross private domestic investment component of the gross national product.[6] Monthly forecasts could be obtained by applying seasonal adjustments to the half-yearly data which effectively allowed for the variation of the sales pattern from month to month. The key to the success of the method devised was the use of the series for gross private domestic investment.

As we have seen, asking salesmen and businessmen what they think is likely to happen is one way of getting a lead on the future. But special techniques are needed to get the best results and care must be taken to avoid getting biased responses. Salesmen may be naturally chary of giving their opinion about the market and if asked about the prospect for sales may be inclined to underestimate possibilities so that their actual performance will stand up well against the apparent difficulty of the task that they were asked to undertake. In placing reliance on the views of businessmen, allowance must be made for the fact that opinions are catching and that it is safer to ask

[5] *National Institute Economic Review* (September 1961).

[6] For definitions see Chapter X, pp. 290-3.

a businessman what he intends to do than what he thinks will happen. The views of businessmen may be determined in some considerable measure by what has been said in official quarters, in financial circles or on television.

Expectations, however, are clearly an important element in forecasting. Research done by Miss Eva Mueller appears to suggest that consumer attitudes to the purchase of consumer goods may be a very good indication of future purchases. But it is desirable not to look too far ahead: expectations are often short run. A number of techniques are available for assessing consumer attitudes. It is possible, for example, to get some indication of buying intentions of consumers by asking them about their financial expectations in the coming year, their views of the long-term outlook, and so on. Another approach is to ask consumers what they intend to buy and this technique is used in the 'Quarterly Survey of Consumer Buying Intentions', published in the *Federal Reserve Bulletin*, as an indication of the prospects for consumer sales in the United States during the next half-year. Some of the work in this field promises well, but it is important fully to assess the reliability of new forecasting techniques before great weight is put upon them, and this is what research workers are trying to do.

The choice of what methods to use is partly a question of the technical performance of the various alternatives available and partly economic. It should not be assumed that the most complicated forecasting model is necessarily the best. At first sight complicated relationships between a large number of variables might appear to hold out the greatest chance of success, and it may be possible to establish such relationships more easily in the future with the development of new statistical series and the use of computers. But there are good reasons for believing that forecasts will be better if they are reasonably simple. All economic series are subject to unobservable and indeterminate error. These errors may not only accumulate when a large number of statistical series are combined in calculation, but interact and multiply. Of smaller importance is that apparent connections between variables may in some cases be derived from errors incorporated in the data used and not represent any real economic significance. Another difficulty is that the more variables are used to 'explain' some series, the easier does it become to fabricate an explanation in statistical terms even though that explanation may not really represent the causal factor at work.

ERRORS INVOLVED IN FORECASTING

Since the susceptibility of forecasts to error is often advanced against attempts to chart the future it may be useful to examine how it is that forecasts go wrong before reviewing the success that has been achieved in practice. Errors can arise for fundamental reasons inherent in the methods of forecasting in use. Many forecasts start off with the assumption that some variable can be expressed as a linear relationship of some other variables: that sales, for example, will vary proportionally with income or that sales will be equal to some fraction of income plus a constant. In the first place this relationship will be established from past data. Even if the relationship postulated is in fact a true one in the sense that it correctly represents economic relationships, it does not follow that it will emerge from a consideration of data relating to past periods. These data are subject to error and the relationship calculated from them is almost certain to be only a rough approximation to the true relation that it was hoped to observe. Secondly, it is unlikely that the form of the relationship postulated between sales and income is the true one between these variables; it may well be only an approximation to the relationship that actually exists. Thus, in addition to saying that sales are equal to some proportion of income, plus a constant, we have to make allowance for the fact that the relationship with which we are working is inexact in some measure and insert a term representing error in the equations with which we are working. Thirdly some variables that are liable to affect the relationships between sales and income may lie outside our system of prediction, and in effect be unpredictable (exogenous variables). Changes in hire purchase regulations may fall into this category, for while it may sometimes be possible to anticipate changes in Government regulations it is seldom possible to anticipate the exact form that they will take.

Another possible source of error may be described as economic. Errors of this kind may arise partly out of inadequate formulation of the relationships between the variable in which we are interested and the other variables in the economy that we might study. In an effort to do something an inappropriate relationship may be selected. In the earlier explanations advanced of the trade cycle it was suggested that cycles were closely correlated with the activity of sunspots. There were reasons for thinking that there might be some connection between the two, but in fact the connection is of slight importance. Forecasts of economic activity related to sunspot activity would obviously be doomed to failure if the relationship postulated in the first place was incorrect. Another class of economic errors arises in what is measured or what it is possible to measure. Income as measured may not be the variable that we would like to consider in forecasting sales, but the nearest we can get to a variable that would give an exact relationship. In some instances also we may be forced to leave out of consideration certain variables that we would like to take into account if they were available. In addition to considering income we might like to consider buying intentions expressed by consumers, but these may be impossible to compile.

Statistical errors also require consideration. Estimating procedures used to establish the connection between two variables may be based on the assumption that the errors in variables are independent of the values that the variables assume. If, in fact, the errors are larger for larger incomes rather than for smaller ones, appropriate methods of estimation will have to be used. Many statistical techniques that are used rest on the assumption that the observed values of variables are independent, that the choice of one does not affect the other; if this is not the case, serious errors may result. Errors in statistical data have already been touched upon; they may be caused by clerical mistakes, by a failure of those compiling data to interpret their instructions correctly or even in some instances by a disregard for what is required.

Very frequently it is necessary to collect data by sampling procedures. This can introduce its own quota of errors. The sample may not be well drawn and be unrepresentative of what is being measured. In the case of questionnaires the sample may become unrepresentative, some of those asked to fill in the questionnaire do not respond. There is generally some systematic reason for non-response; so that non-respondents often prove to have different characteristics from those who complete the questionnaire. A second request for the completion of a questionnaire may sometimes improve the response rates of those who failed to return the questionnaire on the first appeal. It is possible that those who respond eventually will be more representative of those who fail to make any response than those who replied in the first place, and this may enable a more representative sample to be compiled. If, however, no means can be found of getting any response from those who are reluctant to answer the questionnaire, the sample is bound to remain unrepresentative.

Even if the sample has been correctly drawn and response to it is complete, the characteristics of the sample may not be the same as the characteristics of the population from which the sample was drawn. To question twenty housewives about whether they would buy a product will not necessarily give the same proportion of would-be buyers as would emerge if 200 housewives were questioned, or all housewives in the country. It might be that all the twenty housewives first questioned were potential buyers, even though if all housewives had been consulted it would have emerged that only half of them were ready to buy. It would be most unlikely that a sample of 200 housewives would be misleading in the same degree. Up to a point the larger the size of sample the more representative it is likely to be. Unlike errors due to non-response which lie largely hidden, errors due to samples not being completely representative of the population from which they are drawn can generally be estimated within certain limits by statistical methods.

It might be inferred from the foregoing that accuracy of estimates based on samples can always be improved by enlarging the size of the sample. Formally, this is true; but in practice other considerations have to be taken into account. A small sample can be taken with great care, perhaps by a team specially selected and trained for the purpose. For larger samples, it may not be possible to maintain the same care and attention to detail so that errors of observation are increased at the same time as sampling errors are being reduced. The net effect of increasing the coverage of the sample may be to reduce its accuracy, and more money may have been spent in an effort to improve the sample only to have the opposite result in practice. Thus, when only limited resources are available, it may pay to concentrate on taking a good sample rather than to attempt to spread inquiries too widely with a loss of accuracy.

ACCURACY IN PRACTICE

In the face of such a formidable array of sources of error it might seem impossible to make forecasts of any value. Before

TABLE 9.1

CHANGES IN DEMAND, FORECAST AND ACTUAL

1959 Fourth Quarter to 1960 Fourth Quarter

	Per cent change over 1959 Fourth quarter		
	Change forecast in		*Actual*
	January	*May*	*change*
Consumers' expenditure	+3½	+3½	+1½
Of which durables	+9	+6	−21½
Public authorities' current spending	+4	+3½	+6
Gross fixed investment	+8	+7	+6½
Exports of goods and services	+6½	+5	—
Total demand excluding investment in stocks	+4½	+4	+2½
Total final demand	+4	+3½	+3
Less imports of goods and services	+7	+7	+8
Less factor cost adjustment	+6	+6	+6
Gross domestic product (from expenditure)*	+3½	+3	+1½
Gross domestic product (from output)*			+2½
Industrial production	+6 or 7	+6	+2½

Source: *National Institute Economic Review* (May 1961).
* The difference is due to statistical discrepancies in the method used.

considering what constitutes a valuable forecast for various purposes it may be useful briefly to see what accuracy has been attained by some economic forecasts in the post-war period.

The National Institute of Economic and Social Research examines the economic situation at two-monthly intervals in its *Economic Review* which is a very useful source of information about the economy; every January it presents a full-length review of the economic situation. The Institute is staffed by economists and statisticians who are experienced and skilled in forecasting work and have adequate resources for the purpose. In one of the reviews an appraisal was made of the accuracy of some previous forecasts: Table 9.1 summarizes a number of comparisons of what actually transpired with the forecasts of the Institute.

The forecasts were made for less than a year ahead for both the January and May forecasts; yet both the forecasts show substantial differences from what actually transpired. Other forecasters fared no better and a forecast based on a mathematical model developed at Oxford, similar to that described earlier for the Dutch economy, was no improvement. It may be unfair to judge the accuracy of forecasting on the basis of only a few comparisons. There is a good deal of luck in it and the Institute may have been unlucky in this instance and some of the assumptions that it was necessary to make did not turn out to be true in the event, but there is an acknowledged need to improve forecasting techniques for this country's economy. Some measure of success appears to have been achieved by the Dutch forecasters using their economic model. Dr Theil has shown that the percentage change of various economic indicators forecast for the Dutch economy averaged about 0.7 of the percentage changes actually recorded.[7] The corresponding figure for forecasts made for Scandinavian countries was generally somewhat smaller, typically about 0.5. There was, however, in all cases, a considerable variation in the accuracy of individual forecasts. Nevertheless, the forecasts were invariably better than the results that would have been attained if it had been assumed that the changes of the previous year would exactly repeat themselves. The tendency to underestimate the amount of change taking place appears to be a usual feature of forecasts. The recognition of this tendency does not mean, however, that this error can be corrected by the simple expedient of increasing all forecasts in some proportion. While this would improve the average performance it would make some forecasts worse and it might destroy the basis on which the forecasts were constructed in the first place.

In assessing forecasting performance it is always necessary to distinguish between future projections that are in the nature of targets and forecasts that are expected to be realized. In the post-war period the United Kingdom Government was much more concerned with the preparation of targets than of forecasts and there was an element of wishful thinking in the

[7] H. Theil, op. cit., Chapter 3.

projections made. It is scarcely surprising that there were often appreciable differences between what was anticipated and what transpired.

Forecasts particularly likely to be in error are those concerned with capital goods. One reason for this is that many capital goods take a long time to make and most are extremely durable. Forecasts are likely to be of decreasing accuracy the longer the period they are expected to cover, and those concerned with the profitability of capital goods must cover some considerable span of time. The durability of capital goods also makes the demand for them difficult to forecast because the replacement demand for capital goods may be rather small and a moderate increase in the demand for products requiring particular types of capital goods for their production may represent quite a large proportion of normal output.

Estimates of the state of the market for ships, prepared early in 1959, indicated a strong possibility that almost as much as 15 million gross tons of shipping might be laid up in 1961. In the event, laid up tonnage amounted to less than 3 million tons due to a much greater increase in world trade than had been anticipated and to somewhat enhanced rates of scrapping.[8] The estimates might have been improved if they had paid greater attention to the rate of increase in world trade that was likely in the short term and less to the customary life of ships, which was more of a long-term relationship, though interrelated with the level of world trade through the level of freight rates.

Forecasts of energy requirements in Western Europe over two decades again illustrate the difficulty of making accurate forecasts over long periods. An expert committee examining Western Europe's requirements of imported fuels in 1975 increased its estimates by over 25 per cent within 2 years.

The very factor that caused the revision of the committee's estimates of oil requirements—a readiness to allow cheaper sources of energy from overseas to compete with domestic fuel resources—was instrumental in increasing world trade in oil more rapidly than had been assumed. In relation to these forecasts the Government decisions to allow greater oil imports were to be regarded as an exogenous factor that could not easily be

[8] See J. R. Parkinson, 'The Demand for Ships', *Scottish Journal of Political Economy* (June 1959).

taken account of in the model used for prediction purposes. Both the forecasts of energy requirements and of the state of the market for ships rested in the last resort on assumed rates of increase in national income, which, as we have seen earlier, is not easy to forecast with success. Difficulties in forecasting national income over an extended period of time—in the case of the oil estimates, 20 years—would have been quite sufficient to disturb both forecasts substantially with the passage of time.

If shorter forecasts are all that is needed, there is a greater chance of achieving an acceptable standard of accuracy. The estimates of paint sales prepared by Holt *et al.* were found to show an average forecast error for the first half of the year of less than 2 per cent and in the second half of the year of less than 4 per cent. The average for the year as a whole was less than 3 per cent with a maximum of 6 per cent. This suggests that there is a good opportunity for developing useful short-term forecasts of the demand for certain types of consumer durables. In some cases the best estimates might result from combining statistical estimates of the above kind with the results of attitude surveys.

CONCLUSIONS

Few business decisions have consequences only for the present. Many are concerned largely with the future and inevitably involve the formation of some view, explicit or implicit, about the course of events. It is seldom possible to take a decision about the future that will be optimal in all circumstances; and decisions once taken involve commitments that generally cannot be modified or avoided without cost. There are thus good reasons for taking forecasting seriously and for being ready to go to considerable trouble and expense to make sure that the best methods are being used. It does not, of course, follow that the best methods are always the most sophisticated. If experience shows that the forecasts of someone knowledgeable in business are as good as, or better than, those produced by specialists using advanced techniques, the former are to be preferred. But it is as well to establish such superiority before deciding against the use of alternative methods; and it might be worth while exploring whether the experience of those in the trade could be drawn upon to produce even better forecasts by analysing it in some systematic way. It may be, of course, that improvement is not possible or that superior methods of forecasting would cost more than they were worth. In that case there would be no point in attempting to develop the forecasting function.

This is not, however, how the matter has appeared to business in the present century. The value of forecasting has become more apparent with the spread of organized planning and as the more progressive business firms have demonstrated the usefulness of forecasts competitive pressures have stimulated the others to follow suit.[9] The fact is that many business decisions depend on what view is taken of the future, and forecasts of sales, for example, may virtually regulate a factory's operations.

In using forecasts it is important to recognize their limitations; no forecast is exactly right except by chance. Thus business plans must take into account the uncertainty that is attached to a forecast and provide for a degree of flexibility in operation that will take account of a range of outcomes. It may be cheaper to provide for this flexibility than to improve the accuracy with which forecasts can be made.

The accuracy of forecasts depends on the length of period for which the forecasts are required. Short-term forecasts stand a better chance of being right than ones for very long periods. There is some tendency for forecasts that have been constructed for a medium period ahead to be valid for a shorter period, say for the next quarter of the year rather than for the quarter after that.

It is desirable to consider what forecasting horizon should be adopted. It is seldom as far ahead as the whole life-span of an operation that is being considered. If it is planned to build a dam, it may appear natural to consider the whole life-span of the dam in estimating its profitability. But this is not really necessary. The results of operating the dam must be increasingly heavily discounted the more we attempt to peer into the future. Unless the rate of interest is really low it is the first 20 years of the dam's operation that really count; and if the rate of

[9] See Charles C. Holt, 'Forecasting Requirements from the Business Standpoint', *The Quality and Economic Significance of Anticipations Data* (National Bureau of Economic Research).

interest is really low the decision to build the dam is likely to be taken on other than purely economic considerations. When the installation of plant and machinery is at stake there will be no point in preparing forecasts beyond the life of the assets being considered. And, in practice, the relevant period to consider is probably far shorter than this, both because it is necessary to discount the more distant future rather heavily, and because the reliability of the forecasts will almost certainly decrease as they are extended into time.

Rather different methods are needed for short-term estimates than for those for longer periods. Long-term forecasts must look to the establishment of trends; short-term forecasts, on the other hand, may be concerned largely with deviations from trends. This does not prevent some long-term forecasts from being greatly influenced by the conditions ruling at the time they are made. Very often there is a strong subjective streak in forecasting and a tendency to picture the future as being related to the immediate present rather than to a sequence of years. Errors of this kind might be reduced if greater reliance were placed on relationships established mathematically and less on adjustments involving personal judgment. But it is to these elements of personal judgment and to knowing when to reject or modify a mathematical model, that the Dutch planners attribute some of the success of their methods. Clearly the root of all these difficulties is that long-term forecasting is very uncertain.

There is room for much improvement in forecasting techniques. But prediction can be carried out in a number of business situations with sufficient accuracy to make a sizeable contribution to profits by improving the quality of business decisions. The uncertainties that remain are reasons for attempting to improve forecasting techniques rather than for complaining that they do not always give the right results.

Chapter X

QUANTITATIVE METHODS

Figures are the raw material of business decisions. Qualitative information is also important, but it is never a substitute for quantitative measurement. In the last resort it is figures that convince.

The raw material of business decisions may come from within the firm or from outside sources. It is not necessary to live in ignorance of what is happening in the economic world or of what one's competitors are up to. In 1800 it was; the first regular censuses of population had still to be taken and statistics bearing on business problems were rudimentary; but by 1900 the position had improved and today it is comparatively easy to describe economic events in this country and many other parts of the world.

GENERAL STATISTICAL SOURCES

Figures relating to the economy of this country are collected mainly by Government departments. Such figures are often a by-product of administrative processes. But increasingly they have been collected with the object of improving the Government's knowledge of the economic situation. There is not the space in this book to describe in any detail the scope of official statistics. Those who need to know more about this are referred to the *Guide to Official Statistics*; and to *British Economic Statistics* by C. F. Carter and A. D. Roy (Cambridge University Press); M. G. Kendall (ed.), *The Sources and Nature of the Statistics of the United Kingdom* (Oliver and Boyd); Robin Marris, *Economic Arithmetic* (Macmillan); and Ely Devons, *British Economic Statistics*, (Cambridge University Press). It may be helpful, however, briefly to refer to a few examples of the statistics that are compiled and the publications that contain some of the key series.

Statistics relating to labour conditions are published in the *Ministry of Labour Gazette*. They include figures of employment and unemployment, distinguishing main industrial classifications and regions; figures showing changes in wage rates and average earnings according to industry; and an index of retail prices.

Statistics relating to trade are published in *the Board of Trade Journal*. Figures of the value and quantity of imports and exports are published and analysed at monthly intervals in the Journal; they are also given in much greater detail in the Trade and Navigation Accounts prepared each month. It is not always known that the Board of Trade is prepared, where possible, to furnish figures in greater detail than is available in the published returns to assist those in industry. The *Board of Trade Journal* also publishes figures of wholesale prices, import and export prices, retail trade, hire purchase debt and new orders for some industries

The *Monthly Digest of Statistics* is probably the most important single source of figures. The March 1962 issue contained 164 tables and covered such broad areas as national income and expenditure, population and vital statistics, labour, agriculture, production, major industries, distribution, transport, finance, wages and prices and the weather. Each year the tables in the *Digest* are brought together with some others in the *Annual Abstract of Statistics*, which is a useful standby when historical series of figures are required. For a quick appreciation of the economic situation *Economic Trends* is particularly useful. The movements of certain key economic indicators are shown in graphical form. The *Treasury Bulletin for Industry* is also to be recommended as a source of information about the current situation.

The compilation of statistics relating to the national income is now an important responsibility of the Central Statistical Office. In simple terms the national income is the sum of all the incomes of individuals and firms in the country, including Government income of comparable kind. There must be no double counting in this enumeration; thus, wages paid by a firm to an employee count as the income of individuals, not as the income of the firm. It can be seen in Table 10.1 how estimates of the national income are arrived at. First of all the value of people's incomes and profits of companies and corporations are added together. The incomes of firms and some

TABLE 10.1

NATIONAL INCOME AND EXPENDITURE 1961

Shares in the gross national product	£ million	*Expenditure generating gross national product at Market prices*	£ million
Income from employment	15,111	Consumers expenditure	16,608
Income from self-employment(1)	2,007	Public authorities' current expenditure on goods and services	4,189
Gross trading profits of Companies(1)	3,606	Gross fixed capital formation at home	4,103
Gross trading surpluses of public Corporations(1)	522	Value of physical increase in stocks and work in progress	591
Gross profit of other public enterprises(1)	177	Total domestic expenditure at market prices	25,491
Rent(1)	1,122	Exports and income received from abroad	6,475
Total domestic income before providing for depreciation and stock appreciation	22,547	Less imports and income paid abroad	−6,734
Less stock appreciation(1)	−127	Less taxes on expenditure(2)	−3,405
Residual error	−283	Subsidies(2)	489
Gross domestic product at factor cost	22,137	Gross national expenditure at factor cost (gross national product)	22,316
Net income from abroad	179		
Gross national product	22,316		
Capital consumption	2,015		
National income	20,301		

Notes (1) If prices rise traders benefit because the stocks they own at the beginning of a trading period can be sold at higher prices. While profits from such sales can be regarded as a form of income it is probably better to treat them as windfalls and not include them as part of the national income. Similar considerations apply if prices fall.

(2) The gross national product is measured at factor cost, that is, according to the amounts spent on factors of production. Expenditure is recorded at market prices, that is, after indirect taxes have been paid with the effect of increasing prices, or after subsidies have reduced prices. To get from market prices to factor cost we have to deduct indirect taxes and add back subsidies.

self-employed persons may include some profits (or losses), which stem from the fact that stocks of materials and goods in progress have been sold at higher (lower) prices during the year than the prices originally paid for them. Since this is to be regarded as a paper gain (or loss) it is deducted from the sum of incomes. After an adjustment for error which is necessary to make both sides of the account balance (the nation's double-entry book-keeping does not always meet and tie because of statistical difficulties) we arrive at an adjusted total of incomes which is described as the gross domestic product and is the value of goods and services produced in this country. We are paid for what we produce so it is quite correct to regard a sum of incomes as the same thing as the value of what is produced. If a company pays us more than we really produce this is reflected in the company's income which stands the loss.

Some part of the incomes generated in this country and some part of the goods and services produced here belongs to non-residents who may, say, receive dividends on investments; similarly, some part of the things produced abroad belong to residents in this country. On balance we receive more than we pay out and what we have to spend is greater to this extent. Thus, in our case the gross national product is greater than the gross domestic product.

Part of what we have to spend is needed to make good the deterioration of capital due to using it for production, normal and predictable natural loss, such as that caused by fire, and to obsolescence. We are no better off until this has been made good. Thus, an estimate of capital consumption[1] is deducted from the gross national product to arrive at the national income, what in other words is earned or can be spent without damaging the national capital. The estimate is as near as can be got in practice to the economist's concept of depreciation but there is a strong element of conventional calculation in it.

The left-hand side of Table 10.1 shows the country's income; the right-hand side shows how this income is spent. Part goes on consumption by private individuals and a further portion comprises the expenditure of public authorities on goods and services which are consumed; this includes expenditure by the

[1] The estimation of capital consumption involves theoretical and practical considerations which are not considered in detail here.

Government on civil servants' salaries and expenditure by the national insurance funds on the health service, for example. Expenditure, on buildings, machinery, dams and so on is included under the heading gross fixed capital formation at home, while additions to stocks and work in progress, which is also a form of investment, is recorded separately. The total of all these items shows the value of what has been consumed or invested in this country. The money spent in this way may have been used to purchase home-produced goods and services or spent on imports. If it has been spent on imports it will not have contributed directly to generating income in the United Kingdom and therefore needs to be deducted in moving from figures of expenditure to figures of income. Against this, it must be remembered that some of the incomes generated in this country flow from the expenditure of countries abroad on goods produced in this country for export. This has to be added in as an income-generating activity. It will be noticed in the table that both income from abroad and income paid abroad is included in the items for exports and imports respectively. The difference between income received and income disbursed in this way can best be regarded as matching the item, net income from abroad on the income side of the account. Finally it will be noticed that taxes on expenditure are deducted from the total, and subsidies added. The reason for this is that money spent on things we buy pays for taxes as well as production costs, and sometimes we pay less than the cost of production of the things we buy because the Government pays part of the cost in the form of a subsidy; the incomes paid to persons or companies, however, do not include taxes which are raked into the Government's coffers, but do include subsidies which are paid out as an addition to purchaser's expenditure by the Government. Adjusting for taxes and subsidies thus enables us to make the two sides of the account balance.

We have discussed these concepts at some length because figures of the gross national product have some bearing on a number of business problems. We have already mentioned one instance where a sales forecast proved to be closely linked with gross private investment; and assumptions about movements in the gross national product underlie a good many forecasts. Tables relating to the national income are published separately once a year in a blue book called *National Income and Expenditure*. These tables give information about different sections of the economy, about Government expenditure, the purchases of one group of industries from another and the changing pattern of consumption. We have room for only one table which shows some key figures and concepts.

The annual reports of Government departments, regular statistical returns made by them to Parliament, and the regular reports of nationalized industries are also useful sources of information of a more specialized kind.

With the integration of Europe, international aspects of business require increasing attention. Most industrial countries match the compilation of statistical material carried out in this country; and their official publications have to be referred to whenever detailed information is needed. But for many purposes the statitistical publications of the United Nations, and the International Monetary Fund, are sufficient to give preliminary answers to simple questions. The Organization for European Co-operation and Development (previously the Organization for European Economic Co-operation) also publishes statistical bulletins relating to trade and general economic matters.

Trade associations and similar organizations often function as statistical agencies for the industries that they represent. Sometimes the statistics they compile are published, sometimes not; but they are generally available to members of the associations if they do not include confidential material relating to individual firms. The Iron and Steel Federation is an example of an exceedingly effective statistical agency and the figures that it compiles and publishes are a very important source of statistical information. The figures of new orders for ships published by the Shipbuilding Conference are an example of the compilation by a trade organization of statistical information that would not otherwise be available. Such figures are of wide use but they are generally of most use to those in the industry concerned. Figures relating to the operations of firms rather than industries are generally reserved for the use of the firms concerned and are not published. Secrecy restricts publication, sometimes unnecessarily; but often the reason why such figures are not published is that they are not of much interest outside the firm for which they are compiled. There is little to add to what we have already said in Chapter VIII about the information that should be compiled from a firm's own records. Firms' requirements differ, but it is within their own powers to collect and analyse data relating to their operations.

THE ANALYSIS OF DATA

We are concerned in this chapter with the use of data as an aid to the formulation of policy. Before data can be used in this way it must generally be analysed in order to tell us what has been happening in the firm, how the various operations of the firm are related, and what must be done to attain further objectives of the firm. Why is course A better than course B? What do we do when we are not certain about the outcome of alternative courses of action? These are some of the questions that can be tackled along the lines discussed in this chapter.

Consider, for example, the question whether a firm ought to recruit labour all the year round or concentrate its requirement into certain periods of the year. The main issue in such a decision may be whether the demand for the products of the firm is seasonal,[2] and, if so, what the pattern is. One simple device for doing this (not necessarily the best) is to take the total of all the sales made in January over the past few years, and to do the same for February and March and all the other months. Expressing these totals as a percentage of the total sales made in all the years added together gives a picture of how sales vary from month to month on the average. If it appears that substantially more than one-twelfth of the sales were made in any month a seasonal pattern begins to emerge and production and employment can be geared to it.[3] It is very necessary to apply seasonal corrections to economic data collected for the whole country. Take, for example, the Index of Industrial Production which is supposed to show what is happening to production on the average for the whole of the country. In February, the index is observed to be down on the figure shown for December and much below that recorded in November. But is this a sign of falling production and perhaps a recession, or is it just due to the fact that production is always low in

[2] For a discussion of seasonal matters see C. T. Saunders, *Seasonal Fluctuations*.

[3] If the movement is ill-defined or erratic, statistical testing may be necessary in order to see whether the pattern could have been caused by chance fluctuations in the figures.

February, a short month, and always high in November when the full brunt of production for the Christmas trade is felt? Knowledge of the seasonal variations to which such figures are subject enables one to judge what is really happening with greater confidence.

There are occasions when too much data can render interpretation of what is happening difficult. A long list of all the price movements of articles and services that affect the cost of living is very interesting; but it may leave us very much in doubt. Suppose some things have gone up and other things down; what has really happened to the cost of living? We attempt to answer this question by asking in effect: what has happened to the cost of some representative basket of commodities that were bought in some base year? Would more or less have to be paid for these? In working out this sum we give in effect more weight to the things that figured largely in the budget in the base year and less weight to those that constituted a proportionately smaller amount of expenditure. Thus, we have the concept of a weighted average, that is to say an average in which particular price (or other) changes are counted more often or given a greater weight than items of lesser importance in determining an average.

Such comparatively simple manipulations can help us to interpret the data and to decide whether sales are seasonal, or prices rising, even though neither of these conclusions was at all clear in the original figures. Equally simple manipulations may lead to quite significant conclusions for business decisions, as happened when an analysis was made of merchandise rejected by customers of a mail-order firm. This firm found that 30 per cent of its goods sent cash on delivery were being returned, with serious effects on profits. Analysis showed that when merchandise was dispatched on the day the order was received, only 20 per cent of the merchandise was returned; when there was a delay of 10 days the percentage of rejections reached 60 per cent. The implications of this conclusion for policy decisions was clear, it was worth while incurring extra expense on production, stocking and dispatch in order to reduce the percentage of rejections.[4]

[4] See Horace C. Levinson, 'Experience in Commercial Operations Research', *Operations Research for Management*, p. 265.

No advanced statistical techniques were needed for establishing the conclusions reached in this case. Very often, quite simple numerical techniques will enable the import of figures to be understood and appreciated. But this is not always the case. Figure 10.1 draws on an article by Benjamin and Maitland to illustrate how expenditure on advertising and the response it provokes may be related.[5] In this case the response to advertisements for radio equipment in newspapers is shown on the vertical axis and the amount of advertising is shown along the horizontal axis. It will be noted that the amount of advertising is not plotted on the usual kind of scale. It is in fact plotted on a logarithmic scale where proportional increases are given the same distance along the axis. Thus, the distance from 100 to 200 is the same as the distance from 1000 to 2000. It appears that the relationship between the amount of advertising and the response follows a straight line. In effect, in order to get equal *absolute* increases in sales, say, from S to $S+a$ and then to $S+2a$, expenditure on advertising has to be increased in the same proportions from e to er and from er to er^2. This means that in order to keep on increasing sales, advertising expenditure will have to be increased by rather large amounts after a time. If the relationship between advertising expenditure and sales is known and if the marginal cost of producing the article that is being sold is constant, it is a comparatively easy matter to decide at what point advertising no longer pays at the price that is being charged. The fact that sales appear to be related to advertising in the way we have described is consistent with other reactions to stimuli. For example, it is known that the intensity of a sound to a listener increases in proportion to the logarithm of its intensity as measured by instruments. This is why the volume controls of wireless sets are designed to fit a logarithmic law. In practice, it might be possible to predict the effects of an advertising campaign from the initial reactions shown to it.

It is sometimes possible to estimate marginal cost curves by statistical means. Professor J. Johnston has investigated a considerable number of cost curves in this way. In a multiple-products food-processing firm it was possible to compare the

[5] B. Benjamin and J. Maitland, 'Operational Research and Advertising', *Operational Research Quarterly*, Vol. 9. No. 3, p. 207.

costs of producing different products as recorded by an elaborate and efficient accounting system with weekly output. Production costs were measured in terms of constant prices by correcting actual expenditure with an index of the price changes of raw materials, etc. Graphical presentation of the data gave a good indication of the relationship and statistical analysis suggested that marginal costs could be regarded as sensibly constant.[6]

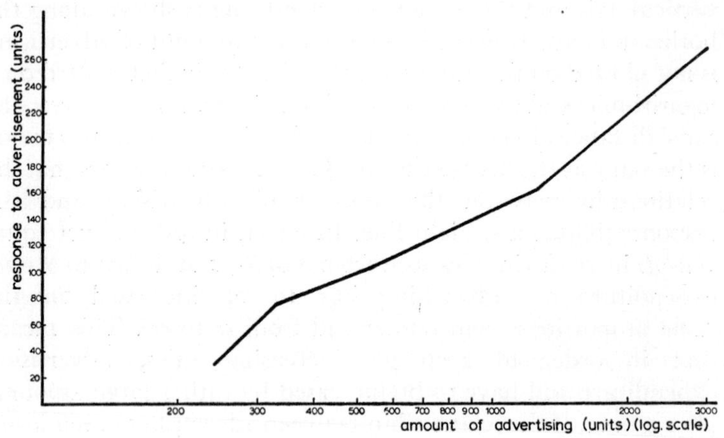

Figure 10·1. Sales of Radio Equipment in relation to Advertising.

OPERATIONAL RESEARCH

The studies of the causes of goods being returned to the mail-order firm, of the effectiveness of advertising and of the relationship between cost and output, described above, come under the heading of operational research. Operational research has been defined in various ways but it is probably best described as the scientific study of the effectiveness of operations, an operation being defined as any human activity in which a certain set of means is directed towards the achieving of a given set of ends. The business applications of operational research can be regarded as an attempt to translate the subject matter and study of economics into practical recommendations.[7] The methods of

[6] *Statistical Cost Analysis*, pp. 87–9. See also Chapter III.

[7] Compare the definition of economics proposd by Robbins in *The Nature and Significance of Economic Science*: 'Economics is a science which studies human behaviour as a relationship between ends and scarce means which have alternative uses'.

operational research are scientific: they are a combination of observation, experiment and deductive and inductive reasoning about relevant quantitative items. These methods are applied to optimizing the effectiveness of operations with the intention of aiding those who manage an operation to make effective decisions.

Although this kind of approach to business decisions has many antecedents, operational research can be said to have been developed during the war when the British and American military services began to look at operations in the way we have described above. In war the need was felt for a scientific examination of the best ways of deploying resources. Florence N. Trefethan has described some of the early operational research assignments concerned with the effectiveness of warning systems against enemy attack from the air and the establishment of a research section by the R.A.F.[8] The teams assembled to carry out operational research in the war were drawn from many disciplines. Partly because of this tradition, partly by intention, mathematicians and econometricians, economists and accountants, psychologists and biologists, scientists and engineers, have come to be associated in operational research teams now operating in industry with growing success.

One of the new techniques that has emerged as a powerful tool in business is that of linear programming. This is a development of economic thinking: it is an aspect of the allocation of scarce resources with alternative uses between different ends. The principles that govern such allocations have been discussed in economics under the heading of marginal analysis. In Chapter III, for example, it is explained that output depends on marginal costs and the prices of factors of production on the marginal product that they produce. But the analysis is designed to illustrate economic principles rather than to provide the businessman with a ready way of deciding what products to produce. In economic analysis very often only two products are considered, but an oil refinery, for example, may be able to produce a multiplicity of products. How is a businessman to be guided in the choice he makes between the various alternatives that are open to him?

[8] 'A History of Operations Research' in *Operations Research for Management*, p. 3.

LINEAR PROGRAMMING

Linear programming enables us to go some way in answering this kind of problem. Consider a simple example. Suppose that in a textile mill there are seventy-seven looms and 100 finishing machines. Assume further that there is a market for two kinds of cloth, one requiring 2 weaving and 1 finishing hour per yard of cloth, and the other requiring 1 hour and 2 hours respectively. Suppose that after allowing for the costs of labour, materials and fuel used for each type of cloth, the profit made per yard of them is the same in each instance. How many yards of each type of cloth should be produced in order to maximize profit?

Graphically the solution can be reached in the following way (see Figure 10.2).

Line AB shows how the limited weaving capacity available affects production possibilities. With seventy-seven looms (and unlimited finishing machines) we could produce 38½ yards per hour of the first type of cloth, represented by point A. The same number of looms employed weaving the second type of cloth would produce 77 yards per hour. Any point on the line AB represents different combinations of the two types of cloth that can be woven with the seventy-seven looms available. Similarly, line CD represents different quantities of the two types of cloth that could be finished using the existing number of machines, that is 100 yards and 50 yards per hour for the first and second types respectively. We cannot produce quantities of cloth represented to the right of lines CD and AB on the diagram because we should not have either enough looms (AB) or finishing machines (CD). It follows that our production possibilities are limited and are to be found within the shaded area OAED. The choice within this area is large; it ranges from not producing anything (O) to producing as much as possible of the first cloth (A) and none of the second cloth or producing the maximum quantity of the second cloth (D) and none of the first. There are also a great many combinations of the two cloths that we could produce with the available machinery. Since in this example we have assumed that we make the same profit per yard of cloth irrespective of the types of cloth we are producing, the problem is to produce as many yards of cloth as possible. If we were to produce OA yards of the first cloth we should find that finishing machinery was left unused; since the

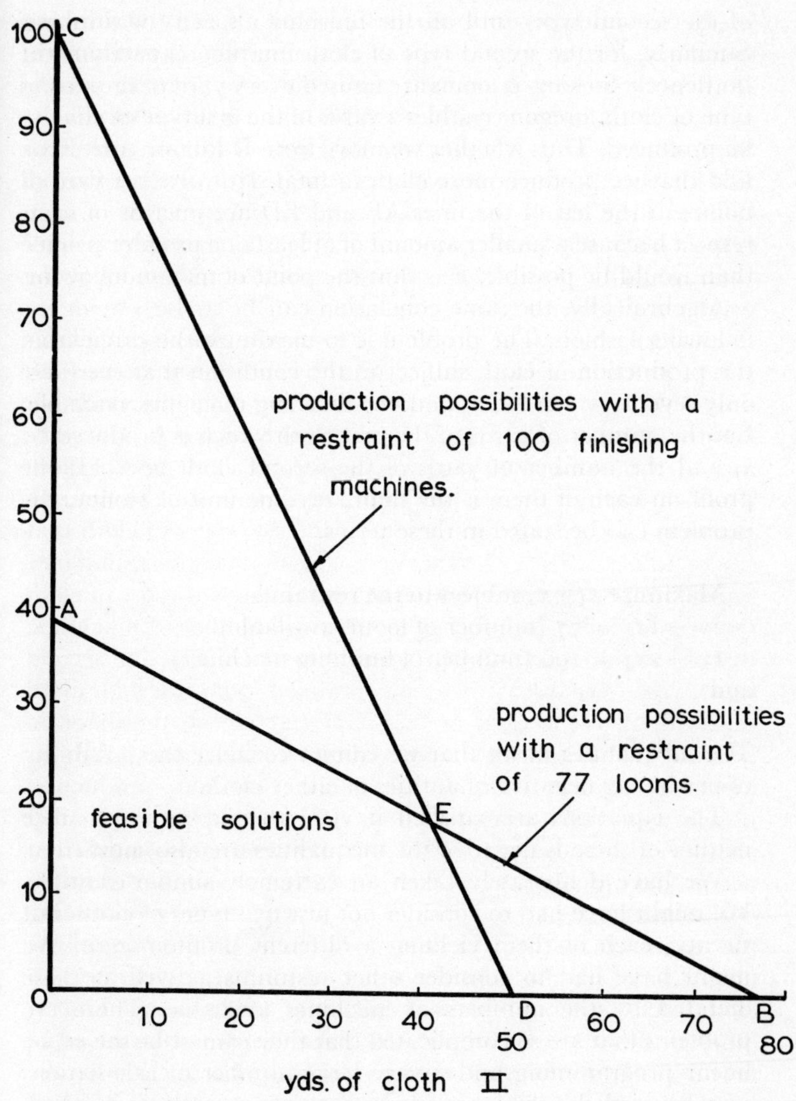

Figure 10·2. Simple Linear - Programming.

second cloth requires only 1 weaving hour per yard against the 2 needed for the first cloth it would pay us to cut down on the production of the first type of cloth and produce twice as much of the second type until all the finishing capacity was in use. Similarly, for the second type of cloth finishing capacity is the bottleneck. So long as looms are unused every yard of the second type of cloth foregone enables 2 yards of the first type of cloth to be produced. Thus whether we move from D to E or A to E we find that we produce more cloth in total. It is obvious that all points to the left of the lines AE and ED are inferior in some respect because a smaller amount of at least one product is made than would be possible. E is thus the point of maximum profit.

Algebraically, the same conclusion can be arrived at in the following fashion. The problem is to maximize the profit from the production of cloth subject to the condition that there are only seventy-seven looms and 100 finishing machines available. Let the number of yards of the first cloth which is produced be x_1 and the number of yards of the second cloth be x_2. If the profit on each of them is the same, say one unit of money, the problem can be stated in these terms.

Maximize x_1+x_2 subject to the restraint.

$2x_1+1x_2 = 77$ (number of looms available)

$1x_1+2x_2 = 100$ (number of finishing machines)

and $x_1 \geqslant 0$ $x_2 \geqslant 0$

The inequalities mean that we cannot consider the possibility of producing negative quantities of either cloth.

The equations are satisfied if $x_1 = 18$ and $x_2 = 41$, since neither of these is negative the inequalities are also satisfied.

We have deliberately taken an extremely simple example. We might have had to consider not just two types of cloth, but twenty, each of them yielding a different profit margin. We might have had to consider other restraints as well as those dictated by the numbers of machines available. There are problems that are so complicated that they cannot be solved by linear programming and a very large number of calculations may be needed if there are a large number of products involved and a large number of restraints. But the method is a powerful one and it has been applied successfully to quite complicated cases. If we wanted to extend our simple example to the consideration of twenty products rather than two we could proceed by comparing one product with another until we found the best of all combinations. A general way of doing this is known as the Simplex method. A description of this method lies beyond the scope of this book but it is well suited for the use of computers and can provide answers to linear programming problems that involve large numbers of variable factors and restraints. One solution to linear programming problem showed, for example, how the cost of transporting coking coal from 154 collieries to sixty-five coke ovens in England and Scotland could be minimized.[9]

In the example we considered, the assumptions made about the course of action that could be followed were quite restrictive. We were considering the production plant only as it existed. Thus, in terms of the economic textbooks we were confining ourselves to the short-period. Linear programming can be equally useful in guiding us in relation to long-term considerations: the kind of plant it would be best to install and what combination of products it would be most profitable to cater for. In fact linear programming has been used to give answers to a wide variety of industrial problems. Apart from the transportation problem that we touched upon, it has been applied to calculating the optimum mix for cattle food, having regard to the need to provide nutrients in the right proportions and the cost of the raw materials required; to the composition of the refined products to be produced in a refinery; and to marketing problems.

Solutions based on experience are often applied where linear programming offers an advantage. An interesting study by J. K. Wyatt compared the utilization of recovered metal in making up alloys to specification when decisions were taken on the basis of experience with those suggested by linear programming. It appeared that linear programming increased the use of recovered metal by 5 per cent and produced a worth-while financial saving. At the same time the process of deciding on alloy specification was greatly simplified by being reduced to a routine and systematic procedure.[10] The study of the

[9] A. H. Land, *Journal of the Royal Statistical Society*, Series A, Part III, 1957, p. 300.
[10] *Operational Research Quarterly*, Vol. 9, No. 2, p. 154.

movement of coking coal showed that a saving of 10 per cent could be made in the transport of coking coal.

One interesting result that comes out of the application of linear programming is that the number of products required to enable full use to be made of productive capacity is no more than the number of restraints involved. In the example we discussed profits were maximized by producing no more than two types of cloth; producing three or more types would not have increased profits. This conclusion follows of course, from the way in which the problem and its solution are formulated. It was assumed, for example, that the profit made per yard of cloth was always the same irrespective of the quantity that was produced and offered for sale. No account was taken of the danger of selling only two products or the fact that an attempt to sell more of one product often reduces prices. Nevertheless, the result is instructive in suggesting that maximum profits can be earned with a limited range of products, giving some encouragement to specialization.

QUEUEING THEORY

In business it is frequently difficult to decide the proportions in which productive facilities should be provided. The problem is simple to solve if there is no element of uncertainty in the operations that are undertaken. But generally uncertainty is present. Consider the operation of doffing spinning machines, that is removing the full bobbins and replacing them with empty reels. The machines stop when the bobbins are full, at intervals that cannot be predetermined. If a large number of the machines stop within a short period of each other it will not be possible to service them at once unless the doffing team is very large, while, if this is the case, there may be long periods when the doffing team is underemployed. On the one hand there will be a queue of machines waiting to be serviced; on the other, there will be a queue of doffers waiting for work.[11] The same type of problem arises in getting a taxi at a station: there may be either taxis on the rank waiting for fares or would-be passengers waiting for transport. It rarely happens that the flow of taxis exactly corresponds with the arrival of passengers

[11] See A. W. Swan, 'Operational Research in Industry', *Productivity Measurement Review*, 196.

so that neither the one nor the other is kept waiting. Other examples of queueing problems include the flow of traffic at traffic lights, the stacking of aircraft for landing or take-off, service at cash desks or in shops, and the arrival of ore-carriers at ports with limited unloading facilities.

The lack of balance between the provision of some service, such as checking-in at an airport, and the demand for the service arises because one or other is unpredictable or intermittent in some way. Thus, passengers to be checked-in arrive at varying intervals and take varying times to be serviced. The provision of additional check-in points reduces the waiting time for passengers but it increases the cost of the clerical labour needed for the purpose. The problem of the airport officials is to provide an acceptable service at minimum cost. In order to do this it may be necessary to consider such factors as the number of clerks to be employed; the system of check-in to be adopted, whether to have different desks for different flights or the same desks for all flights or some combination of the two; the time that passengers must report before take-off; and so on. Acceptable service from the point of view of the passenger depends on how long he is kept waiting before being attended to, how long he has to report before the departure of his flight and the chance that even if he does report on time the queue will be so long that registration will not be completed in time for him to catch the flight before closing-out time. Acceptable service from the point of view of the airline depends on the number of clerks that have to be employed, the risk that delays in registrations due to queues will hold up the departure of flights, and on the danger that customer goodwill will be lost if the wait for the service is protracted.[12]

The relation between the average rate of arrival (of passengers) for service and the average time to carry out the service are important factors affecting the size and duration of queues that develop. It is obvious that if the average time taken to provide the service exceeds the rate at which service can be provided, a queue will eventually build up and may continue to grow almost indefinitely. In practice the size of the queue may be held in check by people leaving it because they cannot

[12] For a discussion of the whole of this problem see A. M. Lee and P. A. Longton 'Queueing Processes', *Operational Research Quarterly*, Vol. 10, p. 56.

face the wait entailed or deciding not to join it for the same reason. Machines requiring service may not be so discriminating, the size of the queue being limited only by the fact that all available machines are out of order. Similarly, the speed of service itself may be affected by the size of the queue, decreasing when the queue is less pressing. If the average service time is less than the rate of arrival the queue will not grow indefinitely and may disappear entirely at some times, though not at all times. The reasons that a queue is to be expected from time to time are that the arrivals for service may be bunched and that the time taken for service may be protracted on occasions. Thus, the sudden arrival of a number of individuals to be checked in at the airport at the same time as previous passengers are taking an unusually long time to complete their business may result in a queue forming and being maintained for some period of time.

The first step in analysing queueing problems in practice consists of observing what happens and measuring such things as arrival rates, service times and queuing times. The next step is to consider alternative arrangements and if these hold out promise of success to try them on a small scale before finally deciding on an acceptable system. The whole of this procedure might be conducted on a trial-and-error basis. But it is not always possible to proceed in this way when, for example, the modifications proposed may be costly on even a small scale, or when it may be too complicated to conduct experiments, such as re-scheduling the arrival times of aircraft. The use of a mathematical model of the performance of the arrangements may enable good operating procedures to be devised without the difficulty of experimenting. It may be possible to describe the varying intervals between the arrivals of passengers at an airport by a frequency distribution showing the proportions of them that exceed various intervals of time and to build up a similar distribution for service times. From two such equations it is possible to build up a picture of the average length of queue that will emerge, and the chance that a customer will have to queue; and to deduce the effects of increasing service facilities. It is not always possible to handle queueing problems in this way; the mathematical solution may be difficult or impossible and it may be easiest to carry out a kind of paper experiment. This is known as simulation.

Table 10.2 illustrates what this means. We take the case of patients queueing for a consultation and assume that patients arrive for appointment exactly on time at the rate of one every five minutes. Suppose, however, that the time taken for a consultation is variable and is as likely to last for any number of minutes 1, 2, 3, etc., up to 10 minutes. We could decide for the purposes of our experiment how long the consultation took by throwing a ten-sided dice and seeing what side it came up. The picture we might get is shown in the Table. It may be

TABLE 10.2

SIMULATION OF A QUEUEING PROBLEM

Patient's number	*Time of patient's arrival*	*Numbers in queue on arrival, including patient in consultation*	*Length of time in queue (min)*	*Length of time of consultation (min)*
1	0	0	0	7
2	5	1	2	4
3	10	1	1	2
4	15	0	0	4
5	20	0	0	7
6	25	1	2	9
7	30	1	6	5
8	35	2	6	6
9	40	2	7	8
10	45	2	10	1
11	50	2	6	4
12	55	2	5	4
13	60	2	4	5

observed that over the period for which we have simulated the working of the arrangements the length of the queue was quite short, averaging 1.2 persons, the average waiting time being 3.8 minutes. For most of the period the consultant was fully occupied, but patients four and five arrived to find no one ahead of them in the queue and the consultant waiting. The maximum length of time spent waiting was 10 minutes. The intervals between the arrivals of patients and the average length of a consultation were the same. The reason that a queue developed was that the time for a consultation varied and that for a period the consultant was not occupied. It is characteristic of models in which service and arrival times are the same to find that there is on the average some positive waiting time.

Depending on the time needed for successive patients, this waiting time can grow very large. Generally the accumulation of a queue can be justified on the ground that the provision of the service is relatively expensive in relation to the cost of the time spent waiting by the patient. There is no reason to suppose that this always applies, however; the time of a business magnate may be worth more than that of the consultant and the services that he employs. In the case of a consultant with a number of wealthy patients it could be argued that it was economical to keep the consultant waiting rather than the patients, though a consultant in this position might find it possible to charge fees such that the value of his services exceeded those of his patients!

We cannot be sure that the brief simulation illustrated in the table correctly portrays the working of the appointments system. In order to be sure that we had got a characteristic picture we should have to continue the process of simulation for some time. In this process we should get an indication of the various kinds of situations that might arise from time to time. If we found on further simulation that the system it was proposed to adopt left too much of the consultant's time unoccupied, we might be inclined to ask patients to come earlier than there was any prospect, on the average, of their being seen. Or if we found that waiting times tended to lengthen beyond a satisfactory figure, we might consider making the appointments at less frequent intervals. In the case of the relation between spinning machines and the size of the doffing team it is possible to balance the costs involved and strike an optimum position. In the study referred to a doffing team of five seemed to be the best choice.

The example we have taken is an extremely simple one. Many actual problems are very complex and may involve several stages of queueing and methods of service. In such cases it may be best to use an electronic computer to simulate the operation, and this makes it possible to gain experience of several years' working of the system in a very short time.

INTEGRATED DATA PROCESSING

In this book we have only enough space to touch on the techniques used in operational research, and our object has been to illustrate what can be done rather than to attempt to teach the application of such techniques. But it should be possible to see that a number of business decisions can be made on the basis of objective tests.

This suggests that many of the decisions made in business can be taken in the form of successive numerical calculations. Thus, sales might be forecast on a relationship shown by operational research techniques to exist in the past between successive sales figures; inspection of inventory figures would indicate by how much they differed from the level shown to be desirable on the basis of a queueing analysis; the consequences for production and purchases would follow and would be related to the labour force needed. If the production programme involved batch production the lot sizes for different products would be determined according to decision rules based on the cost structure of the processes, again determined on the basis of past studies of the costs recorded in the plant. Procedures of this kind might seem to be far removed from practical possibilities if Messrs. Holt, Modigliani, Muth and Simon had not paved the way in their fascinating study by showing that mathematical techniques can be applied to business decision-making.[13] With the use of electronic computers in business there are real possibilities of integrating the normal recording of business operations with the provision of the information needed for decision-taking and even of getting the computer to 'take' the decisions, though always of course according to the rules laid down to govern the computer's operations. Thus, the record of a customer's order fed into a computer might be used to check whether the goods were in stock, to locate stocks and to allocate sufficient from them to fill the customer's order, and issue appropriate orders for dispatch of the goods. At the same time invoices might be prepared, the stock position brought up to date and actual orders compared with a previous forecast. Adjustments to the production programme might follow, and revised estimates for raw material needs and production schedules be prepared. This in turn might be linked to the anticipated cash position and so on. Thus, looking many years ahead, the control and planning of business operations can be seen largely as a mathematical exercise conducted partly

[13] Op cit.

automatically with the aid of high-speed computers. It will be so, of course, only as a management aid to decisions that lend themselves to the kind of analysis that we have been exploring on these pages. But the trend is already evident in the work carried out by LEO, the computer operated by Lyons. LEO holds approximately 30,000 daily standing orders and every day approximately 8,000 revisions to these are received by telephone. Within an hour of receiving the last standard orders, revisions are collated by LEO to produce the total production orders, the sub-totals required for the movement of goods in bulk for dispatch and the details required for packing goods for each branch. In addition deliveries to each branch are valued and cash totals accumulated. Stock control totals are provided and statistics are produced for management.[14] On stock control LEO is equally useful at preparing statements showing the quantities needed to bring stocks up to minimum levels and comparing actual and standard costs for each branch.

[14] D. T. Caminer, 'Some Remarks on Data Processing on LEO', *Journal of the Royal Statistical Society*, Series A, Part III (1957), p. 297.

INDEX